SECURITIES OPERATIONS GLOSSARY

A comprehensive, easy-to-understand guide to securities operations terms

By
Hal McIntyre

Second Edition
Updated For 2001!

ISBN: 0-9669178-3-9

Printed in the United States of America

Published and distributed by The Summit Group Press, a division of The Summit Group

For general information on The Summit Group Press or for permission to photocopy items for corporate, personal or educational use, please call our Wall Street Office at (212) 328-2500.

Cover photo and design: Lee Titone

INTRODUCTION

In 1998, The Summit Group published its first industry glossary, and received a wide approval. Because of that success, we have updated and expanded that information into this new book.

We created our initial glossary because the securities industry, like most other industries, has its own distinct vocabulary. Some words are often used in the industry in a very specific way, and frequently take on meanings that differ from their common usage. In our role as an industry trainer in *Securities Operations Forum*, and through various consulting assignments by *The Summit Group*, we have found that people don't always know the correct definitions of some frequently-used words. This glossary has been compiled to help everyone better understand the major terms that are used daily throughout the securities industry.

Most glossaries that have been created for the securities industry were written *by* brokers and *for* brokers. This glossary has a broader view. It contains terms that are used by brokers, as well as by banks, investment managers and other participants in the securities industry. When a term has more than one usage, the different definitions are shown.

This glossary focuses primarily on the terms that are most often used by the operations and technical staff as well as the front office. Front office and investment terms have been defined in the context of how an operations or technical person might view them.

Any ambitious effort, such as an industry glossary, is by its nature a collaborative work. I would like to thank the staff of The Summit Group and Securities Operations Forum for their support, and would especially like to recognize the continuous editing and feedback that was provided by Kim McIntyre for this edition and by William Juliano, Elizabeth Stone, John Sandman, Hayley Green, Heidi Brown, Deborah Goldstein and Scott Porter for the first edition. Their contributions were invaluable. Any errors are mine alone.

I would also like to thank the self regulating organizations that allowed us to use some of their standard definitions in order to improve the accuracy of this book.

If you come across any terms that are not included in this glossary and that are used frequently in securities processing, please send me an e-mail (hal@tsgc.com). I'll define the term for you by return e-mail and will include it in the next update of this glossary. Also, if you think that a specific definition can be clarified, please let me know since we plan to update this glossary periodically.

Hal McIntyre
Managing Partner
February 1, 2001

The Summit Group
63 Wall Street / 19th Floor
New York, NY 10005
(212) 328-2500

Also from the Summit Group Press

How the US Securities Industry Works

Order copies from www.soforum.com

Glossary of Securities Operations Terms

$A

Abbreviation for Australian dollars

1099

See *IRS Form 1099*

10b-13

See *SEC Rule l0b-13*

10b-2

See *SEC Rule l0b-2*

10b-21

See *SEC Rule 10b-21*

10b-4

See *SEC Rule 10b-4*

10b-6

See *SEC Rule 10b-6*

10b-6A

See *SEC Rule 10b-6A*

12b-1

See *SEC Rule 12b-1*

13d

See *SEC Rule 13d*

144A

See *SEC Rule 144A*

15c3-1

See *SEC Rule 15c3-1*

15c3-3

See *SEC Rule 15c3-3*

15c6-1

See *SEC Rule 15c6-1*

17a-3

See *SEC Rule 17a-3*

17a-4

See *SEC Rule 17a-4*

1933 Act

See *Truth in Securities Act of 1933*

1934 Act

See *Securities and Exchange Act of 1934*

19b-4

See *SEC Rule 19b-4*

33 Act

See *Truth in Securities Act of 1933*

34 Act

See *Securities and Exchange Act of 1934*

401 (h)

See *IRS Section 401(h)*

401(k) Plan

See *IRS Section 401(k) Plan*

403(b) Plan

See *IRS Section 403(b) Plan*

501 (c)(9)

See *IRS Section 501(c)(9)*

80/20 Rule

See *Pareto's Principle*

A.G. Edwards, Inc.

A.G. Edwards, Inc. is a US-based broker/dealer.

www.agedwards.com

ABA

Abbreviation for American Bankers Association

ABA Number

The ABA Number is a US-based numbering scheme to identify banks, which is used for check processing and Fed Wire settlement.

Fed Wire

ABN AMRO

ABN AMRO is a Netherlands-based Universal Bank.

www.abnamro.nl

Above Face Value

See *At a Premium*

Above Par Value

See *At a Premium*

Above the Market

Above the Market is a sell order that has been placed at a price that is above the market's current price for that security.

ABS

See *Asset Backed Security*

ACATS

See *Automated Customer Account Transfer Service*

ACATS-Fund/SERV Interface

The ACATS-Fund/SERV Interface electronically links two of NSCC's services, ACATS and Fund/SERV. Through this interface, mutual funds can electronically update their account registrations when a customer's Mutual Fund account is transferred from one broker to another.

Automated Customer Account Transfer Service

Acceleration Clause

An Acceleration Clause is a standard provision in a mortgage or private loan that allows the issuer the right to demand that the outstanding balance be due immediately.

Access Time

Access Time is the time it takes a PC application to access its Hard Drive and obtain the requested data, or for a mainframe to access one of it's hard drives.

Hard Drive

Account

An Account is:

- A formal record of a client's transactions, cash position, and securities positions
- A category of a general ledger that accumulates information about similar transactions or balances

Account Balance

The Account Balance is the net of the debits and credits in an account.

Account Executive

The Account Executive is an individual assigned to be responsible for a customer's account.

Account Statement

An Account Statement is a report that is typically generated monthly and which lists a client's transactions, cash balances, and securities positions.

Accounting Cycle

The Accounting Cycle is the period of time during which transactions are recorded and reported while complying with standardized procedures. The cycle could be daily, weekly, monthly, quarterly, or annually. Different categories of accounts are typically reviewed after different periods of time.

Accounting Period

The Accounting Period is normally a 12-month period that can be a calendar year or a fiscal year.

Accretion

Accretion is the increase in the value of a bond that occurs steadily from the time it was purchased at a discount until it is redeemed at the Market Value or matures at Face Value.

Market Value, Face Value

Accrual

In accounting, an Accrual is a method for recognizing an expense in the period in which it was incurred.

For bonds, interest is accrued daily from the latest interest payment until the bond is sold, matures, is redeemed or reaches its next payment date. Interest accrues at the coupon rate of the bond.

Accrued Interest

Interest on fixed income instruments is calculated on a daily basis, and Accrued Interest is the amount of unpaid interest that has become due on a fixed income instrument since the last interest payment was made. When a bond is sold, the buyer of the bond pays the market price plus the accrued interest to the seller.

When customer statements are prepared for certain types of accounts, accrued interest is also reported.

Accrual

Accumulated Interest

Accumulated Interest consists of interest payments which were not paid on the anticipated payment date and are therefore past due.

Accumulation

Accumulation is:

- The trading process of assembling block of securities by buying in such a way as to avoid increasing the price
- The accounting process of retaining profits in a capital account rather than distributing them to shareholders as dividends
- The investment process with Mutual Funds whereby investors make a fixed amount investment on a regular basis

ACES

See *Advanced Computerized Execution System*

ACH

See *Automated Clearing House*

ACK

An ACK is an abbreviation for a positive acknowledgment, sent by S.W.I.F.T. to the sender of a message. It indicates S.W.I.F.T.'s acceptance of a message for onward transmission to addressee. An ACK does not indicate that the message has been received by the addressee.

NACK, NCK

ACT

See *Automated Confirmation Transaction Service*

Active Account

An Active Account is one in which securities are bought and sold frequently.

Active Management

An account is Actively Managed when an investment manager tries to obtain the highest possible return relative to a market index, typically by buying and selling frequently.

Passive Management

Active Market

An Active Market occurs when there is a high volume of buying and selling of securities.

Actual Price

The Actual Price is the price at which a transaction that transfers ownership is completed.

Add by Seller

An Add by Seller form is submitted by the selling firm on trade date plus two (T+2) to the NSCC to enter trades that were not previously submitted for comparison.

Added Trade Contract

The Added Trade Contract, the last of the daily contract reports that are prepared by the NSCC, contains the totals of trades that were previously entered and compared to the:

- Regular Way contract sheets
- Supplemental contract sheets
- NSCC's Questionable Trade and DK processing streams

Additional Paid-In-Capital

Additional Paid-In-Capital is the amount shareholders invested in the corporation beyond the amount of the par value of any capital stock.

Additional Voluntary Contributions

Additional voluntary contributions are after-tax contributions made by an employee to their 401(k) plan beyond either:

- The amount matched by the employer

- The maximum pretax investment

Adjustable Rate Mortgage

An Adjustable Rate Mortgage (ARM) is a mortgage agreement between the lending institution and the borrower for real estate that allows predetermined interest rate adjustments at specific intervals during the loan's time frame.

Variable Rate Mortgage

Adjustment Bonds

See *Income Bonds*

Adjustment Interval

On an ARM loan, the Adjustment Interval is the period of time that has been specified between changes in the interest rate or monthly payment.

Adjustable Rate Mortgage

ADR

See *American Depository Receipt*

See *Automatic Dividend Reinvestment*

Advance/Decline

The Advance/Decline report is the number of stocks that rose compared to those that fell over a stated time period on an exchange. This is a measure of the market that indicates a positive investor sentiment when advances outnumber declines.

Advanced Computerized Execution System

The Advanced Computerized Execution System (ACES) is an NASD application that is used by broker/dealers to automate their internal execution and record-keeping functions.

Advice

An Advice is a document that is sent by a bank to its customers verifying that a transaction has taken place. If the advice refers to a securities transaction it is called a confirmation.

Confirmation

Advisor

An Advisor is the individual or organization employed by a fund or individual to advise on investments. An advisor will usually not have the discretion to make investment decisions.

Investment Advisor, Investment Manager

Advisor Communications

Advisor Communications is an organizational unit of a custodian bank that is responsible for working with investment managers and treating them as if they were paying customers.

Advisory Processing

Advisory Processing is the NSCC's process where the counterparty's version of a trade is accepted by the originating firm.

AEX Index

The AEX Index is a stock index derived from equities listed on the Amsterdam Stock Exchange.

Affirm

See *Affirmation*

Affirmation

Investment advisors are required to send an Affirmation of their trades through the DTC's Institutional Delivery System to authorize settlement. An affirmation is established as a positive response to a broker's confirmation.

Confirmation, Executing Broker

Affirmative Obligations

Affirmative Obligations are the requirements that are established by the NASD for Nasdaq Market Makers. They include:

- Quoting firm prices
- Making two-sided markets on a continuous basis
- Participating in the Small Order Execution System
- Reporting price and volume data for each transaction involving a Nasdaq security within 90 seconds of execution

Aftermarket

The Aftermarket for an IPO begins immediately after an issue has been initially offered to the public. This is also called the secondary market.

Initial Public Offering

Against the Box

An investor trades Against the Box when they sell borrowed shares while also holding a long position in the security. This practice is often used to minimize income taxes.

Short Sale

Agency Cross

An Agency Cross occurs when a single broker acts as the agent for the buyer and for the seller. If a broker simultaneously receives an identical buy and sell order from two different customers, the firm's floor broker can match the orders.

To complete the transaction, the floor broker must go to the designated trading post for that stock and announce the bid in case another broker is prepared to offer a better price.

The brokers make their profit from their commission on the trade rather than on the spread.

Trading Post

Agency Order

An Agency Order is an order from a customer that a broker executes with another professional or retail investor and for which the broker charges a commission.

Principal Order, Agency Transaction

Agency Securities

Agency Securities are those that are issued by an agency of the US government.

Agency Transaction

An Agency Transaction occurs when the executing brokerage firm acts as an agent and charges a commission for its services.

Agency Order

Agent

An Agent is an entity that acts on behalf of another as a participant in a transaction. Agents have no legal responsibility and are usually paid for their services. Banks are frequently appointed as agents.

Sub-Agent, Clearing Agent, Clearing Broker

Agent Settlement

An Agent Settlement is a settlement that is performed through an agent as opposed to directly with a depository.

Aggressive

An investor's risk tolerance is Aggressive when they emphasize return on investment over preservation of principal.

Risk Tolerance

Aggressive Investor

Aggressive Investors are willing to risk a loss of principal in order to obtain a greater return. They seek above average returns by accepting above average risks.

Aging Report

An Aging Report is used to categorize events by time period. It can be used to ensure that the oldest exceptions are not ignored, or to transfer very old events from one department to another, etc.

Management Information System

Agreement of Sale

An Agreement of Sale is a legal contract that has been signed by the buyer and the seller, which states the terms and conditions for the sale of real estate or other property.

AIMR

See *Association for Investment Management and Research*

AIMSE

Abbreviation for Association of Investment Management Sales Executives

AKV

See *Ausland Kassenverein*

Alberta Stock Exchange

The Alberta Stock Exchange is a computerized exchange in Canada.

All or None

All or None has two meanings:

- In trading, it is an instruction to fill all of the order or none of it.
- In the primary market, it is an instruction to the underwriter to take all of an upcoming issue or none of it.

All Ordinaries Index

The All Ordinaries Index is a stock index derived from equities listed on the Australian Stock Exchange.

Allocation

Investment advisors frequently buy a single block of shares from a broker in order to keep their transaction costs lower and to distribute, or Allocate, the acquisition cost across multiple portfolios.

Block Trades

Allocation Priority

An operations manager uses an Allocation Priority when they allocate their available resources to multiple events, rather than concentrate all of their resources on one event.

Alpha

Alpha is the amount by which a portfolio either exceeds or falls below its performance goals.

Alternative Trading System

An Alternative Trading System is a system that offers a way to find counterparties other than the exchanges or Nasdaq.

Electronic Crossing Network

AMA

Abbreviation for Asset Management Account

See *Cash Management Account*

American Depository Receipt

American Depository Receipts are certificates issued by a US bank or trust company against the deposit of the original (foreign) share certificates with a sub-custodian in the country of original issue. As foreign shares are deposited abroad, the equivalent ADR's are issued in US dollars to buyers in the US markets.

ADR's trade, clear and settle in the US just as any other registered US security.

American Stock Exchange

The American Stock Exchange (AMEX), located at 86 Trinity Place, New York, NY is one of the US's leading securities exchanges. It has increasingly become a market for options as its traditional equities business has decreased. The AMEX merged with the NASD's Nasdaq in 1998.

www.amex.com

NASD

American Style Option

An American Style Option is an option contract that may be exercised at any time between its purchase date and its expiration date. Most exchange-traded options are American-style.

Option, European Style Option, Capped Style Option, Asian Option

AMEX

See *American Stock Exchange*

AMEX Composite

The AMEX Composite is a stock index derived from equities listed on the American Stock Exchange.

Amortization

Amortization is:

- The process of repaying an entire debt through a series of regular payments rather than in a lump sum
- An accounting method to regularly eliminate a balance sheet liability, deferred charge, or capital expenditure by assigning a portion of the amount as an expense in subsequent periods
- A method of pricing a money market fund that determines the current NAV by calculating the current value of short term debt instruments relative to their maturity value

AMS

See *Automatic Matching and Execution System*

Amsterdam Stock Exchange

The Amsterdam Stock Exchange is the primary stock exchange in the Netherlands.

www.xs4all.nl/~hebels

Amtlicher Handel

The Amtlicher Handel is the Frankfurt Stock Exchange.

Analyst

An Analyst is a person who is trained to investigate a security or an industry and makes recommendations regarding investments

Analytics

Analytics is a term that covers the process of analyzing securities as well as the tools that are used in the analysis.

Annual Percentage Rate

The Annual Percentage Rate is the total cost of a mortgage, expressed as a yearly interest rate. The annual percentage rate is often not the same as the interest rate since it results from an equation that includes the amount that has been financed, the finance charges, and the term of the loan.

Annual Report

An Annual Report is:

- A corporate financial statement that is issued annually to the SEC which identifies assets, liabilities, earnings and other year-end statistics. This type of annual report is called a 10K.
- A glossy presentation of the company's achievements and philosophy, accompanied by the same data that is presented in the 10K

Annual Yield

Annual Yield is the profit or income that an investment or property will return in one year. It is calculated over a one-year period as a ratio of income to cost or market price

Annualize

To Annualize is to extend any actual ratio or balance relating to a partial year to a full year.

Annualized Return

An Annualized Return is one that defines a security's yearly rate of return.

Annuity

An Annuity is an investment program that is designed to provide a series of payments over a specific period of time.

Fixed Annuity, Variable Annuity

Answerback

An Answerback is the identification that is sent by a fax machine or telex to inform the sender of the identify of the machine that received the transmission.

AON

See *All or None*

API

An Application Program Interface is used in a client/server system by one program when accessing another program.

Application

An Application is:

- A set of programs that can complete a task. An application has input, processing and output capabilities.
- An initial statement of personal and financial information that is required to open an account or apply for a loan

Application Development

Application Development is the process by which a programmer creates a set of programs that are designed to meet a user's requirements.

Application Fee

An Application Fee is a fee that is charged by a lender to a borrower to cover the initial costs of processing a loan application. The fee may include the cost of obtaining a property appraisal, a credit report, and a lock-in fee or other closing costs incurred during the process.

Application Maintenance

All applications have to be maintained, whether to update them for changes in legal or regulatory requirements, to repair bugs that were not previously disclosed, or to make minor enhancements. This process is called Application Maintenance.

Application Topology

The Application Topology for a firm is a chart that shows the various programs that are used and their relationships to each other.

Appraisal

An Appraisal is a written estimate of a property's current market value by an impartial party with knowledge of market values of similar property.

Appraisal Fee

An Appraisal Fee is a fee that is charged by a licensed, certified appraiser to render their opinion on the market value of a property as of a specific date.

Appreciation

Appreciation is an increase in an investment's value over time.

APR

See *Annual Percentage Rate*

APT

See *Automated Pit Trading*

APTC

See *Association of Publicly Traded Companies*

Arbitrage

Arbitrage is a:

- Technique that is employed to take advantage of price differences in the same or very similar instruments in separate markets. This is accomplished by purchasing an instrument in one market while simultaneously selling it in another market at a higher price.

- A process that identifies and exploits these price anomalies, which is intended to be risk-free.

Derivative

Arbitration

Arbitration is a formal process that has been established to resolve conflicts between two or more parties. The process is based upon the use of an impartial person, an arbitrator, who understands the issues related to the dispute, and the prior agreement of both parties to be bound by the decision of the arbitrator.

Arbitrator

Arbitrator

An Arbitrator is a disinterested person who has been accepted by both parties to settle a dispute.

Arbitration, Litigation, Mediation

Archival Microfiche Service

The NSCC's Archival Microfiche Service stores archived microfiche records of daily processing activity for users of ACATS, CNS, and non-CNS settlement and NSCC's trade comparison services.

Archive

An Archive is a place where historic records are stored. An archive can be on-site, or off-site in a secure facility. These records are rarely accessed, but are needed to satisfy regulatory requirements, and to support customer inquiries and potential legal actions.

Archival Microfiche Service, Iron Mountain

ARM

See *Adjustable Rate Mortgage*

Arm's Length

An Arm's Length transaction is one that occurs at free market rates.

Arrears

When a financial obligation is in Arrears, it is past due.

As Of Date

The As Of Date is the date upon which a transaction is effective or data maintenance takes effect.

ASE General Index

The AMEX Composite is a stock index derived from equities listed on the American Stock Exchange.

Asian Option

An Asian Option is an option with a settlement value based upon the difference between the strike price and the average price of the underlying security on selected dates over the life of the option.

Option

Asked

The Asked (or Ask) price is the lowest price that a seller is willing to accept at a given point in time. It is also called the Offering Price.

Bid, Quote, Offering Price

Asking Price

See *Offering Price*

Assembler

See *Machine Readable Language*

Asset

An asset is any item of value that is owned by an individual or a business.

In accounting terms, there are several different classifications of assets, including:

- Current Assets
- Long Term Assets
- Prepaid and Deferred Assets
- Intangible Assets

In the securities industry, assets are the securities that are held in a portfolio.

Balance Sheet, Asset Class

Asset Allocation

Asset Allocation is an important portfolio management concept that identifies how investments should be distributed and weighted among different asset classes.

Asset Allocation Models, Asset Class

Asset Allocation Models

Asset Allocation Models are derived as a result of the Modern Portfolio Theory which says that an investor should invest in different classes of securities, such as equities, bonds, cash, etc., over a long period of time in order to maximize profit and minimize risk.

Asset Allocation, Asset Class

Asset Allocator

An Asset Allocator is an investment manager who bases their investment philosophy on the cyclical behavior of the economy and market price trends by using asset allocation techniques.

Asset Allocation

Asset Backed Security

An Asset Backed Security is a securitized instrument that has some other underlying assets (usually loans) that are used as collateral.

Mortgage Backed Securities, Collateralized Mortgage Obligation

Asset Category

See *Sector*

Asset Class

An Asset Class is a group of similar investments, such as equities, bonds, cash, real estate, international equities, etc. Asset classes are further divided into sectors or asset categories.

Sector

Asset In-Kind

An Asset In-Kind is an asset transfer whereby assets are contributed into or withdrawn from an account free of payment. This typically occurs when a new account is established and assets are moved into it from another account.

Asset Management Account

See *Cash Management Account*

Asset Sector

See *Sector*

Asset Servicing

See *Issue Servicing*

Assets Under Management

When a firm or portfolio manager has discretion over the assets in the portfolios they are managing. The total of these assets constitute the firm's Assets Under Management.

Discretion

Assignment

An Assignment is the legal transfer of ownership, rights, or interests in property by one person, the assignor, to another who is called the assignee.

For options, it is a notice sent by the option clearing house to the option writer informing him that the option has been exercised.

Uniform Practice Code

Association for Investment Management and Research

The Association for Investment Management and Research (AIMR) and its subsidiary organizations, the Financial Analysts Federation (FAF) and the Institute of Chartered Financial Analysts (ICFA), have established common performance presentation standards for investment managers. These standards are now accepted as a set of principles that fairly represent and fully disclose investment managers' performance results.

Association of Publicly Traded Companies

The Association of Publicly Traded Companies (APTC) provides publicly traded companies with a forum for addressing regulatory and legislative issues that affect them. This association is not connected to any other industry association.

At a Discount

A security trades At a Discount when:

- Its market price is below its par value
- The market price of a bond is lower than the redemption or face value of the bond

At a Premium

A security trades At a Premium when:

- Its market price is above its par value
- An extra amount is charged to borrow a security to make delivery on a short sale. The more scarce a security is, the greater the premium
- The market price of a bond is greater than the redemption or face value of the bond
- An option trades at a price above the strike price

At Par

See *Par*

At the Close

When an order is placed At the Close, it will be executed at the best price that can be obtained at the close of the market on the day it is entered.

At the Market

An order that is placed At the Market will be executed at the best price that can be obtained after it is received by a broker on the trading floor or entered by a Nasdaq trader. This is the same as a Market Order.

Limit Order, Market Order

At the Money

An option is At the Money if the option's strike price is equal to the underlying security's current market price.

Also called an ATM option.

In-the-Money, Out-of-the-Money, Strike Price, Underlying Security

At the Opening

An order placed At the Opening is one that is intended to be executed at the best price that can be obtained when the market opens. No actual price limit is set.

Athens Stock Exchange

The Athens Stock Exchange is the primary stock exchange of Greece.

www.ase.gr

ATM

ATM is used in the following contexts:

- Banks have established Automated Teller Machines to service retail customers.

- In telecommunications, Asynchronous Transfer Mode is a very fast way to move data.
- An ATM option is At the Money

ATOM

See Automated Trading and Order Matching

ATS

See *Alternative Trading System*

Auction Market

In an Auction Market, buyers compete with other buyers while sellers compete with other sellers by verbal outcry to get the best price. This is the system of trading securities through brokers or agents on an exchange such as the New York Stock Exchange and the American Stock Exchange. At the exchanges, the auctioneer is the specialist.

In the over-the-counter market, the price is a negotiation between a market maker and a buyer or seller and is not an auction.

Specialist, Market Makėr, Stock Exchange

Audit

An Audit is a systematic examination of a firm's records and processes to ensure that the firm's transactions have been legal, accurate, and the processes are in control.

Audit Trail

An Audit Trail is a record of exactly how a transaction was processed. The record can be documented on paper or in a recoverable electronic file.

AUM

See *Assets Under Management*

Ausland Kassenverein

The Ausland Kassenverein is the German central securities depository that is responsible for processing cross-border trades into the German market.

Depository

Australian Stock Exchange

The Australian Stock Exchange is the primary stock exchange of Australia.

www.asx.com.au

Authenticating Agent

An Authenticating Agent certifies that a bond is valid when it is issued.

Bond Trustee

Authentication

Authentication is:

- Verification that a document is correct by the use of a signature

- Verification that a person has the authority to process a transaction
- The process by which two machines determine that the sending machine is an authorized sender

Authorization

Authorization is the final step in processing a transaction. The authority to authorize a transaction is normally held by someone other than the person who entered the transaction into a manual or automated system.

Authorized Common Stock

The Authorized Common Stock is the total number of shares that have been approved by a corporation's charter or the Board of Directors. It consists of shares issued and shares held by the firm.

Automated Clearing House

US Banks established the Automated Clearing House (ACH) to improve the movement of funds transfers among themselves. ACH's allow banks to initiate electronic credits and debits, and exist in many countries to clear domestic transfers.

Recission, S.W.I.F.T.

Automated Confirmation Transaction Service

The Automated Confirmation Transaction (ACT) Service is the NASD service that supports the completion of a transaction when the counterparties to a trade have communicated over the telephone.

Automated Customer Account Transfer Service

The Automated Customer Account Transfer Service (ACATS) is NSCC's process and system that is used to electronically transfer a customer's entire account or a single position from one broker to another.

Automated Delivery Instructions

In order to settle a transaction, the buyer must tell the seller where to deliver the securities. This delivery information can be included in a database of Automated Delivery Instructions that increases the level of electronic processing. This information is often contained in a Standing Instruction Database.

To be effective, the relevant data must be collected from all of the affected firms, and the data must be maintained.

Automated Delivery Instructions also need:

- Reliable connectivity
- Multiple, easy ways to access the data
- Critical mass

Delivery Instructions, Standing Instruction Database

Automated Pit Trading

LIFFE's Automated Pit Trading (APT) system is an automated trading system that is capable of handling 100 transactions per second that emulates the principles and characteristics of trading by open outcry.

LIFFE

Automated Trading and Order Matching

The Automated Trading and Order Matching (ATOM) system is a major function in the Automated Pit Trading process used by LIFFE. It provides a central limit order book with orders stored in price/time priority. Orders can be automatically executed on the opposite side of the market, aggregate bids can be seen along with market volumes at best prices.

LIFFE

Automated Trading System

An Automated Trading System is usually a screen-based trading system that provides a market in which participants can come together to buy and sell securities.

Automatic Dividend Reinvestment

Automatic Dividend Reinvestment is an automatic investor-authorized purchase of additional shares using dividends and capital gain distributions.

Dividend Reinvestment Program, DRIP

Automatic Investment Plan

An Automatic Investment Plan is one where the investor authorizes a mutual fund to automatically debit their checking, savings or Money Market Fund account for a fixed amount at specific periods. This allows an investor to Dollar Cost Average.

Dollar Cost Averaging

Automatic Matching and Execution System

The Automatic Matching and Execution System is used by the Hong Kong Stock Exchange for trading.

Automatic Reinvestment

See *Automatic Dividend Reinvestment*

Availability

See *Available Date*

Available Balance

The Available Balance is the amount of money in a cash account that is available for use. It is different from a Ledger Balance because it includes only cleared funds.

Ledger Balance

Available Date

The Available Date is the date that funds are available for use.

Value Date, Cleared Date

Available Funds

See *Available Balance*

Average

An Average can be:

- Arithmetic averages consist of the mean, median and mode
- Securities averages are used to measure trends of securities prices, such as the Dow Jones Industrial Average, and the Standard and Poor's 500 stock index. These averages are more correctly called indices.

Index, Dow Jones Industrial Average, Mean, Median, Mode

Average Cost

The Average Cost is an accounting method that is used to calculate the cost of securities for tax purposes when they are being sold. It is the arithmetic mean of the purchases.

Average Monthly Balance

The ending Average Monthly Balance is the arithmetic mean that is determined by adding the balances on each business day and dividing the total by the number of business days in the month.

Average Price

The Average Price is the mean, or average, price obtained in the purchase or sale of a security over a period of time.

Average Cost

Averaging Up or Down

Averaging Up or Down is the practice of purchasing the same security at various price levels, thereby establishing a higher or lower average cost.

Dollar Cost Averaging

Away from the Market

An option is Away from the Market when the strike price is very different from the market price of the underlying stock.

In-the-Money, Out-of-the-Money

b.p.

See *Basis Point*

Back End Load

A Back End Load is a fee that a mutual fund charges to an investor when they remove their investment from the fund.

Load

Back Months

On the futures and options market, Back Months are the future months being traded that are furthest from expiration.

Back Office

The term Back Office is a historic one which is still used to identify the operational functions of a financial firm.

Middle Office

Back Value

A Back Value process is one where a transaction is recorded as if it happened on some date in the past.

Backdating

Backdating is a process that allows a mutual fund shareholder to use previous purchases of a fund's shares to qualify for reduced commission charges on subsequent purchases.

Background

A program can run in Background when other programs are being accessed by users on-line. The background program does not require any user interaction, nor does it affect the user's ability to work with the system, although it might slow the system's response time.

Back-to-Back Trades

Back-to-Back Trades are a pair of transactions for the same security that are linked and must be received and redelivered on the same day.

BACS

See *Bankers Automated Clearing Service*

Balance of Payments

The Balance of Payments is the net of all of the funds flowing in and out of a country.

Balance Sheet

A Balance Sheet is a standard financial statement that shows the type and amount of a company's assets, liabilities, capital and net worth on a given date. In a standard balance sheet, Assets equal Liabilities plus Net Worth.

Asset, Liability

Balanced Funds

Balanced Funds are mutual funds which have been designed to include a wide list of stocks and bonds. Generally the investment goals are moderate income and moderate capital.

Balanced Manager

Balanced Manager

A Balanced Manager is an investment manager who manages a portfolio containing a variety of classes of investments, such as bonds, stocks, and cash.

Balanced Funds

BAN

See *Bond Anticipation Note*

Banca d'Italia

Banca d'Italia is the central bank of Italy and provides clearing and depository related services to the Italian capital markets.

Bank

There are several different types of banks, including:

- Retail Bank
- Commercial Bank
- Wholesale Bank
- Investment Bank
- Trust Bank
- Universal Bank
- Savings and Loan

Retail Bank, Investment Bank, Universal Bank, Savings and Loan Association

Bank Certificate of Deposit

See *Certificate of Deposit*

Bank Check

See *Cashier's Check*

Bank Draft

See *Cashier's Check*

Bank Identifier Code

The Bank Identifier Code (BIC) is a universal method of identifying financial institutions. The BIC consists of 8 or 11 characters, comprising a bank code (4 characters), a country code (2 characters), a location code (2 characters) and an optional branch code (3 characters).

Bank of America

Bank of America is a US-based bank.

www.bankamerica.com

Bank of Montreal

Bank of Montreal is a Canadian-based bank.

www.bmo.com

Bank of New York

Bank of New York is a US-based bank.

www.bankofny.com

Bank of Tokyo-Mitsubishi

Bank of Tokyo-Mitsubishi is a Japanese-based bank.

www.btm.co.jp

Bank One Corporation

Bank One Corporation is a US-based bank Holding Company.

Holding Company

www.bankone.com

Bank Trust Department

The Bank Trust Department is one that handles estate planning, guardianships and trusts for individuals or families with a high net worth.

Bankers' Acceptance

A Bankers' Acceptance is a debt instrument that represents a bank's guarantee of a future payment. Bankers' Acceptances are usually issued by banks on behalf of firms involved in the export/import business and are used to facilitate the transfer of funds. Once issued, Bankers' Acceptances can be traded over-the-counter in the secondary market, and have a maturity of 30 to 270 days.

Bankers' Acceptances, while initially issued in bearer form, are now DTC eligible.

Bankers Automated Clearing Service

The Bankers Automated Clearing Service was established to operate as a clearing house for the 17 major banks and building societies in the UK. It handles low value, bulk clearing, similar to the Automated Clearing Houses in the US.

Bankers Trust

Bankers Trust was a US-based bank that was acquired by Deutsche Bank.

Banking Act of 1933

Also known as the Glass-Steagall Act, the Banking Act of 1933 established the Federal Deposit Insurance Corporation and codified the open market operations of the Federal Reserve.

The Banking Act of 1933 also established the regulatory framework of the banking industry and prohibited banks from engaging in both investment and commercial activity.

Federal Deposit Insurance Corporation, Glass-Steagall Act

Banking Act of 1935

The Banking Act of 1935 established and defined the responsibilities of the Federal Reserve Board of Governors and extended the federal deposit insurance program.

FDIC, Federal Reserve System Board of Governors

Bankruptcy

A Bankruptcy is a formal proceeding in a federal court that relieves the debts of a person or a business that is unable to pay them.

Bankruptcy Act

The National Bankruptcy Act of 1898 (repealed and passed in 1978 as the Federal Bankruptcy Reform Act) identified the priority of claims in the event of a corporate bankruptcy, which are: US Government, secured creditors, bond holders and common stockholders. The Act also established a bankruptcy-court system.

Banque Paribas

Banque Paribas is a Swiss-based Private Bank.

www.paribas.com

Barclays Bank

Barclays Bank is a UK-based Universal Bank.

www.barclays.com

Bargain

A Bargain is the term used in the UK for a trade.

Trade

BAS Price Index

The BAS Price Index is a stock index derived from equities listed on the Brussels Stock Exchange.

Base Currency

The Base Currency of a portfolio is the currency in which the investor wants to calculate the overall increase/decrease in the value of the investment. Local currencies are converted to a single base currency, and the gain or loss is calculated on the market action and on the change in the relative values of the currencies.

Market Action

Basis

In futures trading, the Basis is the difference between the underlying product price and the futures price.

Basis Point

A Basis Point is a measurement equal to 1/100 of one percent (0.01%) used to express differences in the interest rates of fixed-income securities.

Batch

In the 1960's, as financial firms began to use the power of computers, the most common form of processing available was by Batch. In a batch process, the users input their transactions throughout the day, but the actual processing of the transaction occurs at the end of the day in a single process that automatically manipulates each transaction. The opposite of batch processing is real-time processing.

On Line

Baud

Baud is a unit of measure that is used to describe the speed of data transmission. In the mid-seventies the typical baud rate across a phone line was 300, and today speeds of less than 19,200 baud are considered slow, with most internet access currently using speeds of 56,000 baud.

Baud Rate

See *Baud*

BBO

The abbreviation BBO has two definitions:

- Best Bid and Offer
- Best Bid, Best Ask

BBS

See *Bulletin Board Service*

BD

See *Broker/Dealer*

Bear

A Bear is someone who believes that the prices of individual securities or markets as a whole will soon experience a general deterioration.

Bull

BEAR

See *Bonds Earning Accrued Returns*

Bear Market

A Bear Market is a market where prices decline steadily. Markets decline when sellers outnumber buyers.

Bull Market

Bear Spread

See Vertical Spreads

Bear Strategies

A Bear Strategy is based on the belief that prices will fall.

Bearer

The Bearer is the person or entity that possesses a negotiable bearer instrument in physical form.

Bearer Bond

A Bearer Bond is a bond with individual certificates payable to the holder. As of 1982, Bearer Bonds have no longer been issued in the US. Long-term bonds issued before this date that have not matured are still being redeemed.

Registered Bond

Bearer Form

Any note or bond that is payable to the bearer of the instrument is in Bearer Form. The holder of the instrument is considered to be the legal owner.

Bearer Instrument

A Bearer Instrument is any security that is issued in bearer form, where the owner's name is not registered in any way.

Bellwether

A Bellwether stock is one whose performance reflects the market's overall direction.

Below Par

Below Par is any price for an instrument that is below the face value (par value) of a security.

Par

Below Par Value

See *At a Discount*

Benchmark

A Benchmark is a standard against which things are measured. Indices are benchmarks.

Index

Benchmark Bond

A Benchmark Bond is the most recently issued and most liquid government bond. The most commonly used is the US Government's 30 year bond.

Beneficial Interest

A person or a firm that has a Beneficial Interest in a security has some right to some of the benefits of ownership, but is not the real owner of the security. When a security is used as collateral, the lender has a beneficial interest in the asset.

Beneficial Owner

The Beneficial Owner of a security is supposed to receive the benefits derived from ownership of the security, including income, voting rights, power to transfer, etc. Since a customer's assets are often registered in the name of the brokerage firm or the central depository, the customer does not have registered ownership, but is the real owner.

Beneficiary of Securities

Beneficiary

A Beneficiary is an entity that is legally entitled to the funds or assets that are distributed from a trust.

Beneficiary of Securities

Beneficiary of Securities is a term that is used in a sell transaction to identify the counterparty's account name and number at their clearing agent. It is usually part of the broker delivery instructions and frequently equates to the executing broker.

Beneficial Owner

Bequest

A Bequest is a gift of personal property that is made through a will.

Best Asked

The Best Asked is the lowest quoted offer at any one time from competing Market Makers to sell a specific stock.

Market Maker

Best Bid

The Best Bid is the highest quoted offer at any one time from competing Market Makers to buy a specific stock.

Market Maker

Best Efforts Basis

When an investment banker receives an assignment to distribute a new issue on a Best Efforts Basis, they agree to do their best to sell the security into the primary market.

They do not guarantee the sale of all of the security.

Best Efforts Underwriting

A Best Efforts Underwriting occurs when an underwriter agrees to participate in the issuance of a security, but does not obligate itself to distribute the entire issue. In this instance, the underwriter may return the unsold portion of the issue to the issuer at no cost to the firm.

Underwriter, Investment Bank

Best Execution Requirement

The Best Execution Requirement was established by the NASD and the exchange to ensure that Market Makers, broker/dealers, and others execute customer orders at the best price available at the time a trade is entered.

Best of Breed

Firms generally need many different types of applications to satisfy all of their business needs. While some vendors offer a suite of applications for these needs, the firms will often pick some applications from one vendor and some from another.

These firms are selecting what they see as the Best of Breed from each vendor, rather than one complete set of applications from one vendor.

BET Index

The BET Index is a stock index derived from equities listed on the Bucharest Stock Exchange.

Beta

The Beta coefficient is a measure of the market risk (volatility) of an individual investment in relation to the risk of investing in the market as a whole. A value of 0.5 indicates that the security has historically been half as sensitive to price changes as the average for the market. A value of 1.0 indicates that the investment has the same risk or response as the market, and a value of 2.0 indicates that the security has historically been twice as sensitive to price changes as the rest of the market.

BET-C Composite Index

The BET-C Composite Index is a stock index derived from equities listed on the Bulgarian Stock Exchange.

BIA

See *Broker Internal Account*

BIC

See *Bank Identifier Code*

Bid

The Bid is the highest price that a prospective buyer will pay for a security at a specific moment of time.

Asked, Quote

Bid and Asked

See *Quote*

Bid and Asked Spread

See *Spread*

Big Board

The Big Board is a name that is often used for the New York Stock Exchange.

Bilateral Netting

Bilateral Netting is the netting that occurs between two parties.

Netting

Billing Cycle

A Billing Cycle is the period of time that routinely passes before an invoice is rendered for orders and unpaid receivables.

Binary

Something is Binary when it can only exist in one of two states. For example, basic computer code is written in a binary language consisting of either a 1 or a 0, which represent a switch being in either an on or off position.

Bit

A Bit is the smallest element of data processing. It consists of a 0 or a 1, and is either on or off. Groups of eight bits form a byte which is one character.

Byte

Black-Scholes Model

The Black-Scholes Model was developed by Fischer Black & Myron Scholes in 1973. This is the options pricing model that is most often used for the valuation of European-style options.

Blanket Recommendation

A Blanket Recommendation is a buy or sell recommendation that is sent to all of a brokerage firm's customers, regardless of their investment objectives.

Block

A Block is a large purchase or sale of a specific stock usually representing at least 10,000 shares or a transaction over $200,000. Investment advisors will frequently combine their portfolio requirements for the same security into a single purchase. When an order for a large number of shares is received, a broker may have to 'shop the trade' to locate several different counterparties to assemble all of the required shares.

The assembled shares constitute the block. When the block is assembled, the broker either reports to the buyer the average cost of the shares or the individual trades that constitute the block.

Allocation

Block Trades

See *Block*

Blotter

A Blotter is a trade-by-trade list that is maintained for each trader or broker, either manually or electronically.

Blue Chip

A Blue Chip stock is a historic term for a company that is known for having excellent management and a conservative financial structure. These stocks traditionally have low associated risk.

Blue Sky Laws

Blue Sky Laws are state laws that define specific state regulations for many areas, such as mutual funds and securities. The laws are passed by individual states to:

- Authorize state commissions
- Require licensing of firms and representatives
- Mandate filing on new securities
- Define trade practice standards
- Define and prohibit frauds

Blue Sky Laws can be different for each state, and are usually more extensive than the laws enforced by the Securities and Exchange Commission.

Board of Directors

A Board of Directors is elected by the stock holders to oversee the activities of a corporation. The Board selects key managers and votes on issues that affect the overall corporation, as specified in the firm's corporate charter.

BOGA

BOGA is the trade confirmation system that is used by the Frankfurt Borse.

Bolsa Boliviana De Valores S.A

The Bolsa Boliviana De Valores S.A is the primary stock exchange of Bolivia.

Bolsa de Bogotá

The Bolsa de Bogotá is the primary stock exchange of Colombia.

Bolsa de Comercio de Buenos Aires

The Bolsa de Comercio de Buenos Aires is the primary stock exchange of Argentina.

www.bcba.sba.com.ar

Bolsa de Comercio de Santiago

The Bolsa de Comercio de Santiago is the primary stock exchange of Chile.

www.bolsantiago.cl

Bolsa de Madrid

The entire Bolsa de Madrid consists of the various Spanish electronic exchanges, which are located in Madrid, Bilbao, Barcelona, and Valencia.

www.bolsamadrid.es

Bolsa de Medellin

The Bolsa de Medellin is a stock exchange of Colombia.

Bolsa de Occidente

The Bolsa de Occidente is a stock exchange of Colombia.

cali.cetcol.net.co/~bolsaocc/index.html

Bolsa de Valores de Caracas

The Bolsa de Valores de Caracas is the primary stock exchange of Venezuela.

www.caracasstock.com

Bolsa de Valores de Lima

The Bolsa de Valores de Lima is the primary stock exchange of Peru.

www.bvl.com.pe

Bolsa De Valores De Lisboa

The Bolsa De Valores De Lisboa is the primary stock exchange of Portugal.

www.bvl.pt

Bolsa de Valores de Montevideo

The Bolsa de Valores de Montevideo is the primary stock exchange of Uruguay.

Bolsa de Valores de Quito

The Bolsa de Valores de Quito is the primary stock exchange of Ecuador.

Bolsa De Valores de Rio De Janeiro

The Bolsa De Valores de Rio De Janeiro is a primary stock exchange of Brazil.

www.embratel.net.br/infoserv/bvrj/index.html

Bolsa de Valores de São Paolo

The Bolsa de Valores de São Paolo is a primary stock exchange of Brazil.

www.bovespa.com.br/indicei.htm

Bolsa Mexicana de Valores

The Bolsa Mexicana de Valores is the primary stock exchange of Mexico.

www.bmv.com.mx

Bolsa Nacional de Valore

The Bolsa Nacional de Valore is the primary stock exchange of Costa Rica.

www.cool.co.cr/usr/bolsa/bolsa.html

Bolsa Valori de Milan

The Bolsa Valori de Milan is the primary stock exchange of Italy.

www.robot1.texnet.it/finanza

Bombay Stock Exchange

The Bombay Stock Exchange is a stock exchange located in India.

Bombay Stock Exchange Sensitive Index

Bombay Stock Exchange Sensitive Index is a stock index derived from equities listed on the Bombay Stock Exchange.

Bona Fide

Bona Fide is Latin for "in good faith."

Bond

A bond is a debt instrument that represents a loan where the issuer is an institutional or governmental borrower. The bond has a stated interest rate and will mature on a stated future date, usually 10 to 30 years in the future, at which time the principal of the bond is due.

Although the denominations can vary widely, most bonds are sold in $1,000 denominations.

Bondholder, Bearer Bond, Registered Bond

Bond Anticipation Note

A Bond Anticipation Note (BAN) is a short to medium-term debt instrument that has been issued by a municipality.

Bond Call Date

The Bond Call Date identifies the date on which an issue can be called.

Bond Call Price

The Bond Call Price identifies the price at which an issue can be called.

Bond Counsel

The Bond Counsel is the lawyer or law firm that drafts the covenants, indenture and other legal documents that are required to issue a bond.

Covenants, Indenture

Bond Indentures

See Indenture

Bond Insurers

Bond Insurers are firms that offer insurance coverage to issuers, and which provide some protection to investors in the event of a bankruptcy.

Some of the leading bond insurers and reinsurers are:

- American Municipal Bond Assurance Corp. (AMBAC)
- ACA Financial Guaranty
- Asset Guaranty Insurance Co.
- AXA Re Finance
- Capital Guaranty Insurance Co.
- Capital Markets Assurance Corp. (CapMAC)
- Capital Reinsurance Co. (Capital Re)
- Enhance Reinsurance Co. (Enhance Re)
- Financial Guaranty Insurance Co. (FGIC)
- Financial Security Assurance (FSA)
- Municipal Bond Insurance Association (MBIA)

Bond Market Association

The Bond Market Association represents securities firms and banks that underwrite, trade and sell debt securities, both domestically and internationally. These debt securities include: Municipal bonds; US Treasury securities; Federal Agency securities; Mortgage and other asset-backed securities, Corporate Debt securities; Money Market instruments; and Repos.

www.psa.com

Bond Paying Agent

See *Paying Agent*

Bond Power

A Bond Power is the form that is used as a power of attorney to substitute for the formal endorsement on the back of a certificate in the sale and transfer of registered bonds. The security can be delivered or transferred after the Bond Power is properly completed and attached to the certificate.

Bond owners must issue Bond Powers whenever registered bonds are pledged as collateral.

Bond Ratings

Bond Ratings are a measurement system that defines the relative investment qualities of bonds, which range from the highest investment quality (least investment risk) to the lowest investment quality (greatest investment risk). This helps investors determine the issuer's relative ability to meet the stated interest and principle payments in a timely manner.

These ratings, according to Standard & Poor's Corp., are:

- Al+, highest grade
- Al, high grade
- A, upper medium grade
- Bl+, medium grade
- B1, lower medium grade
- B, speculative
- Cl+ and Cl, outright speculations
- C, income bonds paying no interest and the best defaulted bonds
- D1 and D, in default, with the D symbol assigned to issues which appear to have little recoverable value.

The primary rating agencies in the US are:

- Standard & Poor's
- Moodys
- Fitch
- Dun and Bradstreet

Bond Registrar

See *Registrar*

Bond Strip

See Strips

Bond Trustee

A Bond Trustee is an agent for the holders of the debt instrument and has a fiduciary responsibility to the bond holders, although they are paid by the issuer.

A bond trustee must:

- Certify validity of the bond when issued
- Ensure that all of the indenture provisions are met
- Monitor payment of interest and principal
- Administer a sinking fund, if applicable
- Monitor performance of any assets pledged as collateral

- Periodically report to the bond holders
- Maintain records
- Act as a fiduciary

Bondholder

A Bondholder is the person or entity that has invested by buying a bond. A bondholder is a creditor of the issuer and, unlike a stockholder, does not own any portion of the company.

Bonds Earning Accrued Returns

Bonds Earning Accrued Returns are zero coupon bonds.

Zero Coupon Bond

Book Entry

Book Entry is a settlement system which uses an electronic transfer of information about a security and/or cash between counterparties rather than physical delivery of the actual certificate. A receipt may be generated.

In practice, for a book entry process to occur when certificates are required by law, the certificates need to be in some form of general name, or street name, and immobilized in a depository.

The only true book entry securities in the US are US Government Bills, Bonds and Notes, for which no physical security exists.

Immobilization, Dematerialization, Street Name, Depository

Book Manager

See *Syndicate Manager*

Book Value

The total Book Value for a firm is calculated by adding up all of a company's assets and then deducting all of its debt and liabilities. This sum is then divided by the number of outstanding common shares.

Book Value for a security in a portfolio is determined by adding the cost of each security in the portfolio, and is different from the market value.

Market Value

Book Value Per Share

Book Value Per Share is calculated by subtracting the total liabilities from the total assets on the balance sheet, then dividing by the number of common shares.

Book-to-Book Proof

A Book-to-Book Proof is used to determine if the correct number of shares or bonds is in a portfolio. Disregarding market value, the proof looks at the opening number of shares (or bonds) for a specific security, adds purchases and subtracts sales, adjusts for Corporate Actions and calculates an ending number of shares (or bonds).

Borrower

A Borrower is an individual or an institution who applies for and receives money as a loan and is obligated to repay the loan in full under the terms of the loan.

BOSS

BOSS is the order routing and reporting system that is used on the Frankfurt Borse.

Boston Stock Exchange

The Boston Stock Exchange (BSE) is a stock exchange located in Boston, Massachusetts.

Bottleneck

When too many transactions are vying for the same resources at the same time (either in a system or a manual process) the result is a Bottleneck where the overall process slows down and errors typically occur.

A Bottleneck can exist in:

- A system when there are too many demands on a single resource, such as a printer or data storage, causing the performance of the entire system to slow down
- A process when too many transactions try to get through a single point in a specific amount of time.

Bovespa

The Bovespa is the Central Securities Depository in San Paulo, Brazil.

CSD

Box

The Box is:

- Slang for a broker's vault, which is where certificates are stored for the firm
- Shorthand for saying the broker's position in a particular security

Segregation, Trading Against the Box

BPR

See *Business Redesign*

Branch Office

A Branch Office is any physical location that has been established by a firm to be closer to its customers.

Bratislava Stock Exchange

The Bratislava Stock Exchange is the primary stock exchange of Slovakia.

www.ljse.si/cgi-bin/slo

Breach

A Breach is a violation of a trustee's fiduciary responsibility.

Break

A Break occurs during securities processing and is a mismatch between trades.

Breaking Market

A Breaking Market is usually one that is rapidly falling.

See *Bear Market*

Breakpoint

A Breakpoint is:

- The incremental threshold with an open-end mutual fund that is large enough to entitle the buyer to a lower sales charge
- A point at which a trend begins to change direction or momentum

Bridge (The)

The Bridge is the name of the telecommunications link between Euroclear and Cedel. The Bridge was developed to simplify settlements between participants in one of the two primary International Central Securities Depositories with a participant in the other ICSD.

ICSD, Cedel, Euroclear

Broker

A Broker is:

- An agent who buys and sells for his customer's account, and where the broker's compensation is the commission paid by the customer for the broker's services
- An individual who brings real estate buyers and sellers together and assists in negotiating contracts for a client

Broker Booth Support System

The Broker Booth Support System (BBSS) is a NYSE order management system that allows brokers to integrate many different applications, services, and functions into a single unit. BBSS is one application of the NYSE's Integrated Technology Program (ITP).

Broker Delivery Instructions

Broker Delivery Instructions identify the Executing Broker's Clearing Agent, account name and number, and any special instructions that are needed to settle the transaction.

Custodian Delivery Instructions, Delivery Instructions

Broker Internal Account

Through cross-referencing, brokers often attach their own account number to an investment manager's account or fund. The BIA is used widely in the industry to retrieve delivery instructions.

Cross Reference

Broker/Dealer

A Broker/Dealer is a firm that acts both as a broker and as a dealer. A broker acts as an agent for their customers and a dealer acts on his own behalf.

Broker, Dealer, Over-the-Counter Market

Brokerage

Brokerage is the fee charged by a broker to execute a transaction. It can be calculated as an amount per transaction or a percentage of a total value of the transaction, and is usually called a commission.

Brokerage Firm

A Brokerage Firm is a business that has been established to help customers buy, sell and maintain securities. A brokerage firm may trade as an agent on behalf of their clients, and/or may act as a dealer and trade for their own account.

Broker, Agent, Dealer

Broker's Call Rate

The Broker's Call Rate is the rate banks charge for loans to brokerage firms to finance the broker's margin accounts and inventory.

Brown Brothers Harriman & Co.

Brown Brothers Harriman & Co. is a US-based Private Bank and Global Custodian with its headquarters at 63 Wall Street, New York, NY, 10005.

www.bbh.com

Browser

A Browser is software that allows a user to identify where they want to go on the internet and to move from point to point on the internet.

Brussels Stock Exchange

The Brussels Stock Exchange is the primary stock exchange of Belgium.

BSE

See *Boston Stock Exchange*

BT Alex Brown & Sons

BT Alex Brown & Sons is a US-based brokerage subsidiary of Bankers Trust Company.

www.alexbrown.com

BTANs

See French Trésor

Bucharest Stock Exchange

The Bucharest Stock Exchange is the primary stock exchange of Romania.

bse.ccir.ro

Bucketing

Bucketing is a form of asset and liability management, where interest rate risk matches the interest rate exposure of future inflows and outflows, with offsetting interest rate exposure at pre-determined future dates.

Budapest Stock Exchange

The Budapest Stock Exchange is the primary stock exchange of Hungary.

www.fornax.hu/fmon/index.html

Bulgarian Stock Exchange

The Bulgarian Stock Exchange is the primary stock exchange of Bulgaria.

Bull

A Bull is a person who believes the value of securities in a market will rise.

Bear

Bull Market

A Bull Market is a market where buyers outnumber sellers and the prices of securities in the market rise.

Bear Market

Bull Strategy

A Bull Strategy is a strategy that is based on the belief that prices will rise.

Bulletin Board Service (BBS)

A Bulletin Board Service (BBS) is a computer, or a portion of a computer, that has been dedicated to manage incoming requests and messages, and to store information that can be downloaded to the requesting computer. BBSs are used by firms to advertise their products, to distribute software, and to answer frequently asked questions.

Bund

A Bund is a German Government bond.

Bundesanleihen Future

A Bundesanleihen Future is a futures contract that is based on a notional German Government bond with a 4% coupon and with an 8.5 to 10.5 year maturity.

Bundesbank

The Bundesbank is the Central Bank of Germany and is the equivalent to the US Federal Reserve Bank.

Federal Reserve Bank

Buoni del Tesoro Poliennali (BTP) Future

The Buoni del Tesoro Poliennali (BTP) Future is a futures contract that is based on a notional Italian Government Bond with a 6% coupon and with an 8.0 to 10.5 year maturity.

Business Cycle

An economic Business Cycle is a regularly recurring sequence of events that includes expansion, recession (or depression), and recovery. The concept of an inevitable business cycle was routinely accepted until the most recent period of expansion which indicates that the greatest ups and downs of the business cycle can perhaps be managed through an effective Monetary Policy.

A Business Cycle for a firm refers to the period of time where a business develops, manufacturers, markets, sells and collects payment for goods sold.

Monetary Policy, Inflation

Business Redesign

Reengineering can focus on either of two areas:

- Business Redesign requires the redesign team to look for radical changes to how the overall business operates, and how its supporting process is changed.
- Process Redesign looks for incremental ways to improve the existing process.

Reengineering, Process Redesign

Butterfly Option

The Butterfly Option is an option strategy with the purchase of one put (or call), the sale of two puts (or calls) at a higher exercise price, and the purchase of one put (or call) at an equally higher price.

Buy Order

A Buy Order is an order that is given by a customer or a customer's agent to a broker or a bank authorizing the purchase of a specific amount of securities or commodities. Buy Orders can be day orders, good until cancelled, or good for a specific period of time.

Day Order, Good-til-Cancelled Order

Buy Side

The Buy Side consists of institutional investors, pension funds, mutual funds, etc., who buy services from brokers.

Sell Side

Buy Side Trader

A Buy Side Trader is an individual who initiates trades for a buy side firm or an institutional investor.

Sell Side Trader

Buy Stop

A Buy Stop order is entered above the current market price in order to limit losses or protect a profit. It is a memorandum order that becomes a buy order when the set price is reached.

Sell Stop

Buy-Back Agreement

See *Repurchase Agreement*

Buyer's Option

A Buyers Option gives the buyer the right to set the settlement date, using one of the available forms:

- Regular Way
- Cash Settlement
- Next Day Settlement
- Future Settlement

Seller's Option

Buying Power

The Buying Power in a margin account is the maximum dollar amount of securities that the client can purchase or sell short without having to deposit additional funds.

BVL General Index

The BVL General Index is a stock index derived from equities listed on the Bolsa De Valores De Lisboa.

Byte

A Byte is a group of eight bits, and usually equals one letter or two numbers. Bytes are a unit of measurement used to denominate a computer's storage capacity.

Bit

CA

The abbreviation CA can have two meanings:

- A Chartered Accountant is the UK equivalent of an American CPA (Certified Public Accountant)
- Abbreviation for the software vendor, Computer Associates

CAC 40 Index

The CAC 40 Index is a stock index derived from equities listed on the SBF Paris Bourse.

CAES

See *Computer Assisted Execution System*

Cairo Stock Exchange

The Cairo Stock Exchange is the primary stock exchange of Egypt.

www.elrowad.com.eg

Caja de Valores

Caja de Valores provides securities depository services as well as services related to the clearance and settlement of transactions in Argentina.

Calendar Year

The Calendar Year is the twelve month period from January through December.

Fiscal Year

Calispa

Calispa is the clearing organization and central depository for transactions on the São Paulo Stock Exchange in Brazil.

Call

The term Call can be used in two ways:

- A Call occurs when the issuer of a bond issues a call notice in accordance with the terms of the bond indenture. A call could include all of the outstanding bonds or a portion of the outstanding issue. The owners (or the selected sub-set of the owners) of the bond must present the bond for redemption. Bonds are usually called at a premium to the current market price. Preferred Shares can also be called.
- A Call is a form of Option.

Callable, Option

Call Center

A Call Center is a centralized department that receives telephone inquiries, investigations or orders from customers, or which is used for telemarketing.

Call Market

A Call Market is a form of exchange process where all of the securities traded in a single issue are exchanged at the same price.

Call Money Market

The Call Money Market is a sector of the money market which provides brokers and dealers with callable funds that are secured by government securities. The funds are used by the brokers and dealers to meet their margin requirements.

Call Option

A Call Option is:

- A legal agreement that provides the owner of the option the right, but not the obligation, to buy a contracted amount of the underlying security at a set price, which is called the strike or exercise price, for a predetermined period of time prior to the expiration date after which the option is obsolete.
- A provision in a note which gives the lender the right to demand repayment of a loan before the loan matures. The option may be exercised by the lender if the terms of the loan are violated, or at their discretion.

Strike Price, Exercise Price

Call Premium

The Call Premium is:

- A dollar amount that is paid by the issuer as a penalty for the exercise of a call provision. It is usually stated as a percent of the principal amount that is being called.
- The difference between the call price and the par value of a callable preferred stock.

Call Risk

Call Risk is the risk that a high-yielding bond will be called by the issuer prior to maturity.

Callable

The term Callable can be used in two ways:

- When a firm issues debt or preferred shares, they may include a Callable feature that allows them to recall the security under predetermined conditions prior to the maturity of the issue.
- A Callable covenant in a bond indenture allows the Issuer to retire the issue at their discretion at a predetermined premium over the face value of the bond before the maturity date.

Canadian Depository for Securities

Canadian Depository for Securities Ltd. is the central depository and securities clearing house for the Montreal and Toronto Stock Exchanges.

Canadian Depository for Securities Link

The Canadian Depository for Securities (CDS) Link provides book entry clearance and settlement services to CDS participants trading equities and corporate bonds with US participants.

Canadian Derivatives Clearing Corporation

The Canadian Derivatives Clearing Corporation is the clearing agent for the settlement of derivative contracts that trade on the Montreal Exchange, the Toronto Stock Exchange, the Toronto Futures Exchange and the Vancouver Stock Exchange.

Canadian Imperial Bank of Commerce

The Canadian Imperial Bank of Commerce is a Canadian-based commercial bank.

www.cibc.com

Canadian Market Portfolio Index

The Canadian Market Portfolio Index is a stock index derived from equities listed on the Montreal Stock Exchange.

Cancellation

Cancellation of a bond occurs when an issue matures or is redeemed.

CAO

Abbreviation for Chief Administrative Officer

Cap

A Cap is a term that can be used in two ways:

- The top interest rate that can be paid on a floating-rate security
- An option strategy that sets a ceiling on the holder's interest rate exposure

See Capitalization

Capital Appreciation

Capital Appreciation is the increase in the market value of an investment from the time the security was purchased.

Capital Commitment

The value of a Market Maker's inventory is their Capital Commitment.

Market Maker, Inventory

Capital Debenture

A Capital Debenture is an unsecured instrument that must be converted into the debenture issuer's common stock by a specific date.

Capital Gain

A Capital Gain is a profit that results from the purchase and sale of a security.

Capital Gain Tax, Capital Loss

Capital Gain Tax

Capital Gains Tax is levied on the profits gained from the sale of an investment. Short term capital gains occur when an investment is held for six months or less; long term capital gains occur when an investment is held longer than six months. Short term and long term capital gains are treated differently for tax purposes.

Capital Gains Distribution

Capital Gains Distributions are made by a mutual fund to their participants, and are often taxed differently from payments that are made to distribute income.

Capital Loss

A Capital Loss is a loss of value due to trading or holding a security.

Capital Gain

Capital Stock

A firm's Capital Stock includes all of the shares that represent ownership of a business, including preferred and common shares.

Capital Structure

The Capital Structure of a firm consists of the stock and bonds that have been issued to finance the firm's activities.

Capitalization

A firm's Capitalization is the total value of various securities issued by a corporation calculated to be the current market price per share, multiplied by the total number of shares outstanding. Capitalization may include bonds, debentures, preferred stock, common stock and capital surplus. This is often referred to as the "Cap" or "Market Cap" for the firm.

Capped Style Option

A Capped Style Option is an option with a pre-defined profit cap or cap price. The cap price is determined by the option's strike price plus a premium for a call option or the strike price minus an amount for a put option. A capped option is automatically exercised when the underlying security closes at or above a call's cap or at or below a put's cap.

Exotic Option

Caracas Stock Exchange's General Index

The Caracas Stock Exchange's General Index is a stock index derived from equities listed on the Bolsa De Valores de Caracas.

Case Study

A Case Study is a narrative summary of a real life problem, along with a solution.

Cash Account

There are two types of Cash Accounts:

- For international institutional activity, the Cash Account is the account name and number at the Custodian or Sub-custodian where a client's cash is held. There may be separate cash and securities accounts for the customer.
- For US retail brokerage activity, the Cash Account is a specific type of an account, and is different from a margin account. In a cash account, securities purchased in the US must be paid for in full, normally by the third business day, but no later than the fifth business day after trade. The actual settlement date varies by instrument type and by country.

Securities Account, Safekeeping Account, Margin Account

Cash Basis

Cash Basis is an accounting method whereby transactions are not recorded until cash is exchanged. When used for determining the capital gain (or loss) earned on a securities position, cash basis is determined by multiplying the number of units held by the average acquisition price and subtracting that figure from the current market valuation of a position once it is sold.

Cash Concentration Account

A Cash Concentration Account aggregates the balances of several other accounts through automatic funds transfers.

Cash Pooling

Cash Correspondents

Cash Correspondents are banks:

- That are used by a Securities Settlement System in a country to send or receive payments
- That are used by other banks to settle local cash transactions

Securities Settlement System

Cash Deposit Risk

Cash Deposit Risk is the credit risk involved when a firm temporarily holds funds with an intermediary to settle securities transactions.

Cash Dividend

A Cash Dividend is a dividend that is paid for each share that is outstanding from the earnings of the corporation to the holders of an equity in cash or by check.

Dividend

Cash Equivalents

Cash Equivalents are investments of very short maturity, high liquidity and safety and are therefore virtually equal to cash in terms of risk. These include money market instruments, STIF and US Treasury bills.

Money Market Instruments, STIF

Cash Flow

Cash Flow is:

- A firm's net income plus bookkeeping deductions such as depreciation which are not paid out in actual dollars
- The net flow of funds in or out of a mutual fund

Cash Forecast

A Cash Forecast is a prediction of how much cash will be available in an account at a point in time. The forecast is used as a tool to improve cash management.

Cash Instructions

Cash Instructions are the delivery instructions for the cash side of a securities trade and involve a specific Cash Account. These instructions usually include an account name, account number and a bank agent name and number.

Cash Account

Cash Management

Cash Management is used to maximize the return on liquid assets. A firm's objective is to have enough cash on hand to meet immediate funding requirements plus regulatory reporting while simultaneously investing as much cash as possible in short term assets.

Cash Management Account

A Cash Management Account is a single account that is offered by a financial firm that offers banking and brokerage products in a single consolidated package.

Cash Market

See *Spot Market*

Cash Pooling

Cash Pooling is a summary of the available cash in multiple accounts. It is used to calculate interest and to determine net overdrafts. Cash does not actually move between accounts.

Cash Concentration Account

Cash Sale

A Cash Sale is one that settles on its trade date, rather than on the regularly scheduled settlement date.

Cash Trade

Cash Settlement

Cash Settlement occurs when the settlement is scheduled for the same day the trade is made. All cash trades in the US are usually completed by 2:00 PM.

Cash Sweep

A Cash Sweep is an automated process whereby all, or a portion, of the available cash is moved from a non-interest bearing account into an interest bearing account or an interest bearing instrument.

STIF

Cash Trade

A Cash Trade is one that usually settles on trade date, rather than on the regular way settlement date.

Trade Date, Settlement Date, Cash Sale, Regular Way

Cashier's Check

A Cashier's Check is a check whose payment is drawn on the bank's account and is guaranteed by the bank since it has already been paid for in advance by the customer who purchases the cashiers check.

Cashier's Department

The Cashier's Department is responsible for a variety of brokerage functions, including:

- Receive and Deliver
- Trade Clearing
- Bank Loans
- Securities Borrowing/Lending
- Reorganization
- Stock Transfer

Cash-In-Lieu

An investor might receive Cash-In-Lieu of the actual instrument:

- When the instrument is no longer available
- When the value of the instrument has increased and the amount due was based upon an old price
- When less than a whole share is due

CATS

See *Certificates of Accrual on Treasury Securities*

CBOE

See *Chicago Board Options Exchange*

CBOT

See *Chicago Board of Trade*

CBT

See *Chicago Board of Trade*

CD

The term CD can be used in three ways:

- Canadian Dollar
- See Certificate of Deposit
- See CD ROM

CD ROM

CD ROM stands for Compact Disk Read Only Memory. A CD ROM is used to store approximately 550 megabytes of data on a single disk that can be read by a computer.

Read Only Memory

CDSC

See *Contingent Deferred Sales Charge*

Cede

Cede is the nominee name for the Depository Trust Company.

Nominee

CEDEL

CEDEL is an international clearance and settlement depository (ICSD) located in Luxembourg. CEDEL's primary competitor is Euroclear.

CEDEL is dominant in Global Custody transactions, and processes approximately $1.0 billion annually and has deposits of over $1 trillion.

www.cedel.lu

Euroclear, ICSD, STP, Intersettle

Central Asset Management Accounts

Brokers and Banks have been offering Central Asset Management Accounts to their customers since Merrill Lynch pioneered the concept in 1980 with their CMA product. These accounts combine securities products and bank-like products to deliver a consolidated view of a client's financial position.

Asset Management Account, Cash Management Account

Central Computer Complex

The Central Computer Complex in Trumbull, Connecticut, is Nasdaq's data center. The data center supports more than 3,400 Nasdaq terminals in securities firms and financial institutions. It processes more than one million transactions per day.

Central de Valores Mobiliários e Sistema de Liquidação e Compensação

Central de Valores Mobiliários e Sistema de Liquidação e Compensação (CVM) is the central depository and securities clearing house of Portugal.

Central Depository Ltd.

Central Depository Ltd. (CDP) is a subsidiary of the Stock Exchange of Singapore, which provides clearing and book entry settlement of trades in the SESDAQ market in Malaysia.

Central Gilts Office

The Central Gilts Office is the computerized book entry settlement system operated by the Bank of England for gilt transactions.

Gilt

Central Processing Unit

The Central Processing Unit (CPU) of a computer is the actual brain of the computer.
In a mainframe it can be a group of physical entities that collectively manage the computer's processing. It allocates resources and directs the flow of information inside of a computer.

In a PC it is the chip that controls the computer.

Central Registration Depository

The CRD is an NASD system that maintains the employment, qualification, and disciplinary histories of the securities industry professionals who deal with the public.

Central Securities Depository

A Central Securities Depository is an institution which holds immobilized or dematerialized securities in a book entry form for a specific market, and is responsible for the centralized transfer against payment by entries on its books and records. Most local CSDs only maintain securities accounts and allow banks to maintain the related cash accounts.

Depositories are charged with safekeeping the physical certificates that have been issued for equities and bonds.

A Depository has several primary functions:

- Determining eligibility
- Immobilizing securities
- Re-registration in nominee name
- Book entry movements
- End of day cash settlements
- Collecting and distributing income and dividends
- Multiple Depositories that are interconnected

Book Entry, International Central Securities Depository

Central Securities Depository SA

Central Securities Depository SA is the central depository and securities clearing house of Greece.

Centralized Securities Depository of Chile

Centralized Securities Depository of Chile is the central depository and securities clearing house of Chile.

CEO

Abbreviation for Chief Executive Officer

Certificate

A Certificate is the physical document that establishes the ownership of an equity or a debt instrument.

Increasingly, stocks and bonds that are actively traded are immobilized in a depository, and the actual paper is no longer moved when purchases or sales occur.

Certificate of Deposit

A Certificate of Deposit (CD) is a short term debt instrument issued by banks or Savings and Loan Associations. CDs are established for a fixed amount, for a fixed period of time and usually for a fixed rate of interest. Larger denominations (usually over $25,000) are often negotiable and can be traded in the secondary market.

Negotiable CD's are issued by banks with maturities of 30-360 days in amounts generally over $100,000. In the secondary market, large denomination CD's can be sold through financial intermediaries to other investors before the CD matures, and without a pre-payment penalty.

Certificates of Accrual on Treasury Securities

Pronounced Cats

Certificates of Accrual on Treasury Securities are Zero Coupon Bonds that have been issued by Salomon Smith Barney.

Zero Coupon Bond

Certified Check

A Certified Check is created by a bank when it processes a customer's check by debiting the amount of the check from the customer's account and holding the amount in escrow until the check is presented for payment. Most certified checks must be exception processed.

CFA

Abbreviation for Chartered Financial Analyst

CFC

Abbreviation for Chartered Financial Counselor

CFO

Abbreviation for Chief Financial Officer

CFP

Abbreviation for Certified Financial Planner

CFSC

Abbreviation for Certified Financial Services Counselor

CFTC

See *Commodities Future Trading Commission*

CGO

See Central Gilts Office

Chaining

Chaining is an automated method of processing trades where the order in which the transfers are received is rearranged in order to increase the number or value of the transfers that can be settled with the available securities and cash.

Chambre de Liquidation

The Chambre de Liquidation is the settlement office of the Luxembourg Stock Exchange where physical delivery is required against payment for trade settlement.

Change Agent

A person or a department can be the initiator of any type of a change in a business, and is called a Change Agent. These changes can include changes to the organization, products, services, processing methods, technical support, etc.

CHAPS

See *Clearing Houses Automated Payments System*

Chapter 11

Chapter 11 is an option under the bankruptcy law where a trustee is appointed to manage the reorganization of the bankrupt firm. In a Chapter 11 bankruptcy, the firm intends to continue operations and hopes to recover and continue in business. Since the investors' existing claims may be reduced or replaced with another obligation, all creditors and owners must approve the plan before the reorganization can be confirmed by the court.

Chapter 7

Chapter 7

Chapter 7 is an option under the bankruptcy law where a bankrupt firm is liquidated after the courts have determined that the firm cannot be successfully reorganized. A trustee is assigned to liquidate the assets and distribute the proceeds to satisfy claims in an order of priority that is specified by law.

Chapter 11

Charter

See *Corporate Charter*

Chartist

A Chartist is a person who uses technical analysis techniques to present a stock's history and to predict future price changes.

Chase Manhattan Corporation

The Chase Manhattan Corporation is a US-based bank holding company.

www.chase.com

Chattel

Chattel is any property that can be moved.

Check Writing Privilege

A Check Writing Privilege is a service that is provided for some types of brokerage accounts and money market funds. It means that a customer receives a checkbook and can write checks against the account.

Cash Management Account

Checkpoint

A Checkpoint is a point in time or in a process where a manager's progress towards a plan can be measured.

Plan

CHF

Abbreviation for Swiss Francs

Chicago Board of Trade

The CBT (or CBOT) is a major commodity exchange, established in 1848, located at 141 East Jackson Boulevard, Chicago, Illinois.

The CBOT offers Financial Futures for US Treasury Bonds and Notes, GNMA, and commodity futures.

www.cbot.com

Chicago Board Options Exchange

The CBOE specializes in listed options, and was the first exchange to trade options, beginning in 1973.

CBOE provides liquidity to the options market and currently lists a wide range of options and futures, and has recently added Latin American instruments such as:

- Mexico 30 Index (Options, futures and options on futures)
- 18 ADRs and ADSs for Latin American firms
- CBOE Mexican Index (includes 10 US listed DR's, and country funds)
- Latin 15 index (tracks leading equities in Mexico, Argentina, Brazil and Chile)

www.cboe.com

Chicago Mercantile Exchange

The CME is a major commodity exchange in Chicago, Illinois that specializes in:

- Commodity Futures
- Foreign Currency Futures
- Stock Index Futures
- Futures Options Contracts

Chinese Wall

Chinese Wall is the term that is used to describe the requirement for a securities firm to separate the firm's trading and underwriting departments in order to restrict access to non-public, material information.

Glass-Steagall Act

CHIPS

Clearing House Interbank Payments System

Churning

Churning occurs when a broker trades excessively in a customer's account in order to increase commissions. This violates the industry's rules.

Rules of Fair Practice

CIC

Abbreviation for Chartered Investment Counselor

CICS

CICS stands for complex instruction set computing, and is the primary method of programming the on-line, real-time portions of mainframe applications.

COBOL

CIEBA

Committee on Investment of Employee Benefit Assets is a committee of the Financial Executives Institute.

CINS

See *CUSIP International Numbering System*

CIO

The abbreviation CIO can be used in two ways:

- Chief Information Officer
- Chief Investment Officer

Circuit Breaker

A Circuit Breaker is a procedure that temporarily halts trading on an exchange when a predefined event occurs such as a large-scale sell-off.

At the New York Stock Exchange, trading halts for:

- Sixty minutes if the DJIA drops by 10% before 1PM

- Thirty minutes if the DJIA drops by 10% between 2PM and 3PM
- Trading halts for the day if the DJIA drops by 10% after 2:30PM or by 20% at any other time.

Other exchanges will also halt trading when the NYSE does. The Chicago Mercantile Exchange has established a set of trading halts for its various stock exchange indices. These procedures are in place to help prevent crisis selling in the markets.

DJIA

Citicorp

Citicorp is a New York-based bank holding company, with its headquarters at 399 Park Avenue, New York, NY 10043.

Citigroup

www.citibank.com

Citigroup

Citigroup is the firm that resulted from the merger of Citicorp and Travelers Insurance.

Citicorp

Claim

A Claim is a formal demand for money or other relief.

Class Action Lawsuit

A Class Action Lawsuit is one where one entity or a limited number of entities sue on behalf of a larger group. Proceeds from the lawsuit, if any, are distributed among all affected entities.

Class of Options

There are several Classes of Options:

- American puts or calls
- European puts or calls
- Capped puts or calls
- Exotic puts and calls

Put, Call, American Style Option, European Style Option, Capped Style Option

Classes of Shares

Classes of Shares can be used to identify mutual funds and equities in the following manner:

- Mutual Funds can have multiple classes in a single portfolio that permit investors to purchase the portfolio in different ways. For example, Class A shares of a fund could give retail investors the option of paying a front-end sales load, Class B shares could give retail investors the option of having a contingent deferred sales charge, etc.

- Equities can have different classes of shares based upon the rights that are offered. For instance, Class A shares might have one vote for each share, Class B shares might have one vote for each ten shares, etc.

CLC

CLC is the clearing organization and central depository for transactions not taking place on the São Paulo Stock Exchange in Brazil.

Clearance

Clearance is the process, prior to settlement, of determining accountability for the exchange of money and securities between the counterparties to a transaction. Clearing occurs between brokers and frequently involves netting, settlement, margin and the provision of a settlement guarantee.

Settlement, Trade Life Cycle, Netting

Cleared Date

See *Cleared Funds*

Value Date, Available Date

Cleared Funds

Cleared Funds is that portion of an account which has been cleared through a cash settlement system and has become available for use. Once funds have been cleared, they cannot be returned.

Ledger Balance, Available Funds

Clearing

See *Clearance*

Clearing House Electronic Sub-register System

Clearing House Electronic Sub-register System (CHESS) is the clearing and settlement system for bonds and equities in Australia.

Clearing Agencies

Brokers have established Clearing Agencies to simplify the movement of securities and payments between firms to settle their trades. The largest Clearing Agency in the US is the NSCC.

Clearing Agent

A Clearing Agent is an intermediary, usually a bank, that works between the buyer and seller to settle transactions. A Clearing Agent is also known as Clearing Broker, Sub-agent, Sub-custodian, or Settlement Agent.

Clearing Broker, Agent Settlement, Sub-Agent, Sub-Custodian

Clearing Broker

A Clearing Broker is a broker who agrees to settle security transactions for another broker for a fee. Also known as a Clearing Agent, Sub-agent, Sub-custodian, or Settlement Agent.

Agent Settlement, Sub-Agent, Sub-Custodian

Clearing Corporation

A Clearing Corporation is a centralized processing center that is operated for its brokerage firm members.

The functions provided by the Clearing Corporations typically include:

- Receive and deliver
- Trade recording, comparison and pricing

Clearing House

A Clearing House is:

- The processing arm of a futures exchange which clears the trades by matching purchases and sales. This type of clearing house will act like a Clearing Corporation.
- A group of banks that work together to process transactions among themselves in an efficient manner

Clearance, Clearing Corporation

Clearing House Comparison

The Clearing House Comparison form is used to submit trades to the NSCC that have missed the normal entry methods.

Clearing House Interbank Payments System

The CHIPS network offers clearing service for high-value, real-time payments between US banks in the US.

Clearing Houses Automated Payments System

The CHAPS network offers clearing service for high-value, real-time payments between US banks in the UK.

Clearing Processing System

The Clearing Processing System is LIFFE's system which supplies all members with their real-time positions and margin calculations. It also maintains accounts and informs members of all account changes and positions.

Clearing Slips

Clearing Slips are pieces of paper with the details of the trade that was just completed. It is filled in by clearing members and sent to LIFFE for input to the Trade Registration System.

See Trade Registration System

Client

A Client:

- In a client/server system is an application that generally interacts with the user and places demands upon other elements of the system, called servers
- Is a customer who repeatedly buys from a firm, thereby developing an on-going relationship. A client differs from a customer who may only buy once or who does not have an on-going relationship with the firm.

Client/Server, Server

Client/Server

A Client/Server system consists of two main parts, a client that requests and uses the output of servers, which often store data and perform certain processing functions.

Clone Fund

A Clone Fund is a mutual fund that is started by a fund manager when one mutual fund becomes so large that its management feels the fund's investment alternatives are limited. When Fidelities Magellan Fund grew too large, a new fund was created for new customers.

Closed End Fund

A Closed End Fund or Closed End Investment Company is an investment company with a fixed number of outstanding shares which are traded on a securities exchange, or via the over-the-counter market.

The number of shares outstanding is limited by the company's charter and their value is determined in the open market. No new shares are available after the initial offering.

Open End Company

Closely Held

A Closely Held issue is one in which there are very few owners of the issue.

Closing Price

The Closing Price is the price of a security's final transaction on a specific trading day. Closing prices are listed daily in the financial pages of many newspapers, and include:

- Number of shares traded
- Opening price
- High price for the day
- Low price for the day
- Closing price
- Net change from the previous day

Closing Purchase

A Closing Purchase is the transaction that is used to eliminate a short position.

Closing Transaction

Closing Sale

A Closing Sale is a transaction where the seller intents to reduce or eliminate a long position in a given series of options.

Closing Transaction

A Closing Transaction is:

- When an option writer purchases a listed option that has the same terms as an option previously sold

- When an investor sells all of the shares or bonds held for a specific security

Closing Purchase, Closing Sale

CMA

See *Cash Management Account*

CME

See *Chicago Mercantile Exchange*

CMO

See *Collateralized Mortgage Obligation*

CNS

See *Continuous Net Settlement*

COBOL

COBOL, an abbreviation for Common Business Oriented Language, is a programming language used primarily for batch applications.

COBOL/CICS

See *COBOL*

See *CICS*

Code

Code:

- As a verb, means to write the instructions in a computer language that will tell a computer what actions it should take under specific circumstances
- As a noun, is the set of written instructions that tells the computer what to do

COF

Abbreviation for Cost of Funds

COLD

See *Computer Output to Laser Disk*

Collar

A Collar is:

The simultaneous purchase of a put and the sale of a call on similar underlying securities.

The upper and lower limits on the interest rate of a floating-rate security. The upper limit is the Cap and the lower limit is the floor.

Put, Call

Collateral

Collateral is an asset that is given by a borrower to a lender to support the borrower's intent to repay the loan. If the borrower defaults on the loan, the lender can keep or sell the collateral as payment for the loan.

Default

Collateral Trust Bonds

Collateral Trust Bonds are bonds that are secured by other securities (stocks and bonds) which are often controlled by the issuer and are deposited with a trustee. These bonds are only as secure as the creditworthiness of the issuer and the market value of the deposited securities.

Sometimes a large company will issue bonds in a subsidiary and use bonds issued by the parent as collateral.

Collateralized Mortgage Obligation

A Collateralized Mortgage Obligation (CMO) is one type of pass-through mortgage-backed fixed income instrument that gives the buyer an interest in, but not ownership of, the underlying assets.

CMOs are divided into various segments called tranches. Each tranche consists of a different group of securities with a similar maturity date. In a typical mortgage-backed security, the investor owns a share of the underlying mortgages proportionate to their investment and receives repayment of principal and interest as it occurs.

In a CMO, the investors in the earlier tranches are repaid in full before the owners of the later tranches are paid principal. This helps the investor determine when they wish to be repaid and eliminates the risk of early pre-payment.

Tranche

Collection Agent

A Collection Agent is a corporate trust function, where the trustee receives coupons and forwards them to the paying agent.

Corporate Trust, Paying Agent, Trustee

Collective Trust

See *Common Trust Fund*

College Construction Loan Insurance Association

College Construction Loan Insurance Association, or Connie Lee as it is known, was established in 1987 to guarantee loans to construct colleges in the US. Connie Lee is owned by the Department of Education and by Sallie Mae.

Colombo Stock Exchange

The Colombo Stock Exchange is the primary stock exchange of Sri Lanka.

www.lanka.net/slweb/slstock.html

Co-Manager

See *Co-Underwriter*

Combination Order

A Combination Order is one where two orders are entered simultaneously for options with the same underlying security.

Option

Combo Trade

A Combo Trade is a LIFFE option trading strategy where the transaction shorts a call and goes long on a put at a lower exercise price.

COMEX

COMEX is the commodity exchange located at 4 World Trade Center, New York, New York.

Comfort Letter

A Comfort Letter is an accounting firm's official statement that is given to a firm that is preparing to go public. The letter reports the accountants' comfort that unaudited financial data in the company's prospectus consistently follows GAAP, and that no material changes have occurred since the report was prepared.

GAAP

Commercial Paper

Commercial Paper is a short term, negotiable, unsecured promissory note that is issued by large corporations in bearer form on a discount or coupon basis to raise working capital for any term up to 270 days. The rate of interest is set when it is issued and can only be realized if held to maturity.

Commercial Paper can be traded in the secondary market.

Commission

A Commission can be:

- The compensation for an account executive for purchasing or selling securities or property as an agent. This fee may or may not be negotiated.
- The amount charged by a broker to buy or sell securities for a customer
- The amount paid to a real estate agent or broker for negotiating a real estate or an transaction

Commission Billing for Listed Equities

Commission Billing for Listed Equities is an automated service that allows participants to debit and credit commissions for other participants. Each firm can submit an automated commission bill file to NSCC thereby eliminating individual checks between participants.

Commission House Broker

A Commission House Broker is a person who executes orders on the exchange floor for their firm and for their firm's customers.

Floor Broker

Commission Settlement and Global Update Service

The Commission Settlement and Global Update Service:

Automates the exchange of commission information for mutual funds between participants and the funds, and centralizes the commission payments into NSCC's settlement system.

Allows participants to provide mutual funds with global update information that affects numerous accounts.

Commitment

A Commitment is:

- A pledge or promise to do something in the future
- A promise to lend under specific terms and conditions

Commodities Future Trading Commission

The Commodities Future Trading Commission (CFTC), established in 1974, is the federal agency responsible for enforcing the futures industry's rules and regulations.

Commodity Futures Trading Act of 1974

The Commodity Futures Trading Act of 1974 established the Commodities Futures Trading Commission (CFTC), which oversees procedures and regulations for future trading.

CFTC

Commodity Trading Advisor

A Commodity Trading Advisor (CTA) is anyone who, for compensation or for profit, exercises trading authority over a customer's commodities account or gives advice on the advisability of buying or selling futures and/or options, whether directly or through written publications or other media.

Common Message Switch

The Common Message Switch (CMS) is the store-and-forward message-switching system that connects NYSE member firms to the systems that are used by different US exchanges. CMS also forwards orders from member firms to the NYSE SuperDot system, which then processes them.

SuperDot

Common Stock

See *Equity*

Common Stock Fund

A Common Stock Fund is a mutual fund that limits its investment to shares of common stocks.

Common Trust Fund

A Common Trust Fund is a trust fund that permits the assets of several trusts to be commingled.

Collective Trust

Company Risk

Company Risk is the risk that the issuer of a security will be unable to meet their obligations.

Comparison

See *Matching*

Clearing Corporation, Trade-for-Trade

Compensating Controls

Compensating Controls are manual or automated controls that are designed to be used instead of a preventive control which is impractical for a specific process.

Detective Controls, Preventive Controls

Competitive Market Makers

See *Competitive Trader*

Competitive Trader

A Competitive Trader is a member of the exchange who trades in stocks on the exchange floor for their own account.

Competitive Underwriting

In a Competitive Underwriting, several different investment bankers will submit bids to be the underwriting manager.

Underwriting Manager, Negotiated Underwriting

Compile

A computer will Compile source code into object code so that it can be understood by the computer.

Object Code, Source Code

Compliance

See *Compliance Departments*

Compliance Departments

Compliance Departments have been established in markets and firms to oversee activity and ensure that trading complies with the appropriate regulations.

Composite Quotation Service

See *Consolidated Quotation System*

Compound Interest

See *Compounding*

Compounding

Compounding occurs when the interest earned on principal is retained in the investment to calculate future interest payments. With compounding, the next interest calculation will be based upon the original principal plus the interest that was already earned.

Interest may be compounded daily, monthly, quarterly, semiannually, or annually.

When a dividend is reinvested in the same equity, it is called a Dividend Reinvestment Plan (DRIP). When an interest payment on a bond is used to buy additional bonds, it is called IRIP.

DRIP, IRIP

Compounding Returns

See *Compounding*

Compression

See *File Compression*

Comptroller of the Currency

See *Office of the Comptroller of the Currency*

Computer Assisted Execution System

The Computer Assisted Execution System (CAES) is an inter-dealer automated execution service for Nasdaq that automates order routing and execution for securities that are listed on domestic exchanges under 19c3 by linking Market Makers with specialists on an exchange floor through the Intermarket Trading System.

Intermarket Trading System

Computer Output to Laser Disk

Computer Output to Laser Disk (COLD) refers to a method of transcribing data onto a laser disk for storage and future recovery.

Computer to Computer Facility

Computer to Computer Facility (CCF) is a batch oriented facility established by The Depository Trust Company for the transfer of data files between DTC and its participants. CCF uses a DTC proprietary protocol.

Computer to Computer Facility II

Computer to Computer Facility II is a batch oriented facility established by The Depository Trust Company for the transfer of data files between DTC and its participants. CCFII uses an industry standard protocol.

Computer-to-Computer Interface

Computer-to-Computer Interface (CTCI) has two definitions:

- Generically, a Computer-to-Computer Interface is a direct electronic connection between two computers.
- CTCI is the name of a high speed communication interface between large NASD member firms' mainframes and the Nasdaq system.

Confirm

See *Confirmation*

Confirmation

Brokers are required to send a Confirmation containing the details of an authorized trade. The Confirmation includes such information as price, security description, settlement money, trade and settlement dates.

Retail customers continue to receive physical (or paper) confirmations. Institutional Investment Advisors receive electronic notification via the DTC's ID system and are required to respond to the trade by issuing an electronic affirmation. Brokers can supplement the electronic notification to Investment Managers by sending paper if the Manager requests such an arrangement.

Affirmation, DTC, Institutional Delivery System

Confirmation Systems

Confirmation Systems are used by brokers and investment managers to exchange trade details followed by legal confirmation of the trade. Delivery methods such as ETC, DTC-ID and Domestic OASYS are included in this category.

ETC, Institutional Delivery System

Conflict of Interest

A Conflict of Interest can arise when:

- A person takes a gift from a supplier when they are in a position to recommend the supplier's services or products
- A fiduciary represents two conflicting interests

Conglomerate

A Conglomerate is a diversified corporation that typically grows by buying businesses in very different industries.

Connectivity

Connectivity is becoming an increasingly important area of interest for firms in the securities business. Automated electronic connectivity is available from vendors of various solutions:

- ETC Solution Providers
- Crossing Networks
- Confirmation Systems
- Clearance and Settlement Systems
- Portfolio Management
- Custody Systems
- Market Data Vendors
- Trade Reporting Systems
- Electronic Communication Networks
- Order Management Systems
- Order Indication Systems
- Order Routing Systems

Conservative Investor

An investor's risk tolerance is Conservative when they emphasize conservation of principal over obtaining a greater return on their investment.

Risk Tolerance, Aggressive Investor, Moderate Investor

Consolidated Financial Statement

A Consolidated Financial Statement is a financial accounting report that combines all of a firm's assets and liabilities, plus the operating accounts of a company and its subsidiaries.

Consolidated Quotation System

The Consolidated Quotation System (CQS) is an electronic service that electronically collects and disseminates current bid and asked quotations and volume for stocks listed on the New York and American Stock Exchanges, regional stock exchanges, and issues traded by NASD member firms in the third market.

Nasdaq processes this data and provides it to subscribers through the Composite Quotation Service.

Third Market

Consolidated Tape

The Consolidated Tape is a high-speed system that continuously provides public information on the last sale price and volume for listed stocks transactions. All NYSE-listed securities traded, regardless of the trading market, are reported on the ticker system.

The following market centers are Consolidated Tape participants:

- American Stock Exchange (AMEX)
- Boston Stock Exchange (BSE)
- Chicago Board Options Exchange (CBOE)
- Cincinnati Stock Exchange (CSE)
- Chicago Stock Exchange (CHX)
- National Association of Securities Dealers (NASD)
- New York Stock Exchange (NYSE)
- Pacific Stock Exchange (PSE)
- Philadelphia Stock Exchange (PHLX)

Consolidated Tape Association

The Consolidated Tape Association (CTA) is the administrative authority for information on exchange-listed securities. It administers the Consolidated Tape System that, for a fee, provides market prices.

See *Consolidated Tape System*

Consolidated Trade System

The Consolidated Trade System (CTS), owned by the exchanges, electronically receives and disseminates last-sale prices on listed stock for all markets in which they trade.

Consumer Price Index

The Consumer Price Index (CPI) is used in the United States and Canadian to measure the composite price of a selected group of goods and services which are typical purchased by urban families.

Contact

A Contract is created for futures and options transactions.

Option

Contingency

A Contingency is a condition which must be satisfied before a contract is legally binding.

Contingency Planning

Firms engage in Contingency Planning when they consider possible future events that could negatively affect their business, and prepare plans to react to these possibilities.

Contingent Deferred Sales Charge

A Contingent Deferred Sales Charge is established for a 12b-1 plan as a back-end load for a fund that is sold by a broker. The sales charge could phase out in increments over a period of years.

SEC Rule 12b-1

Continuous Improvement

Operations Managers generally engage in a process of Continuous Improvement when they routinely examine their process and look for incremental ways to make things work better.

Kaisen

Continuous Net Settlement

Continuous Net Settlement (CNS) is NSCC's automated book entry accounting system that centralizes the clearance of compared security transactions. Throughout each trading day, CNS nets each participant's security obligations into one net position for each issue, and one overall net cash position. NSCC becomes the contra-party to each compared trade and guarantees settlement for eligible transactions.

Trades that fail today will be held by CNS for the next day's activity.

Contra

The word Contra is used to denote the opposite of something or the offset for something. For example:

- The contra-account for account 123 is account 456
- The contra-broker for this trade is Merrill Lynch

Counterparty

Contract Month

The Contract Month is the month in which a futures contract is fulfilled.

Delivery Month

Contract Note

See *Confirm*

Contrarian

A Contrarian is an investor who decides which securities to buy and sell by going against the crowd.

Crowd

Controlled Disbursement Account

A Controlled Disbursement Account is a central account that is used to clear checks and to fund overdrafts in subordinate accounts.

Convergence

Convergence is the movement of the cash asset price towards the futures price as the expiration date of a futures contract approaches.

Conversion

A Conversion occurs when one instrument is exchanged for another instrument, usually with the same company. An example of a conversion is when a convertible bond or preferred shares are exchanged for common shares.

Conversion Agent

A Conversion Agent is a trustee that exchanges one class of security for another.

Trustee

Conversion Clause

A Conversion Clause is a provision in some Adjustable Rate Mortgages (ARMs) that allows the mortgagee to change an ARM to a fixed-rate loan.

Adjustable Rate Mortgage

Conversion Price

The Conversion Price is the price at which a convertible instrument may be converted.

Conversion

Convertible ARM

A Convertible ARM is a type of Adjustable Rate Mortgage (ARM) loan that allows the mortgagee to convert to a fixed-rate loan during a given time period.

Adjustable Rate Mortgage

Convertible Bond

A Convertible Bond or debenture is a fixed income instrument which can be converted into the common stock *of* a corporation at a predetermined price or ratio at the option of the holder of the instrument.

Convertible Debentures

Convertible Debentures

See *Convertible Bond*

Convertible Preferred Stock

Preferred Convertible Stock is an issue which, under certain conditions, can be converted into the common stock of the same company.

Preferred Stock, Common Stock

Convertible Security

See Convertible Bond

See Convertible Preferred Stock

Conveyance

A Conveyance is a document that is used to transfer a deed, mortgage, or other instrument.

COO

Abbreviation for Chief Operating Officer

Cooling-off Period

The Cooling-off Period is the time between the registration statement for a new issue is filed with the Securities and Exchange Commission and the effective date of the offering. The period is usually 20 days.

Underwriting

Copenhagen Stock Exchange

The Copenhagen Stock Exchange is the primary stock exchange of Denmark.

Corporate Action

A Corporate Action is an event, determined by a corporation's Board of Directors, that changes the existing corporate capital structure or financial condition.

There are several different categories of Corporate Actions, including:

- Fully Called
- Future Partial Call
- Partially Called
- Matured
- Name Change
- Converted
- Exchanged
- Merged
- Tendered
- Spin-off
- Split
- Reverse Split
- Rights Offering
- Warrant Offering

- Liquidated

Corporate Agency Services

A financial firm provides Corporate Agency Services when they sell their processing services to another firm for a fee.

Correspondent Clearing, White Label

Corporate Bond

A Corporate Bond is a fixed-income instrument issued by a corporation. A corporate bond carries a fixed rate of interest that the issuer must pay to the bondholder, as well as a promise to repay the principal when the bond matures or is called. Some corporate bonds may be issued as variable rate bonds. The life of a bond may be as long as 30 years.

Bond, Variable Rate Bond, Fixed Rate Bond, Maturity, Call

Corporate Bond Fund

A Corporate Bond Fund is a mutual fund that invests in long-term corporate bonds and generally passes the income on these securities to its shareholders.

Corporate Charter

The Corporate Charter is a legal document that is issued by a corporation at the time of its incorporation. The charter defines the number of shares authorized, limitations of ownership, and other rules that define how the corporation can operate.

Corporate Reorganization

A Corporate Reorganization occurs when a firm makes a change to their capital structure or issues new securities.

Corporate Trust

Corporate Trust is the function of a bank that involves overseeing the administration of bond issues with regard to an issue's indenture terms.

As an agent of the issuer, acting on behalf of the shareholders, a trustee could be assigned any of the following agency roles:

- Paying Agent
- Transfer Agent
- Stock Registrar

Paying Agent, Registrar, Transfer Agent

Corporate Trustee

A Corporate Trustee is a trust company or the trust department of a bank that is responsible for the administration of an issue. The Corporate Trustee is paid by the issuer and is responsible to the bondholders.

Corporate Trust

Corporation

A Corporation is an artificial legal entity, that was established by other entities called incorporators, which has been established by law for some specific purpose as defined by its charter.

Corpus

The Corpus is the principal portion of a bond. The other portion, representing interest, is the coupon.

Coupon

Correction

A Correction is the reverse movement (usually downward) in the price of an individual stock, bond, commodity or index after any long-term move.

Correlation

See Correlation Coefficient

Correlation Coefficient

A Correlation Coefficient is a statistical relationship between two measurable activities. If, when one changes and the other changes similarly, then the two have a positive correlation. If, when one changes, the other changes in the opposite direction, then the two are negatively correlated.

A correlation does not imply a cause and effect relationship.

Correspondent Bank

A Correspondent Bank is one that offers its processing and lending services to other banks for a fee.

Correspondent Clearer

See *Correspondent Clearing*

Correspondent Clearing

Correspondent Clearing is:

- A function provided by brokers to other brokers, where the Correspondent Clearer acts as the back office for the other brokers. These services include back office operations and technology and usually involve real-time front end systems.
- An NSCC process for equity and corporate bond transactions executed by NSCC members on behalf of other participants.

Cost Basis

The Cost Basis of a security is the accounting method that will be used to determine the cost that is used. There are several different types of accounting methods used for determining cost basis:

- FIFO: First In – First Out
- LIFO: Last In – First Out
- Average Cost

First In – First Out, Last In – First Out, Average Cost

Cost of Capital

A firm's Cost of Capital is:

- The interest rate that a company must pay for its capital
- The minimum rate of return that is required to maintain the market value of a company's common stock

Cost of Funds

The Cost of Funds is the rate that a firm must pay to borrow short term money.

Cost of Capital

Co-Transfer Agent

See *Transfer Agent*

Co-Underwriter

A Co-Underwriter assists another underwriter in bringing an initial public offering to market. The lead underwriter and the co-underwriters, also called co-managers, jointly form a syndicate.

Underwriter, IPO, Syndicate

Counterclaim

A Counterclaim is a claim by the defendant against the claimant.

Counterparty

A counterparty is any one party to a trade who is legally bound to make a good delivery of the securities or cash that were involved in the trade.

The term is usually used by one party to the trade to identify the other party.

Counterparty Risk

Counterparty Risk is the potential for a loss that could result from a default on a payment due.

Credit Risk

Country Risk

Country Risk is the risk that an investment in a particular country will lose value due to local economic or political conditions.

Coupon

The term Coupon can be used in two ways:

- The term Coupon is also often used to denote the nominal interest rate on a bond, even if it is a registered bond without coupons.
- For some categories of bonds, a Coupon is a physical document that must be detached from a bond and presented to a specified authority in order to receive the interest that is due.

Coupon Bond, Nominal Interest Rate

Coupon Bond

A Coupon Bond is a negotiable bond where the interest is paid to the person who physically clips the coupon and deposits it with a Paying Agent or Co-Paying Agent. Upon maturity, the bearer is paid the face value of the security.

Paying Agent, Coupon

Coupon Instruments

A Coupon Instrument is a security that has a coupon attached.

Coupon Paying Agent

See *Paying Agent*

Covariance

The Covariance is the correlation between two securities, multiplied by the standard deviation for each.

Covenants

A Covenant is any legally enforceable promise made by one party to another.

Indenture

Covered Call

A Covered Call is a call where the option writer:

- Owns the underlying security
- Owns another call on the same underlying security with an exercise price equal to or less than the exercise price of the call sold
- Owns a security convertible into the underlying security
- Has sold the underlying security short

Option, Call, Option Writer

Covered Option

A Covered Option is one that has been written as the offset to an existing position in the underlying instrument. Covered Options are generally written to increase the writer's yield.

Option, Naked Option

Covered Put

A Covered Put is a put where the option writer:

- Owns a put on the same underlying security with an exercise price equal to or greater than the exercise price of the put written
- Has sold the underlying security short
- Owns the underlying security
- Owns a security convertible into the underlying security

Option, Put, Option Writer

CPA

Abbreviation for Certified Public Accountant

CPI

See *Consumer Price Index*

CPS

See Clearing Processing System

CPU

See *Central Processing Unit*

CQS

See *Consolidated Quotation System*

CRD

See *Central Registration Depository*

Credit

The term Credit is used in two ways:

- A Credit is an accounting term that is the opposite of a debit
- A firm can provide Credit if they grant a loan to a borrower

Debit Balance

Credit Balance

A Credit Balance is:

- The money in a customer's cash or margin account that is available for use
- The net amount that a customer is short in a brokerage account

Debit Balance, Net Position

Credit History

A firm's Credit History is the record of their previous ability to repay debt.

Credit Only When Paid

When an account or an issue is coded as Credit Only When Paid, it indicates that the bank or broker will not credit a customer's account until they have actually received the cash. This term is usually used in the Income Collection process.

Income Collection

Credit Rating

A firm's Credit Rating is the grade established by a recognized credit agency, which defines a borrower's ability to meet their financial obligations in a timely manner.

Credit Report

A Credit Report is a report that is used to help determine a potential borrower's creditworthiness.

Credit Rating

Credit Risk

Credit Risk is:

- The risk that a party to a contract will not be able to pay their obligation
- The risk that a counterparty will not settle an obligation for full value, either when due or at any time thereafter

Credit risk includes replacement cost risk, principal risk and cash deposit risk.

Credit Suisse Group

The Credit Suisse Group is a Swiss-based Universal Bank.

www.credit-suisse.com

CREST

CREST is a UK-based electronic book entry settlement system developed by the Bank of England to replace Taurus.

Crobex Index

The Crobex Index is a stock index derived from equities listed on the Croatian Stock Exchange.

Cross

A Cross is a purchase or sále that involves the exchange of assets between two accounts versus payment. This is also known as Swap.

Swap

Cross Currency Spreads

Cross Currency Spreads are transactions where contracts relating to different interest rate markets are bought and sold simultaneously.

Cross Reference

A Cross Reference file is one that defines the relationships between two lists of data.

Cross-Border Settlement

A Cross-Border Settlement is a settlement that takes place in a country other than the one in which either of the trade counterparties are located.

Crossed Quotations

See *Locked Quotation*

Crossing Network

Crossing Networks, also called Matching Networks, are used by institutional investors to find counterparties without the help of a broker.

Electronic Crossing Network

Crowd

The Crowd is the group of brokers that come to the trading post on an exchange to make a trade.

CS First Boston

CS First Boston is the US-based brokerage subsidiary of the Credit Swisse Group.

www.csfb.com

CSD

See *Central Securities Depository*

CTA

See Commodity Trading Advisors

CTA

See *Consolidated Tape Association*

See Commodity Trading Advisors

CTCI

See *Computer-to-Computer Interface*

Cumulative Preferred Stock

Cumulative Preferred Stock has a provision that if the issuing firm is unable to pay a preferred dividend in any period, it will accumulate until the firm is able to pay it. No dividend for common shares can be paid until all of the obligations of a cumulative preferred share are met.

Cumulative Rate of Return

A compounded rate of return that covers more than one year.

Curb Exchange

See *Curb Market*

Curb Market

Prior to 1800, brokers trading the stock of small firms met in the streets of the financial district to find counterparties. This arrangement became known as the Curb Market. By 1900, they generally met on Broad Street near the existing NYSE building, and in 1921, the Curb Market began trading in a new building on Trinity Place. In 1953, the Curb Market changed its name to the American Stock Exchange.

Currency Conversion

A Currency Conversion occurs when one currency is exchanged for another through a process of buying and selling.

Currency Risk

Currency Risk is the risk that an investor in multiple markets takes that the value of a local currency will decrease relative to the investor's base currency.

Base Currency

Current Assets

Current Assets include cash and other liquid instruments, including accounts receivable. Current Assets have to be convertible to cash within a maximum of one year.

Balance Sheet

Current Income Objective

An investor has a Current Income Objective when they have a preference for investments that generate income rather than capital appreciation.

Current Maturity

Current Maturity is either:

- The length of time before a security matures
- The stated maturity date

Current Price

Current Price is the last price at which a sale occurred.

Current Yield

The Current Yield is a bond's annual interest rate calculated as the annual interest amount divided by its current market price. Current yield is also known as running yield or interest yield.

Cursor

The Cursor is the icon that identifies the user location on the screen of a graphical user interface.

Icon, Graphical User Interface

CUSIP

Pronounced Que-Sip

CUSIP is the system created by the ABA's Committee on Uniform Security Identification Procedures to provide unique identifying numbers for equities and registered debt in the US and Canada. The 9 digit CUSIP number for any given security series is different from the ISIN number.

The CUSIP contains a segment which is unique for each issuer (first 6 digits), and another segment which is unique for each security (next 2 digits, plus a check digit).
CUSIPs are required for all Debt instruments over $500,000 and for any equity that is registered with the SEC.

Because of the limitation of only 100 issues for each issuer, there is a potential problem with Options and Municipal Securities.

www.cusip.com

ABA, ISIN

CUSIP International Numbering System

The CUSIP International Numbering System was developed to establish securities codes for non-US securities using the CUSIP format. A single letter is added to the beginning of a CUSIP-like to number to identify the country of issue. For example, A (Austria), E (Spain, J (Japan), etc.

CUSIP

Custodian

A Custodian is the organization (usually a bank) that keeps custody of securities and provides other value-added services for firms such as Mutual Funds, corporate clients, pension funds and individuals.

Custody, Sub-Custodian

Custodian Delivery Instructions

The Custodian Delivery Instructions identify the Investment Manager's Custodian's Clearing Agent, account name and number and any special instructions that are needed to settle a transaction.

Broker Delivery Instructions, Delivery Instructions

Custody

Custody is the safekeeping and administration of securities and cash provided by one entity on behalf of another. The administrative activities of custody include such issue-servicing activities as:

- Income Collection
- Corporate Actions
- Pricing
- Cash Management
- Foreign Exchange
- Securities Lending
- Reporting
- Performance Measurement
- Statement Generation

Income Collection, Corporate Action, Performance Measurement, Cash Management, Foreign Exchange, Securities Lending

Custody Risk

Custody Risk is the risk of loss of securities held in custody that could result from the insolvency, negligence or fraudulent action of the custodian or of a sub-custodian.

Custody System

Investment Managers link to a custodian's Custody Systems to send trade instructions and receive holdings and transaction positions.

The primary functions of a Custody System are:

- Collect information and instructions from customers, brokers, depositories, clearing corporations, regulators and transfer agents
- Process transactions and update customer files
- Provide information that includes a description of the assets and money received/disbursed, income collected, and trade instructions
- Update master files to provide accurate and updated data
- Produce management and customer reports

Customer

See *Client*

Customer Agreement

See *New Account Information Form*

Customer Complaints

Customer Complaints occur when a customer feels that they have not been treated fairly on a trade or if they feel that an error has been made. Customer complaints are initially made directly to the firm. If they remain unsatisfied, a customer may request arbitration.

Investigation, Inquiry

Customer Protection Rule

See *SEC Rule 15c3-3*

Segregation, Inventory

Customer Service

Customer service is:

- As a verb, the act of responding to a customer's inquiry, investigation or request
- As a noun, either the department that deals directly with customer issues or the process that is involved in responding to a customer's inquiry, investigation or request

Investigation, Inquiry

Customer Side

See *Street Side*

Cutting a Loss

Cutting a Loss is the decision to close out an unprofitable position and take a loss now, rather than hope that the market value will rise.

Cyclical Stocks

Cyclical stocks are those which tend to move in conjunction with the business cycle.

Business Cycle

Dai-Ichi Kangyo Bank, Ltd.

Dai-Ichi Kangyo Bank, Ltd. is a Japanese-based bank.

www.infoweb.or.jp/dkb

Data

The term Data is both singular or plural, and refers to the collection of numbers and words that are categorized and stored in a computer. When organized for a user, data becomes information.

Information

Data Center

A Data Center is the place where large computers are run. It is generally a controlled environment and is secure.

Data Element

A Data Element is a single unit of useful numbers or words, such as a name, telephone number, price, etc.

Data

Data Entity

A Data Entity is a category of data such as customer names, security master file, etc.

Data

Data Mapping

Data Mapping is a process of identifying the purpose of data elements in one system and identifying the corresponding data element name in another. The procedure is done so that a computer programmer can write a program that will move the data from the first system to the second system.

Data

Data Model

A Data Model is a graphical representation of the relationships between data entities.

Data, Data Entity

Data Processing

Data Processing is one term that describes the overall process of developing and maintaining applications and running the computers that support the applications.

Data Storage

Data Storage is the process of putting data into one of several forms for later retrieval. The cost of data storage is directly related to its access time. The faster that the data can be retrieved, the more it will cost.

Dated Date

The Dated Date is the day on which interest begins to accrue on bonds that have just been issued. The issuer receives interest from the buyer from the Dated Date to the Settlement Date. The issuer then reimburses the buyer for this interest with the first regular interest payment.

Day Order

A Day Order is an order that expires at the close of trading if it is not executed on the day the trade is entered.

Day Trade

A Day Trade is the purchase and sale of the same security on the same day.

Day Trader

A Day Trader is an individual who buys and sells for their own account, usually in the same day, and who tries to make a profit on the minute to minute movement in the price of stocks. True Day Traders, as opposed to individuals who trade from home on the internet, rent space and computer time from brokerage firms and clear through the firm.

Day Traders must maintain a minimum balance in their account, and usually cannot hold positions over night to reduce the firm's risk.

Daylight Credit

See *Daylight Overdraft*

Daylight Exposure

See *Daylight Overdraft*

Daylight Overdraft

A Daylight Overdraft occurs when the balance in an account drops below zero during the day. Most accounting systems have determined overdrafts by processing debits and credits during an overnight batch run. Increasingly, banks have begun to manage the balance during the day to ensure that their customers do not transfer out large amount of funds in the morning with the intent of repaying in the afternoon.

Dealer

A Dealer is a firm or an individual who acts as a principal in a trade. A dealer buys and sells securities for their own account. A dealer's compensation results from the difference or spread between ask and bid quotations.

Broker, Agent, Asked, Bid, Dealer Clearance, Government Dealer

Dealer Clearance

When a Bank acts as an agent for Broker/Dealers who are active in the government securities market they are performing Dealer Clearance. To do this, they receive and record securities' positions and process the transactions since Broker/Dealers cannot be members of the Federal Reserve System. The Fed is responsible for processing government securities.

There are high profits and high risks in this business since the market can experience sudden, massive increases in volume, which involve very high dollar amounts.

Dealer Market

The Dealer Market is the third market, and consists of market makers who are trading for their own account. In this market, each dealer can be competing with several other dealers who are also making a market in the same security.

When trading through Nasdaq, each dealer posts their bid and offer prices. The average Nasdaq stock has eleven Market Makers.

When trading over-the-counter off of Nasdaq, dealers talk to each other by telephone and negotiate a price.

Dealer Placed Commercial Paper

Dealer Placed Commercial Paper is commercial paper that is placed through a dealer.

Dealer Spread

The Dealer Spread is the difference between a Market Maker's highest price bid and the highest asked price for a security.

Debenture

Debentures are debt issued by a corporation which are backed by the general credit of the issuer and are not secured by a specific lien on property or income.

Debentures are distinguished from bonds which are backed by some specific asset.

Bond

Debit Balance

Debit Balance is the amount of an outstanding loan in a margin account.

Net Position, Credit Balance

Debt

A Debt occurs when one party has a legal promise to repay a loan.

Debt Restructuring

Debt Restructuring is the exchange by a company of one or more new debt issues for one or more of its existing debt issues. Generally, the new issues will have interest rates and/or maturities that are different from the existing issues. Firms restructure to lower their cost of capital.

Cost of Capital

Debt Security

A Debt Security is a financial instrument that represents borrowed funds that must be repaid according to the terms of the instrument.

Bond

Decimalization

Decimalization is the process by which the US practice of making bid and offer prices in fractions is replaced by decimal bids. As fractions, the size of the spread is often artificially controlled. For instance, when the minimum fraction used was one-eight, the minimum spread was 12.5 cents. With the move to sixteenths, the minimum spread has been reduced to 6.25 cents. This benefits the buyer and seller of a security and reduces the potential profits for dealers.

On Nasdaq, shares under $10.00 generally trade in one-thirty seconds, or for 3.125 cents.

Spread

Decrypt

See *Encryption*

Deed of Trust

See *Indenture*

Deep Discount Bond

A Deep Discount Bond is typically a bond one that sells for more than 20% off its face value.

Default

A Default is a failure to meet the legal obligations that have been defined in a contract, including the failure to make loan payments on time. A default occurs when:

A borrower fails to meet the terms of a loan

There is a failure to complete a funds or securities transfer according to its terms for reasons that are not technical or temporary, usually as a result of bankruptcy. A default is usually distinguished from a "failed transaction."

Delinquency

Default Risk

Default Risk is the risk that the issuer of a security may not be able to pay the principal and/or the interest/dividend on time due to financial inadequacy or bankruptcy. The interest rates on a debt instrument rise as the default risk increases.

Risk is usually defined by a rating agency.

Rating Agency

Defensive Stock

A Defensive Stock is a stock that tends to resist following general stock market declines.

Deferred Delivery

A Deferred Delivery:

- Is one that will take place in the future, and beyond the regular time for settlement of a specific instrument in a specific country
- Can also refer to a distant settlement contract that is beyond any normal futures contract

Defined Benefit Pension Plan

See Defined Benefit Program

Defined Benefit Program

In a Defined Benefit program, the actual amount that a retiree will receive is pre-defined, based upon age at retirement, years of service, and/or pre-retirement salary. The Plan Sponsor must calculate how much it will need to have based upon actuarial tables and its anticipated rate of return in order to determine how much to put into the pension fund each year.

A defined benefit program is a liability for a firm since it must be properly funded regardless of the rate of return on the fund's investments.

Defined Contribution Program

Defined Contribution Pension Plan

See Defined Contribution Program

Defined Contribution Program

In a defined contribution program, which is regulated by the IRS as 403(b), 401 (k) or 457 plans, the individual investor takes responsibility for ensuring how much they will have to retire. The investor decided how much they will put into the program, up to some legal limit, and select the investments from a list of alternatives provided by the sponsoring firm. If the investments do well, the person has a larger amount available for retirement than if they do poorly. The firm sponsoring the program has no liability to the investor.

Defined Benefit Program, IRS Section 401(k) Plan, IRS Section 403(b) Plan

Deflation

Deflation is an infrequently occurring phase of the business cycle when consumer spending is seriously curtailed, bank loans shrink, and the amount of money in circulation is reduced. It is the opposite of inflation.

Inflation, Business Cycle

Delayed Opening

A Delayed Opening is the when trading of an issue on a stock exchange has been postponed because of unusual market conditions, such as:

- Delayed input of either buy or sell orders
- An imbalance of buyers and sellers
- Pending corporate news that could dramatically affect the price of the stock.

Delete of Compared Trade Form

The Delete of Compared Trade Form is used to support NSCC's process to delete trades that were already erroneously compared.

Delinquency

A Delinquency is a failure to make payments according to the schedule in a loan agreement.

Delinquency Report

A Delinquency Report is used to identify payments that are past due, or to follow-up on customer documentation, etc.

Deliver Free

Deliver Free is a trade settlement in which securities move to the opposing settlement party without payment. A custodian is instructed to deliver securities only.

The party delivering the securities is at risk until they are paid.

DVP, Deliver versus Payment

Deliver Versus Payment

Deliver vs. Payment (DVP) occurs when, to complete a trade, there is a simultaneous exchange of securities for cash that ensures that delivery occurs if, and only if, payment occurs. To be true DVP, there must be an element of finality in the process, whereby neither side of the trade can unwind the transaction after settlement.

DVP, RVP, Receive vs. Payment

Deliverer of Securities

The Deliverer of Securities is the institution from which a custodian or agent will receive securities in a buy transaction. A deliver of securities is usually the executing broker's clearing agent and is part of the Delivery Instructions.

Delivery Instructions

Deliverer's Instructing Party

Deliverer's Instructing Party is the term used in a buy transaction to indicate the executing broker who will instruct their clearing agent (Deliverer of Securities) to deliver securities. The Deliverer's Instructing Party is part of the Delivery Instructions.

Deliverer of Securities, Delivery Instructions

Delivery

Delivery is the final transfer of a security or financial instrument from one individual or firm to another to complete a trade contract.

Some instruments, including futures contracts such as stock index futures, are settled by a cash payment rather than by the physical delivery of the asset.

Delivery Instructions

Delivery Instructions identify the data elements that are critical for the efficient settlement of a trade. The instructions generally include such items as: settlement agent, account name and number and any special instructions needed to settle the transaction.

The delivery instructions from both counterparties must match in order for the settlement to occur.

Broker Delivery Instructions, Custodian Delivery Instructions

Delivery Month

The Delivery Month, also called the contract month, is the specified trading month for a particular futures or options contract. For instance, on LIFFE these are March, June, September, December.

Options may also be traded on a 1-2-3 month cycle e.g. January, February, March, in addition to the quarterly cycle.

Delta

Delta is the measure of change in the value of an option compared with a change in the price of the underlying instrument.

Dematerialization

Dematerialization is a process by which physical certificates are eliminated so that securities exist only as accounting records.

Securities are initially immobilized in a depository and through the process of dematerialization, eventually can become book entry only securities.

Physical Security, Immobilization, Book entry

Dematerialized Security

A Dematerialized Security that is a security recorded solely on the books and records or an appropriate intermediary (usually a CSD), without any physical certificate.

Physical Security

Den Danske Bank

Den Danske Bank is a Denmark-based Universal Bank.

www.ddb.dk

Department of Labor

The Department of Labor (DOL) is the regulatory body that is responsible for the administration and enforcement of ERISA.

ERISA

Deployment

Deployment is the allocation of investable funds between alternative asset categories.

Asset Category

Depositary

Same as Depository.

Deposito Central de Valores

Deposito Central de Valores (DECEVAL) is the central depository for securities listed on the Bogotá, Occidente and Medellin exchanges.

Depository

See *Central Securities Depository*

Depository Agent

A Depository Agent is typically a bank or trust company that is appointed by the person or firm making a tender offer to receive any securities that are tendered, and to pay for them when authorized.

Depository Bank

The term Depository Bank is often used when referring to the custodian bank for an ADR.

ADR

Depository Eligible

A security is considered Depository Eligible when it meets the minimum requirements stipulated by the depository in which the security will be held.

Depository Receipt

A Depository Receipt is an instrument that is issued in one country that represents an entitlement of the rights due to an underlying security that is held in custody in another country.

ADR

Depository Trust Clearing Corporation

The Depository Trust Clearing Corporation was established in 1999 as the holding company for the DTC and the NSCC, which will continue operating separate processes for the next few years.

DTC, NSCC

Depository Trust Company

The Depository Trust Company (DTC) is the primary central securities depository for stocks and bonds in the US. DTC is a corporation, owned by banks and brokerage firms and the New York Stock Exchange, that:

- Holds securities such as equities, bonds and UITs
- Arranges for the receipt and delivery of securities
- Arranges for the payments during settlement
- DTC has an electronic book entry settlement system, called the ID system, that is used in settlement.

www.dtc.org

Central Securities Depository, UIT, Institutional Delivery System

Depreciation

Depreciation is:

- A decrease in an investment's value
- The systematic reduction in the value of an asset recorded on a company's balance sheet

Depth of Market

The Depth of Market for a security identifies the number of shares of a security that can be bought or sold without causing a major change in price.

Derivative

See *Derivative Security*

Derivative Security

A Derivative Security is a financial instrument whose value is determined principally from the value and characteristics of an underlying security, reference rate or index.

Some examples of derivatives are:

- Futures
- Options
- Swaps
- Mortgage Backed
- FX Forwards
- Credit Derivatives

Underlying Security, Forward, Option, Warrant, Mortgage Backed Securities

Designated Examining Authority

A Designated Examining Authority is a Self Regulating Organization responsible for examining individual brokers to ensure that they are in compliance with the rules established by the respective SRO.

Self Regulating Organization

Designated Order Turnaround System

The Designated Order Turnaround (DOT) System is the NYSE's order routing and execution reporting system that can automatically process orders of up to 599 shares that have been entered by member firms.

SuperDOT

Detective Controls

Detective Controls, which are designed to detect errors, fraud and mischief after they occur, include:

- Routine Procedures
- Monthly Operating Reviews
- Data Reconciliation
- Data Reasonability Reviews
- Analytic Reviews
- Re-performance of Procedures
- Direct Verification by Comparing to Source Documents
- Preventive Controls, Compensating Controls

Deutsche Bank

Deutsche Bank is a German-based Universal Bank.

www.deutsche-bank.de

Deutsche Börse

The Deutsche Börse is the primary stock exchange of Germany.

Deutsche Terminbörse

The Deutsche Terminbörse was established in 1990 as a physical exchange for the automated trading of financial futures and options contracts in Germany.

Deutscher Aktienindex

The Deutscher Aktien (DAX) Index is a stock index derived from equities listed on the Deutsche Börse.

Deutscher Kassenverein

Deutscher Kassenverein AG is the central depository and securities clearing house of Germany.

DIAMONDS

DIAMONDS is an index that is designed to contain the 30 securities that compose the Dow Jones Industrial Average. DIAMONDS have been sold on the AMEX since 1998.

Index, Dow Jones Industrial Average

Differential

The Differential is the fractional commission that is applied by a dealer or a specialist for handling an odd lot order.

Odd Lot

Digital Interface Service / Character Interface Presentation Server

Digital Interface Service / Character Interface Presentation Server (DIS /CHIPS) is an alternative to Nasdaq's Workstation II service for Level 3 users. DIS/CHIPS connects a participant's computers directly to the Nasdaq network.

Nasdaq Level 3 Service

Digital Video

Digital Video is a video file that can be converted into digital form rather than as a series of frames so that it can be stored in computer memory or on a CD.

CD ROM

Dilution

Dilution occurs when a firm adds to the number of shares outstanding, which reduces the value of earnings and assets for existing shareholders.

Direct Deposit

A Direct Deposit occurs when any firm makes an electronic deposit directly to an account at a financial institution on behalf of a third party. Direct Deposits are used for payroll, accounts payable, tax refunds, etc.

Direct Marketing

Direct Marketing is a form of distribution used by mutual funds to sell their shares directly to the public. Direct marketing makes it possible for investors to purchase fund shares by mail or by telephone.

Direct Member Input

The Direct Member Input (DMI) system allows LIFFE members to bypass the traditional paper clearing slips and input trades directly onto TRS themselves.

Direct Participation Program

A Direct Participation Program (DPP) is a formal partnership agreement that allows participants to receive the tax benefits of an investment.

Directed Trust

A Directed Trust is a trust that does not grant the trustee full managerial authority. ERISA identifies three different types of directed trusts where authority has been moved away from the trustee:

- To plan participants or trust beneficiaries over the assets in their own individual accounts
- To a fiduciary who is not a trustee
- To an investment manager

ERISA

Director

A Director is a corporate board member who has been elected by the stockholders of the corporation.

Board of Directors

DIS/CHIPS

See *Digital Interface Service / Character Interface Presentation Server*

Discount

See *At a Discount*

Discount Bonds

Discount Bonds are bonds which are purchased below par, giving them a higher yield to maturity, which also reduces the risk of the bond being called.

Par, Call

Discount Brokerage

A Discount Brokerage is a brokerage firm that generally charges lower commissions, but which historically has not offered investment advice.

Discount Factor

The Discount Factor is the rate used to derive net present value of a sum of money to be paid at a future date.

Net Present Value

Discount Loan

A Discount Loan is a loan that takes place between the Federal Reserve and a member bank. Member banks borrow from the Federal Reserve only when confronted with short term liquidity needs. As a result, the Federal Reserve has become known as the lender of last resort.

The interest rate on Discount Loans is called the discount rate, and is established and adjusted by the Federal Reserve Board of Governors.

Federal Reserve System Board of Governors, Federal Reserve Bank Discount Rate

Discount Note

A Discount Note is a short-term obligation that was issued at a discount from the face value, with maturities ranging from overnight to 360 days. These notes have no periodic interest payments, and the investor receives the note's face value at maturity.

Discount Rate

See *Federal Reserve Bank Discount Rate*

Discretion

Discretion refers to the arrangement whereby a Registered Representative or Portfolio Manager holds the right to buy and sell securities without receiving specific instructions from their client, usually within some boundaries. The managers are typically not allowed to move cash out of the account.

A Trustee may be given discretion in the Trust Agreement to purchase or sell assets in a Trust.

Trustee, Trust Agreement

Discretionary Account

A Discretionary Account is one where the broker or adviser has the authority to buy and sell without the client's prior knowledge and consent.

Discretion, Rules of Fair Practice

Disintermediation

Disintermediation occurs when a person or firm finds a way to avoid using a financial intermediary in order to save money. This can be for processing, issuance or funding.

Display Book

The Display Book is an application that maintains information on limit orders and new market orders. SuperDot orders that are received from member firm systems are posted on the specialist's Display Book screen.

SuperDot

Disposal Agent

The Disposal Agent is a bank or trust company that has been appointed to destroy and dispose of cancelled securities and coupons after they have been redeemed or transferred.

Dissident Shareholders

Dissident Shareholders are those investors who oppose a firm's management or management policy.

Distribution

Distribution is:

- The payment of dividends and capital gains by a firm

- The sale of securities from a firm's inventory
- The sale of an IPO to a firm's customers or to the general public

Distribution Capability

Distribution Capability is the ability of an investment banker or underwriter to sell shares of an IPO to their customers or to the general public.

IPO

Distributor

A Distributor is a firm that provides mutual fund shares to brokers and investors.

Underwriter

Diversification

Diversification is the term that is used by investment managers and advisors to describe the process of spreading a portfolio's risk by investing simultaneously in several different categories of investments such as stocks, bonds, money market funds, etc. A portfolio can also be diversified by investing in different countries, industry sectors, and capitalization classifications.

Asset Allocation

Dividend

A Dividend is:

- The portion of net earnings paid by a corporation to its stockholders. Preferred stock is supposed to pay a regular and prescribed dividend amount. Common stock pays varying amounts when declared.
- An insurance policy holder's share in the divisible surplus funds of an insurance company apportioned for distribution. Such a dividend takes the form of a refund of part of the premium on a participating policy.

Dividends must be declared by the Board of Directors. There are several types of Dividends:

- Cash Dividends
- Normal Dividend
- Partial Liquidation
- Return of Capital
- DRIP (873 firms offer DRIP)
- Redemption of Unused Rights
- Stock Dividends
- Spin-offs
- Warrant distributions
- Optional Dividends
- Cash dividend with option to receive stock
- Stock dividend with option to receive cash
- Fractional processing

Dividend Payment Frequency

Dividend Notification

Dividend Notification is the process requiring a paying agent to notify the industry of a pending dividend. A dividend notification is usually sent through automated information vendors.

Paying Agent

Dividend Paying Agent

See *Paying Agent*

Dividend Payment Frequency

Dividend Payment Frequency is the interval at which a dividend is paid. Common dividend payment frequencies include:

- No Dividend
- Annually
- Semi-Annually
- Three-times Annually
- Quarterly
- Monthly
- Bi-Monthly
- Variable
- Unknown

Dividend Reinvestment Program

Dividend Reinvestment Program's, or DRIPs, are established by firms that wish to encourage individual investors to buy and hold their securities. The program maintains book entry information about the investor's position and converts cash dividends into fractional shares and adds them to an investor's account.

Dividend Settlement Service

The Dividend Settlement Service (DSS) is the NSCC's claims-processing system that manages the collection of dividends and interest that is owed to participants by other financial institutions. DSS users can claim funds due to them by charging other DSS participants through NSCC's clearance and settlement system.

Dividend Yield

Dividend Yield is the percentage that is calculated by dividing the anticipated dividend that will be paid over the next twelve months by the current market price of a stock.

DJIA

See *Dow Jones Industrial Average*

DK

See *Don't Know (DK)*

DM

DM is the abbreviation for Deutschemark, which is a German unit of currency.

DMI

See Direct Member Input

DNI

See *Do Not Increase*

DNR

See *Do Not Reduce*

Do Not Increase

Do Not Increase (DNI) is a formal instruction that tells a firm's order department not to increase the quantity of shares that has been specified on an order if a stock dividend is declared. A DNI is usually placed on buy limit, sell stop, and stop limit Good-Until-Cancelled orders.

Do Not Reduce

Do Not Reduce

Do Not Reduce (DNR) is a formal instruction that tells a firm's order department not to reduce the price of an order by the amount of dividends received when the dividend is paid by the corporation. A DNR is usually placed on buy limit, sell stop, and sell stop limit GTC orders.

Do Not Increase

DOL

See *Department of Labor*

Dollar Cost Averaging

Dollar Cost Averaging occurs when an investor invests the same amount at regular intervals, regardless of whether the market is up or down. This permits investors to purchase more shares per investment when the market is down and less when the market is up.

Since the equity market has historically risen over the long term, the dollar cost averaging investor expects to show a long term gain. Investors who employ the strategy of dollar cost averaging usually have a long term investment objective.

Domestic Settlement

Domestic Settlement is the settlement that takes place in the country in which both counterparties to the trade are located, and in which the issue being traded is also domiciled.

Domestic Trade

A Domestic Trade is a trade that occurs when both counterparties are located in the same country.

Domicile

A Domicile is a place of residence, or a security's country of origin.

Don't Know (DK)

Don't Know (DK) is an industry term that stands for "don't know the trade." When a bank or corporation cannot match an incoming trade to the instructions to receive that they have on file, they will DK the trade. A trade may be labeled DK because of unmatched differences in price, quantity, etc.

DOT

See *Designated Order Turnaround System*

Double Barrel Bond

A Double Barrel Bond is a municipal bond that is backed both by a special tax or specific revenue, as well as the full faith and credit of the municipality.

Dow Jones Industrial Average

The Dow Jones Industrial Average (DJIA) is an adjusted average of 30 industrial stocks, listed on the New York Stock Exchange, which has been published by Dow Jones & Co. since July 3, 1884.

Dow Theory

The Dow Theory says that the market is in a basic upward trend if one of its averages (industrial or transportation) advances above a previous important high, accompanied or followed by a similar advance in the other.

If both averages move below previous important low points, it is considered to be the confirmation of a basic downward trend.

Down Tick

A down tick is a decrease in price of a security from its last quoted price.

Tick

Downside Risk

Downside Risk is the risk that a specific security will decline.

Downsize

When firms have excess staff or have an inefficient process they may reduce the size of their workforce by Downsizing, or shrinking their staff.

Downstairs Trader

The Downstairs Trader is the trader on the floor of an exchange.

Upstairs Trader

DPP

See *Direct Participation Program*

DR

See *Depository Receipt*

DRIP

See *Dividend Reinvestment Program*

DSS

See *Dividend Settlement Service*

DTB

See Deutsche Terminbörse

DTC

See *Depository Trust Company*

DTC Eligibility

DTC Eligibility refers to a security acceptance in the DTC system, which is determined by whether it meets certain criteria established by the DTC.

Depository Trust Company

DTC Hub

DTC Hub is a mailbox concept that allows participants to select their own frequency of communication with the DTC. The participant can deposit or retrieve information from their electronic mailbox as often throughout the day as they wish.

DTCC

See Depository Trust Clearing Corporation

Dual Currency Bond

A Dual Currency Bond is a bond that is denominated in one currency and is redeemable in a different currency.

Due Bill

A Due Bill is an industry IOU that is used to settle trades during the dividend payment period and when splits occur.

Uniform Practice Code

Due Date

The Due Date is the date when a bond, note, or other evidence of debt matures and becomes payable.

Due Diligence

Due Diligence is the process of investigating a company that is:

- About to go public
- About to be sold to another firm

Dumb Terminal

See *Terminal*

Duration

Duration measures the length of time that an investor who owns the bond will have to wait to be repaid along with the interest rate sensitivity of the bond. It considers the:

- Remaining time until maturity
- Interest rate(s) and payment periodicity
- Potential for a call

Dutch Auction

A Dutch Auction is an auction where the seller makes an initial offer, and then reduces the price until a buyer emerges. When the first buyer commits, the price for the rest of the auction is established.

In the US Treasury's version of a Dutch Auction, each bidder submits a bid that includes a price and an amount of securities they wish to purchase. The Treasury uses the lowest price to establish the price for that sale, but allocates the available number of securities to the bidders who offered the highest prices.

DVP

See *Deliver Versus Payment*

EAFE Index

EAFE is Morgan Stanley Capital's international index for Europe, Australia, and the Far East. It includes over 1,000 major companies.

Early Withdrawal Penalty

See Withdrawal Penalty

Earnings Per Share

Earnings Per Share (EPS) is the firm's net income, less preferred dividends, divided by the number of shares of common stock outstanding.

Earnings Yield

The Earnings Yield of a firm is a ratio that is determined by dividing its earnings by the market price of its stock.

EBV

See *Effectenclearing BV*

EC

See European Community

ECN

See *Electronic Crossing Network*

See *Electronic Confirmation Network*

ECOA

See *Equal Credit Opportunity Act*

E-commerce

E-commerce is the purchase and sale of goods or services over the internet.

Economic and Monetary Union

The Economic and Monetary Union (EMU) creates a single market to allow the free movement of people, goods, capital and services, and the formation of the European Monetary Institute as a precursor to a single EU central bank, and a single EU currency.

Economic Indicators

Economic Indicators are statistics such as unemployment, inflation and factory utilization that analysts use to predict the direction of the overall economy.

EDE

See *Electronic Data Exchange*

EDGAR

See *Electronic Data Gathering Analysis and Retrieval*

EDI

See *Electronic Delivery Instruction*

EDIFACS

EDIFACS (*pronounced eddie facts*) is an Electronic Delivery Instruction (EDI) format that is used pre-dominantly in Europe. It is being promoted by Europeans as a standard that could compete with S.W.I.F.T. and FIX.

S.W.I.F.T., FIX, Electronic Delivery Instruction

Editor

An Editor is a program that checks data as it is being entered, in order to ensure that only correct data is entered into the system. It is possible for data to be correctly formatted and pass the edit, but be incorrect.

Edward Jones Investments

Edward Jones Investments is a US-based brokerage firm.

www.edwardjones.com

Effectenclearing BV

Effectenclearing BV is a wholly-owned subsidiary of the Amsterdam Stock Exchange that provides clearing services for the members of the Exchange.

Effective Date

The Effective Date is:

- The first day after a new issue's cooling-off period when the security can be offered
- The date on which anything is scheduled to occur

Efficient Market

An Efficient Market is one where securities sell for what they are worth, and where all investors (individual and institutional) have an equal opportunity to make a profit.

An efficient market assumes that all investors have an equal access to all available information and that the market adjusted instantly to any new information.

Efficient Portfolio

In theory, an Efficient Portfolio has a mix of investments which offer the highest possible yield at a given level of risk, or the minimum possible risk at a given yield level.

EFT

See *Electronic Funds Transfer*

EIN

EIN is a corporation's Employee Identification Number.

See *Tax Identification Numbers*

El Rowad General Index

The El Rowad General Index is a stock index derived from equities listed on the Cairo Stock Exchange.

Electronic Book

See *Display Book*

Electronic Confirmation Network

An Electronic Confirmation Network (ECN) is any electronic system that widely disseminates orders to third parties that have been entered by an exchange member or OTC Market Maker.

ECNs are used primarily by Institutional Managers to find trade counterparties without going through a broker. Some of the leading ECNs are:

- Instinet
- Bloomberg TradeBook
- Tierra Nova
- Island
- SelectNet

Electronic Crossing Network

An Electronic Crossing Network is a term that has been replaced by Electronic Communication Network.

Electronic Communication Network

Electronic Data Exchange

Electronic Data Exchange is a method that has been used to send transaction data from firm to firm to avoid re-keying information. The related concept in securities processing is Straight Through Processing.

Straight Through Processing, UN/Edifact

Electronic Data Gathering Analysis and Retrieval

Electronic Data Gathering, Analysis, and Retrieval (EDGAR) is the SEC's electronic system that allows firms to electronically file all of the documents that are required for securities offerings and ongoing disclosure obligations.

Electronic Delivery Instruction

Electronic Delivery Instruction (EDI) is a method of electronically exchanging information that relates to commerce and finance.

Electronic Funds Transfer

Electronic Funds Transfer (EFT) is the electronic movement of money between banks.

Automated Clearing House, Bankers Automated Clearing Service, S.W.I.F.T.

Electronic Funds Transfer

An Electronic Funds Transfer is the electronic movement of funds from an account at one bank to an account at another bank, without using cash or any other paper to execute the transfer.

Electronic Pool Notification

The Electronic Pool Notification system, developed by MBSCC in the early 1990's, is a real-time electronic communications network that allows buyers and sellers to transmit MBS pool information more quickly, efficiently and reliably than was previously possible. Before EPN, firms relied on phone and fax to exchange this information.

Electronic Trade Confirmation

Electronic Trade Confirmation (ETC) has two different meanings:

- The IUG (Industry User Group) was formed by a group of brokers and investment managers, who selected several vendors to form the IVL (Inter Vendor Link) in the UK. ETC systems include OASYS Global, SEQUAL, TRAX , I
- S.W.I.F.T.'s new category of participants. S.W.I.F.T.'s ETC vendors provide their customers with connectivity and message routing. Some of the ETC vendors are Bloomberg, Instinet, CrossMar (Citibank), Advent, DTC, PAM, FMC, Shaw, OASYS Global, ID

Electronic Traders Assistance Association

The Electronic Traders Assistance Association is a for-profit organization that will research the time and sales prices for up to five disputed trades for $200.

www.etaa.com

Eligibility Rules

Eligibility Rules can cover:

- Who is eligible to become a registered representative
- Who can become a member of a stock exchange
- What issues can be listed on an exchange

- What issues can be put into a depository
- When a claim can be submitted for arbitration

Eligible Trade Report

The Eligible Trade Report is the final notification step in the DTC notification process. When the DTC sends the ETR to the broker and the custodian, the DTC informs them that unless it is notified otherwise, the trades listed on the report will settle on settlement date.

E-mail

E-mail is the commonly used term for electronic mail. An e-mail system requires:

- Software on the sender's computer that assists in the composition and routing of the message
- A network switch (or switches) that can relay the message to the correct end point server
- A network that carries the message to the intended server
- A server that can store the incoming message until it is accessed by the intended recipient
- Software on the recipient's computer that can access the server, retrieve the message and display it for the reader

Embedded Option

An Embedded Option is a provision included in a bond that gives either the issuer or the bondholder the option to take some action against the other party. The most common embedded option is a call option, which gives the issuer the right to call, or retire, the debt before the scheduled maturity date.

EMCC

See *Emerging Markets Clearing Corporation*

Emerging Market

An Emerging Market is a securities market in a country which does not have a fully developed economy. Investments in these markets are usually characterized by a high level of risk and the possibility of a high return.

Emerging Markets Clearing Corporation

The Emerging Markets Clearing Corporation (EMCC) was established by the ISCC with the assistance of the EMTA to facilitate the clearance, multilateral netting, and risk management of emerging market debt products, including Brady Bonds.

International Securities Clearing Corporation, Emerging Markets Traders Association

Emerging Markets Traders Association

The Emerging Markets Traders Association (EMTA) was formed in 1990 and works to increase cross-border capital flows by clarifying market practices and promoting consistency between local and international trading standards. EMTA member organizations include broker-dealers, commercial banks, investment banks, merchant banks, and other major financial organizations such as law firms, accounting firms, vendors, rating agencies, data providers and consultants.

Employee Retirement Income Security Act of 1974

The Employee Retirement Income Security Act of 1974 (ERISA) is a law that was established to protect the interests of participants and beneficiaries in employee benefit plans. The law created a major new business for banks and other forms of Trust Companies since it requires that persons who administer supervise, and manage pension funds have a fiduciary responsibility. This means that all investment-related decisions are made: "with the care, skill, prudence, and diligence ... [that a prudent expert] familiar with such matters would use ...by diversifying the investments ... so as to minimize risk."

This new wording required two significant changes in traditional investment practice:

The age-old "prudent man" rule has been replaced by the notion of a prudent "expert."

The notion of a prudent investment has been replaced by the concept of a prudent portfolio.

Employee Stock Ownership Plan

An Employee Stock Ownership Plan (ESOP) is a qualified retirement plan in which employees receive shares of the company's stock.

EMTA

See *Emerging Markets Traders Association*

EMU

Economic and Monetary Union

EMU

See *European Monetary Union*

Encryption

Encryption is often used when data is moved from one application to another or from one firm to another across open telecommunication lines. The process involves the coding of the data in such a way that only the receiving party can understand its meaning. Encryption devises and algorithms provide the sender and receiver with a secret key that is unique to the two firms, and which is used to decode the encrypted message.

Key

Endorsement

An Endorsement is a signature that is added to a document:

- To transfer the document to another person
- To increase the level of authorization on a document

Enhancement

An Enhancement is a minor improvement to an existing application.

Maintenance

Enquiry

See *Inquiry*

Envelope Settlement Service

The Envelope Settlement Service (ESS) is used by firms in New York and Jersey City to standardize and control their participant-to-participant physical delivery of securities. Firms outside of the New York areas can use IESS to deliver to NSCC branches.

EPN

See *Electronic Pool Notification*

EPS

See *Earnings Per Share*

Equal Credit Opportunity Act

The Equal Credit Opportunity Act is a federal law that requires creditors to offer credit without discrimination based on race, color, religion, national origin, age, sex, marital status or receipt of income from public assistance programs.

Equipment Trust Bond

An Equipment Trust Bond is a bond, secured within a trust, and backed by equipment collateral, such as railroad cars, trucks, etc.

Equity

Equity is:

- A security defining ownership in a corporation, which is often represented by a certificate. With an equity instrument, the stockholder has:
- A contract with the issuing corporation that defines the stockholders' rights
- A partial ownership position in the firm
- The right to participate in profits
- A claim upon any assets that remain after all debts have been paid
- The difference between the current market value of a property and the total mortgage.

Stock, Common Stock, Preferred Stock, Certificate

Equity Clearing House

Equity Clearing House is a wholly owned subsidiary of the Johannesburg Stock Exchange (JSE) that provides clearing services to members of the Exchange.

Equity Derivatives

Equity Derivatives are futures or options that are based on some underlying equity instruments, which could be individual stocks or stock market indices.

Derivatives

Equity Options

See Options

Equivalent Taxable Yield

The Equivalent Taxable Yield is the taxable return that must be achieved in order to equal, on an after-tax basis, a given tax-exempt return. This is used to compare the yield on tax exempt instruments with taxable instruments.

ERISA

See *Employee Retirement Income Security Act of 1974*

Ernst & Company

Ernst & Company is a US-based brokerage firm and a correspondent clearer.

www.ernst-co.com

Error Rate

An Error Rate measures how many errors are produced by a unit, an application, or a person compared to the total number of units processed.

Escheat

The process of Escheating is governed by the Federal Uniform Unclaimed Property Act or state law, and is used to pass unclaimed funds or property to the state when the legal owner cannot be identified.

Escrow

Escrow is the process that is offered by trust departments and lawyers, where the trust department or lawyer keeps funds or property until certain pre-defined conditions are met, and then properly releases the funds or property.

Escrow Receipt

A guarantee of delivery issued by a qualified bank to a clearing corporation, such as OCC, on behalf of the bank's customer. The member brokerage firm acts as a conduit for this document.

ESOP

See Employee Stock Ownership Plan

ESOP

Abbreviation for Employee Stock Ownership Plan

ESS

See *Envelope Settlement Service*

ETAA

See *Electronic Traders Assistance Association*

ETC

See *Electronic Trade Confirmation*

Euro

The Euro is the new currency of the European Monetary Union.

European Monetary Union

Eurobond

A Eurobond is a bond that has been issued and traded in countries other than the European country in which the bond is denominated.

Eurodollar

Euroclear

Euroclear is an international clearance and settlement system (ICSD) operated by Morgan Guaranty Trust in Brussels. Euroclear, which operates as an International Central Securities Depository, has one primary competitor: CEDEL. Annual transactions processed by Euroclear exceed $25 billion, and deposits exceed $1.9 trillion. Euroclear has been traditionally strong in supporting the needs of broker/dealers.

www.euroclear.com

CEDEL, ICSD, Intersettle

Eurodollar

Eurodollars are US dollar currency held in banks outside the United States (mostly in Europe) commonly used to settle international transactions. While held outside of the US, the dollars are not supervised by the US Federal Reserve System.

Eurodollar-based instruments are not subject to oversight by the US Securities and Exchange Commission.

Fed, SEC

Eurodollar Time Deposit Futures

Eurodollar Time Deposit Futures are futures contracts, offered in increments of $1,000,000 Eurodollars, that reflect the three month LIBOR rate. These futures are extremely liquid, and as much as $1,000,000,000 can be purchased at one time without moving the market.

LIBOR

Eurodollar Time Deposits

Eurodollar Time Deposits are European demand deposits, denominated in Eurodollars, and are similar to a US Certificate of Deposit.

Certificate of Deposit

European Community

The European Community (EC) is a group of Western European countries that have joined together to promote trade, economic and political cooperation. This was formerly called the European Economic Community (EEC).

European Monetary Union

The EMU is a major change in the economic structure of eleven European countries that goes in to effect January 1, 1999. New countries are expected to join in 2002.

From 1/1/99 through 1/1/02, countries and issuers will phase in a number of regulations that are designed to merge multiple independent currencies into a single currency and central bank.

The new currency is called the Euro.

Euro, Target

European Option

See European Style Option

European Style Option

A European Style Option is an option that may be exercised only during a short period of time just before its expiration date.

American Style Option

Event Risk

Event Risk is the risk that some change outside of the market (tax changes, legal action, tender offers, etc.) will affect the value of an investment.

Everen Securities, Inc.

Everen Securities, Inc. is a US-based brokerage firm.

www.everensec.com

Ex Ante

The term Ex Ante is used to categorize predicted variables.

Ex by Ex

Ex by Ex is the process that is used to automatically exercise options that are ready to expire and which are in the money, unless the customer provides other instructions.

Option, In-the-Money

Ex Post

The term Ex Post is used to categorize historical variables.

Exception Based Processing

Firms establish Exception Based Processing as they increase their level of automation and shift their focus from concentrating on processing routine transactions to only those transactions that do not process correctly.

Excess Spread Policy

The Excess Spread Policy is a NASD requirement prohibiting Market Makers from entering quotations on Nasdaq that exceed the limits for maximum allowable spreads.

Excessive Trading

See *Churning*

Exchange

A recognized securities Exchange in the US performs several functions, including:

- Listing securities
- Centralizing buying and selling

- Multiple exchanges, linked by the Intermarket Trading System (ITS)
- Reporting trading activity
- Monitoring compliance

Exchanges have been established to facilitate the matching of buyers and sellers of securities and other products, such as commodities. Each exchange has its own rules that its members agree to follow, and which have been approved by the SEC.

There are several recognized exchanges in the US:

- American Stock Exchange
- Boston Stock Exchange
- Chicago Board of Trade
- Chicago Board Options Exchange
- Chicago Stock Exchange
- Coffee, Sugar & Cocoa Exchange
- Kansas City Board of Trade
- Minneapolis Grain Exchange
- National Association of Securities Dealers
- New York Cotton Exchange
- New York Futures Exchange
- New York Mercantile Exchange
- Pacific Stock Exchange
- Philadelphia Board of Trade
- Philadelphia Stock Exchange

Exchanges also exist in almost every country around the world.

SEC, ITS

Exchange Agent

A Corporate Trust department acts as an Exchange Agent when it supports a reorganization due to a merger or recapitalization.

Ex-Distribution

The Ex-Distribution date is one day after the record date of a mutual fund's dividend. Investors are not entitled to the dividend and the NAV drops by the amount of the dividend, since it will be paid to the investors who held the fund on the record date.

Ex-Dividend Date, NAV

Ex-Dividend

When a stock trades during the Ex-Dividend period, the owner does not receive the recently declared, but not yet paid, dividend.

Once declared by the Board of Directors, dividends are payable on a predetermined date to all of the shareholders who are identified on the books as of a specified date, which is called the record date.

Dividend, Record Date, Ex-Dividend Date

Ex-Dividend Date

The term Ex-Dividend can be used in two ways:

- The Ex-Dividend Date is the first day on which a new buyer of the security is not entitled to receive a declared dividend. On this day, the price of the security drops to reflect the fact that a portion of the company's assets have just been paid out of the company. The owners of the equity as of the record date have not lost value since, while they still own the slightly reduced value stock, they are also entitled to the declared dividend.
- For mutual funds, the Ex-Dividend Date (or ex-distribution date) is the date on which declared distributions (dividends or capital gains) are deducted from the fund's assets before it calculates its net asset value (NAV). The NAV per share will drop by the amount of the distribution per share.

Ex-Distribution, Record Date

Execute

See *Execution*

Execute an Order

When a broker Executes an Order, it completes an order it received from a customer to buy or sell a specific security.

Execute at the Close

See *At The Close*

Executing Broker

The Executing Broker is the broker who finds a counterparty and completes a trade, either on an exchange or over-the-counter.

Execution

An Execution is a completed trade.

Execution Risk

Execution Risk is the risk that is included in completing the final stages of an exchange-traded transaction.

Exercise

The term Exercise can be:

- The process by which an option holder has the right to buy or sell the underlying security.
- The action by a stockholder to take advantage of a privilege offered by the company, such as subscribing to additional stock or bonds, or converting securities into another form.

Exercise Price

The term Exercise Price can be used in two ways:

- *See Stock Price*

- *See Strike Price*

Exotic Option

An Exotic Option is an option style with unusual features such as how the strike price or the expiration date is calculated.

Asian Option

Expense

An Expense is the cost that is incurred in running a business.

Expense Account

An Expense Account can be either:

- A General Ledger account that is used to record and categorize the expenses a firm incurs
- A periodic report submitted by an employee to obtain reimbursement for personal funds that have been used to pay business expenses

Expense Code

An Expense Code is used by most accounting systems to identify the department that incurs an operating expense.

Operating Expenses

Expense Ratio

An Expense Ratio is a mutual fund's cost of doing business which is disclosed in the prospectus as a percent of assets.

It includes the following expenses which, in total, are divided by the fund's average net assets:

- Management Fee
- Administrative Costs
- 12b-1 charges

Expiration

See *Expiration Date*

Expiration Cycle

See Expiration Date

Expiration Date

The Expiration Date is the last day on which a stock option, a future contract, an offer or other contracted security may be exercised. After this date the item is worthless.

For example, at the CBOE, options expire at 10:30 AM on the last Monday of January, April, July or October. Trading of these options stops at 2:00 PM on the prior trading day.

Expiration Month, CBOE

Expiration Month

The Expiration Month is the month in which an option, futures contract or other contracted security ceases to have value.

Expiration Date

Expiration Time

The Expiration Time is the time of day by which all exercise notices must be received on the expiration date.

Expiry

See Expiration Date

Ex-Rights

When a security trades Ex-Rights, it is trading without some rights that have been recently granted to shareholders. This can occur as a result of any one of three circumstances:

- After record date
- Right removed
- Right expired

When a corporation wants to raise funds, they may offer their current stockholder some additional right, such as the right to purchase additional shares at a discount, etc. The rights can then be traded with the shares or separated from them and traded separately.

Right

External Audit

An External Audit is required under a variety of circumstances to be conducted periodically on a corporation by an independent audit firm.

External Controls

External Controls are those that are established as a result of an audit or inspection by external auditors, regulators, or SRO's.

Internal Controls, SRO

External Device

An External Device is any piece of hardware that is outside of a PC's CPU box, and which is attached to the PC. The attachment can be through a serial, SCSI or parallel connection, or directly to a dedicated board in the PC.

CPU, SCSI

Extract Program

An Extract Program is an application that was written to extract specific data from one or more systems, usually in order to move that information to another system either directly or through a specific form of telecommunication.

Extranet

An Extranet is an Intranet that has been opened to outside users.

Intranet, Internet

Face Value

The Face Value is the amount that appears on the front of a debt certificate and that the issuer must pay at maturity, unless the redemption value is specifically indicated by the issuer as other than the amount printed on the certificate.

Face Value is sometimes referred to as the par value of a bond.

Factor

A Factor is:

- The ratio of the principal repayment to the total monthly payment for a pass-through security. This is a decimal value reflecting the proportion of the outstanding principal balance of a mortgage security, which changes over time, in relation to its original principal value.
- A financing technique in which a firm sells receivables or debt to another firm for a fraction of their face value

Factor Table

A Factor Table is the matrix that is used to compute the outstanding principal on pass-through instruments such as Ginnie Maes, Freddie Macs, and Fannie Maes.

Factor, Pass-Through Security, Ginnie Mae, Freddie Mac, Fannie Mae

Fail

A Fail is a transaction that is not settled as scheduled due to:

- A failure by the seller to deliver the securities
- The buyer not having sufficient funds available to complete the transaction
- Fail-to-Deliver, Fail-to-Receive

Fail Float

Fail Float is the interest that is earned on money that should have been used to settle a failed transaction.

Fail-to-Deliver

A Fail-to-Deliver occurs when the selling firm does not deliver a security on the settlement date. This could occur when:

- The firm does not have the security
- Delivery instructions are either incomplete or do not exist

Fail-to-Execute

A Fail-to-Execute occurs when a broker is unable to execute a customer order.

Fail-to-Receive

A Fail-to-Receive occurs when the buying firm is unable to receive, or does not receive the security that was agreed upon at the time of the trade. This could occur when:

- The firm does not have sufficient funds in the account to settle
- Settlement instructions are either incomplete or do not exist

Fair Practice Rules

See *Rules of Fair Practice*

Fair Pricing

Fair Pricing , also called fair value, can be:

- In the futures market this would represent the cash price plus the net cost of carry.

In the options market, it is the value derived from the mathematical equation used (e.g. Black-Scholes model).

Family of Funds

A Family of Funds consists of several different mutual funds, each with its own investment objective, that are managed and distributed by the same company. Typically, the fund managers do not charge any fees to switch from one fund to another within the same family.

Mutual Fund

Fannie Mae

See *Federal National Mortgage Association*

FAQs

Pronounced Facks

FAQS is an abbreviation for Frequently Asked Questions.

Firm Access and Query System

Farm Credit System

The Farm Credit System was established in 1917 and consists of cooperative banks that provide loans to farms and farmer-owned cooperatives.

Farm Credit System Financial Assistance Corporation

The Farm Credit System Financial Assistance Corporation (FAC) was established in 1988 to provide capital to institutions with financial problems within the Farm Credit System.

Farm Credit System

Farmers Home Administration

The Farmers Home Administration (FMHA) was established within the Department of Agriculture to extend loans in rural areas for farms, homes, and community facilities.

FASB

See *Financial Accounting Standards Board*

FAST

See *Fast Automatic Stock Transfer*

Fast Automatic Stock Transfer

Fast Automatic Stock Transfer (FAST) is a service offered by DTC to help participants notify transfer agents of the need to re-register a certificate.

FAX

Pronounced Facks

A FAX is an abbreviation for a piece of telecommunications equipment, called a facsimile machine, that can send the image of a document to another FAX machine.

FDIC

See *Federal Deposit Insurance Corporation*

FDICIA

See *Federal Deposit Insurance Corporation Improvement Act*

Fed

See *Federal Reserve Board*

Fed Eligibility

An instrument is Fed Eligible when it is eligible for deposit and processing in the Fed by meeting certain requirements.

Firms, such as federally chartered banks, can deal directly with the Fed if they are subject to its regulation. As a result, brokers, which cannot be members of the Fed, must use federally chartered banks to access the Fed.

Fed Funds

Fed Funds are same day money transfers sent electronically between member banks of the Federal Reserve System using the Fed wire system. Fed funds are usable immediately upon receipt.

Fed Wire, Fed Funds Rate

Fed Funds Rate

The Fed Funds Rate is the rate that member banks of the Federal Reserve charge each other for short term loans of their excess reserve funds. These are the funds held towards the end of the day in excess of the Fed's reserve requirements which are subsequently loaned to other banks so that they can meet their own end of day reserve requirements without incurring penalties.

Changes in the federal reserve requirements and changes in the Fed's discount rate impact the Fed Funds Rate.

Fed Funds

Fed Regulation G

Fed Regulation G governs credit for margin securities that have been extended by parties other than banks, brokers and dealers.

Fed Regulation T, Fed Regulation T

Fed Regulation T

Fed Regulation T governs credit for margin securities extended by securities brokers and dealers to their customers.

Margin

Fed Regulation U

Fed Regulation U governs lending of money using securities as collateral by banks to their customers.

Collateral

Fed Regulation X

Fed Regulation X extends Regulation G, T and U to additional borrowers and to some types of credit that are not otherwise covered.

Fed Wire

The Fed Wire is the US electronic settlement system for cash, US treasuries and government agency securities. The Fed Wire system is managed by the US Federal Reserve System and is also used to move money between member banks.

Fed Funds

Federal Agricultural Mortgage Corporation

The Federal Agricultural Mortgage Corporation (FAMC), also known as Farmer Mac, was established in 1988 to provide a secondary market for farm mortgages.

Federal Deposit Insurance Corporation

The Federal Deposit Insurance Corporation (FDIC), established under the Banking Act of 1933, charters and regulates State Banks, and it insures deposits in Federal and National banks. The FDIC insures deposits in federally chartered banks up to $100,000 per customer. In the event of a bank failure, the customer will receive a cash payment equal to the amount of their deposit, up to $100,000.

www.fdic.gov

Federal Deposit Insurance Corporation Improvement Act

Section 112 of Federal Deposit Insurance Corporation Improvement Act (FDICIA) was signed into law in May, 1993. This law requires banks to annually report that management is responsible for financial statements, controls and compliance with regulations, and to help assess the effectiveness of their procedures and compliance with regulations.

Federal Financing Bank

The Federal Financing Bank (FFB) was established by the Federal Financing Bank Act of 1973 to consolidate and reduce the government's cost of financing a variety of federal agencies as well as other institutions whose obligations are guaranteed by the federal government. The bank is authorized to purchase any obligation that is issued, sold, or guaranteed by a federal agency.

Federal Funds

See Fed Funds

Federal Funds Rate

See Fed Funds Rate

Federal Home Loan Bank

The Federal Home Loan Bank (FHLB) was established in 1932 to provide short term liquidity and long term credit to Savings and Loan Banks.

Federal Home Loan Mortgage Corporation

The Federal Home Loan Mortgage Corporation (FHLMC), also known as Freddie Mac, was established in 1970 to create a national secondary market for mortgages.

Freddie Mac

Federal Housing Administration

The Federal Housing Administration (FHA) is a federal agency within the Department of Housing and Urban Development (HUD), which insures residential mortgage loans made by private lenders and sets standards for underwriting mortgage loans.

Federal National Mortgage Association

The Federal National Mortgage Association (FNMA), also known as Fannie Mae, was established in 1938 as a government agency to provide a secondary market for FHA and Veteran's Administration guaranteed mortgages. It adds liquidity to the residential mortgage market by buying mortgages from original lenders and selling securities which represent interests in pools of mortgages.

FNMA is still considered a quasi-governmental agency since the government guarantees its bonds; however, as of 1968, Fannie Mae has been a publicly owned corporation and is traded on the NYSE.

Federal Housing Administration

Federal Reserve Bank

The Federal Reserve Bank is a part of the Federal Reserve System which makes loans to members of the system.

Federal Reserve Bank Discount Rate

Federal Reserve Bank Discount Rate is the rate at which member banks may borrow funds directly from the Federal Reserve. Such loans are called discount loans and are intended for short term liquidity needs. The discount rate is determined by the Federal Reserve Board of Governors.

Discount Loan, Federal Reserve System Board of Governors

Federal Reserve Board

See Federal Reserve System Board of Governors

Federal Reserve System

The Federal Reserve System is a government institution created by Congress in 1913 to act as the nations central bank and administer the nation's bank reserves, credit and monetary policies, and oversee the banking industry, as well as certain aspects of broker activity such as credit. The Fed is responsible for monetary policy in the US.

Monetary Policy

Federal Reserve System Board of Governors

Federal Reserve System Board of Governors is the supervisory body responsible for administering to the Federal Reserve System. Established by the Banking Act of 1935, the board is composed of seven members, appointed by the President of the United States, and is divided into six offices and nine divisions.

Federal Reserve System Board of Governors has several responsibilities, including:

- Oversee US monetary policy
- Establish reserve requirements for US federally chartered banks
- Provide participant services
- Make loans
- Facilitate currency transfers outside the US
- Facilitate check clearing
- Facilitate electronic funds transfers within the US

Banking Act of 1935, Federal Reserve System, Monetary Policy

Federation Internationale des Bourses de Valeurs

The Federation Internationale des Bourses de Valeurs (FIBV) is an international organization consisting of the world's stock markets. Located in Paris, FIBV's goal is to stimulate a free flow of capital across national boundaries.

www.fibv.com

FEDI

See *Financial Electronic Data Interchange*

Fences

See *Collar*

FF

FF is an abbreviation for French Francs which are the unit of currency of France.

FHA

See *Federal Housing Administration*

FHLMC

See *Federal Home Loan Mortgage Corporation*

FIBOR

Pronounced Fi Bore

FIBOR is the abbreviation for the Frankfurt Interbank Offered Rate.

London Interbank Offered Rate

FIBV

See *Federation Internationale des Bourses de Valeurs*

Fiche

Fiche is an abbreviation for microfiche.

Fiduciary

A Fiduciary is defined under ERISA as a person or institution that is legally responsible for acting for the benefit of another. Specific duties of a fiduciary are identified in law, while further duties may also be defined in a Trust Agreement.

Trust Agreement, ERISA, Fiduciary Duties

Fiduciary Duties

Fiduciary Duties are the legal obligations of a fiduciary. They include:

- Loyalty to the Trust
- Preservation of Trust assets
- Segregation of assets
- Exercise of skill and care
- Accountability
- Payout of income
- Fiduciary

FIFO

See *First In-First Out*

Fifth Third Bank

Fifth Third Bank is a US-based bank.

www.53.com

Figuration

Figuration is the process conducted by the Purchase and Sale department of a broker to calculate the net amount that is due from a buyer or seller. Figuration considers the price of the security, quantity, commission, taxes, etc.

File Compression

File Compression is used to reduce the overall size of a file in order to save storage space or transmission time for text, images or digital video. Compression is achieved by removing the blank spaces in the data or the image.

File Transfer Protocol

The File Transfer Protocol (FTP) is a standard that is used to send files between computers that use the UNIX operating system.

Fill-or-Kill

Fill-or-Kill (FOK) is a command that specifies that an entire order must either be filled immediately, or cancelled.

Filter

A Filter is a computer program or a methodology that examines data or transactions and only allows specific instances of the data or transaction to pass through. A filter can act as an editor or a router.

Final Transfer

A Final Transfer is an irrevocable and unconditional transfer of funds or a security.

Provisional Transfer, Finality Risk

Finality Risk

Finality Risk is the risk that a transfer of funds or securities can be rescinded.

Final Transfer

Finance Bonds

Finance Bonds are issued by banks, finance companies, Real Estate Investment Trusts, etc., to raise funds in order to make customer loans at a higher rate.

Financial Accounting Standards Board

The Financial Accounting Standards Board (FASB) is an independent, self regulating organization that established the Generally Accepted Accounting Principles which are the accounting rules followed by firms throughout the US, including securities firms.

Generally Accepted Accounting Principles

Financial Assistance Corporation

The Financial Assistance Corporation (FAC) was established in 1988 to support the FSLIC.

Financial Company Commercial Paper

Financial Company Commercial Paper is commercial paper that has been placed through a Finance Company, rather than directly from the purchaser to the buyer.

Financial Electronic Data Interchange

Financial Electronic Data Interchange is the electronic movement of commercial transactions information in a standard format between banks.

Financial Futures

Financial Futures are futures contracts for interest-sensitive financial instruments such as:

- US Treasury bonds
- CDs
- Currencies
- Stock market indices

Financial Industry Numbering System

Pronounced Fins

A Financial Industry Numbering System (FINS) number is created by the Financial Industry Numbering System. It is a unique number for each firm in the financial industry, and consists of an Industry Code (1 digit), and an Institution Code (4 digits).

Financial Information eXchange

FIX is a messaging standard for pre-trade and trade messages that was started by a small group of US Investment Managers and Brokers. This group wanted real-time connectivity and felt that S.W.I.F.T.'s store and forward approach was too slow, and that S.W.I.F.T.'s ability to generate new message standards was too slow to develop the standards needed by the Front Office.

S.W.I.F.T.

Financial Intermediary

A Financial Intermediary is a bank, broker, mutual fund, investment manager, etc., that assists in the flow of funds through the economy by bringing together buyers and lenders.

Financial Leverage

See *Leverage*

Financial Loss

A Financial Loss occurs when a business or operation makes an error that must be reimbursed or which causes an interest payment that cannot be recovered.

Financial Planner

A Financial Planner is an investment professional who analyzes an individual's financial circumstances and personal goals, and prepares a program to meet the investor's objectives.

Financial Printer

A Financial Printer is a printer in the US that works within SEC regulations that cover the way a prospectus is presented. Financial Printers are bonded and are required to keep information confidential until it is released to the public.

FINS

See *Financial Industry Numbering System*

FIPS

See *Fixed Income Pricing System*

Firm Access and Query System

The Firm Access and Query System (FAQS) is the NASD system that helps participating members maintain registration and examination data for their registered representatives in the Central Registration Depository.

Central Registration Depository, NASD

Firm Bid or Offer

A Firm Bid or Offer is a bid or an offer that is made regarding a security at a definite price for a certain period of time which the maker is obligated to meet if accepted.

Bid, Offering Price

Firm Commitment Underwriting

See *Underwriter*

Firm Offer

See *Firm Bid or Offer*

Firm Price

See *Firm Bid or Offer*

Firm Quotation

The term Firm Quotation can be used in two ways:

- See Firm Bid or Offer
- The term Firm Quotation is used by NASD to describe its requirement that a Market Maker execute an order from another broker/dealer at its displayed Nasdaq price for the normal unit of trading, or for its displayed size, whichever is greater.

NASD

Firm Quote

See *Firm Bid or Offer*

Over-the-Counter Market

First Call Date

The First Call Date is the earliest date on which a security may be redeemed by the issuer. The first call date is listed on the bond certificate.

First Call Year

The First Call Year is the specific year before maturity when a bond may be called and redeemed at par.

First Chicago NBD Corporation

First Chicago NBD Corporation is a US-based Commercial Bank.

www.fcnbd.com

First Coupon Date

The First Coupon Date is the initial day that an interest payment will be paid by the issuer to the holders of a fixed income security.

The First Coupon Date is used for interest accrual and cash flow purposes. For example, for a U.S. corporate bond issued on 6/15/99, the First Coupon Date could be 11/15/99.

Last Coupon Date

First Deed of Trust

A First Deed of Trust is a lien on a property that has a first claim because it was recorded first.

First In-First Out

First In, First Out (FIFO) is an accounting standard that says that the first transaction will be considered before any others when any portion of the position is sold. In a rising market, this means that the lots purchased first, and presumably at a lower price will be sold first, thereby maximizing the amount of gain that would be subject to tax.

Last In-First Out

First Mortgage

A First Mortgage is a lien on property that is superior in law to any other.

First Payment Date

The First Payment Date is the first due date for the payment of interest on a bond.

First Principal Payment Date

The First Principal Payment Date is the first day that a principal payment will be paid by the issuer to the holders of a fixed income security. For many bonds, the First Principal Payment Date at maturity. For asset backed securities, there may be a First Principal Payment Date shortly after the security is issued.

The First Principal Date is used for interest accrual and cash flow purposes.

Fiscal Year

The Fiscal Year, often abbreviated as FY, is the twelve-month period that is used by a business for its financial records. This cycle does not have to be the same as the calendar year.

Calendar Year

FITS

See *Fixed Income Transaction System*

FIX

See *Financial Information eXchange*

Fixed Annuity

A Fixed Annuity is an investment contract that guarantees returns during its accumulation period and level (fixed) payments during its pay-out period.

Annuity

Fixed Income

Fixed Income instruments are securities which represent a loan, whereby the issuer is the debtor and the investor is the lender. Classification of fixed-income instruments includes bonds and debentures.

Debt, Bond, Debenture

Fixed Income Pricing System

The Fixed Income Pricing System (FIPS) is a NASD system that centralizes quotations and trade reporting for high-yield and other debt securities.

Fixed Income Security

See Fixed Income

Fixed Income Transaction System

The Fixed Income Transaction System (FITS) was established by the NSCC to provide efficient and standardized processing of municipal and corporate bonds and Unit Investment Trusts, by allowing the submission of trades on trade date. FITS enables timely trade comparisons and early resolution of discrepancies by participants, and also reduces risk.

NSCC

Fixed Rate

Fixed Rate refers to the condition of a loan or security that has a permanent interest rate.

Fixed Rate Bond

Fixed Rate Bond

A Fixed Rate Bond is a bond that has a coupon rate that does not change.

Variable Rate Bond

Fixed Rate Instruments

See *Fixed Rate Bond*

Fixed Rate Loans

A Fixed Rate Loan is a loan where the interest rate does not change over the life of the loan.

Flat

See *Trading Flat*

Float

Float is the time period between:

- The presentation of a negotiable instrument to a financial firm and the actual collection of the funds by the firm.
- When a liability is incurred until the date it is settled.

Float is also defined by the relative number of shares of a stock available for trading by the public compared with the total of the shares issued.

Floating Rate Bond

See *Variable Rate*

Floating Rate Instruments

See *Variable Rate*

Floating Rate Note

See *Variable Rate*

Floor

A Floor can be:

- The place in a recognized exchange where trading is actually conducted
- A call on a futures contract that is sold to protect the investor against a decline in rates
- The lower limit for the interest rate on a floating–rate bond

Floor Broker

A Floor Broker is a member of a recognized exchange who is authorized to trade on behalf of their customers on the floor of an exchange.

Floor Official

A Floor Official is an employee of an exchange who supervises and regulates trading floor activities.

Exchange

Floor Reporter

A Floor Reporter is an employee of an exchange who collects transaction data and inputs it into the exchange's price reporting system.

Exchange

Floor Trader

A Floor Trader is a person who is a member of an exchange who trades only for their own account.

Floppy Disk

A Floppy Disk is the removable medium that is most common today on personal computers. It currently measures 3.5 inches on each side and holds approximately 1.4 megabytes of data.

Removable Media

Floppy Drive

The Floppy Drive is the computer device that is used to access the data on a floppy disk. Floppy drives are either built into a personal computer or can be attached as an external device to a laptop computer.

External Device, Laptop Computer

Flow Chart

A Flowchart is a graphical representation of a process flow or a sequence of events. There are several ways to depict events on a flow chart, but they all use some form of line to show how a transaction in the process moves from point to point.

Fluctuations

Fluctuations are the up and down changes in the price of a stock.

FNMA

See *Federal National Mortgage Association*

FOK

See *Fill-or-Kill*

For Further Credit to

See *Beneficial Owner*

Forced Conversion

Forced Conversion occurs when a call for redemption of a convertible security is made at a price lower than the market value of the underlying asset into which the convertible may be exchanged.

In this case the investor will find it more favorable to exchange the convertible for the underlying asset than to give up the security for cash at the call price.

Forced Settlement

The Forced Settlement of securities or funds is an event that is either mandated or enforced by a third party.

Foreclosure

A Foreclosure is the legal process of enforcing the payment of a debt by taking title to the assets that were identified as collateral.

Foreign Currency Futures

Foreign Currency Futures are established for foreign currencies, and are quoted in the US in dollars. They include futures for Interest Rates, US Treasury Bonds, Notes and Bills, GNMAs, Euro-dollar Deposits, and CDs.

Foreign Exchange

Foreign Exchange is the process whereby firms buy and sell multiple currencies with an institutional counterparty.

Foreign Ordinary Shares

The term Foreign Ordinary Shares was created when the NYSE considered adding securities issued in other countries to the New York Stock Exchange list of eligible securities. The shares were to have been listed in the original currency and settled via the DTC in the country of origin.

NYSE, DTC

Foreign Securities Comparison and Netting System

The Foreign Securities Comparison and Netting System (FSCN) automates the comparison and netting of non-US equity transactions executed by NSCC members. FSCN allows non-US equity transactions to be processed in NSCC's OTC Comparison System, which uses a common price to net and settle compared trades on a participant-to-participant basis.

Foreign Security

A Foreign Security is one that is traded outside of the trader's domicile.

FOREX

See *Foreign Exchange*

ForEx

See *Foreign Exchange*

Form 1099

See *IRS Form 1099*

Form 10-K

Form 10-K is an annual report that all corporations with 500 or more shareholders, and assets of at least $10 million, must file with the Securities and Exchange Commission.

The 10 K includes an income statement, balance sheet, statement of cash flows with a review by auditors, management discussion and analysis of financial results, and other information.

Form 10-Q

Form 10-Q is a quarterly report to the Securities and Exchange Commission filed by most firms with listed stocks. Financial results are unaudited.

Form W-2

See *IRS Form W-2*

Form W-4

See *IRS Form W-4*

Form W-9

See *IRS Form W-9*

Format

A Format is a structured way of organizing data so that both the sender and receiver can use the data in the same way.

Message

Forward

See *Forward Contract*

Forward Contract

A Forward Contract is a cash market transaction in which two parties agree to the purchase and sale of a commodity at some point in the future under some agreed upon conditions. Unlike futures, forwards are not traded on an exchange.

Contract terms for forward contracts are not standardized, they are not transferable and usually can be canceled only with the consent of both parties.

Some countries without a futures exchange use forwards as their only method of trading against a future date. Forward contracts have more counter-party risk than futures contracts.

Futures Contract

Forward Interest Rate

The Forward Interest Rate is the interest rate for a specific futures contract.

Forward Yield Curve

The Forward Yield Curve is typically derived from the zero coupon yield curve and shows the implied forward interest rate as points on the curve.

Forwarding Agent

A Forwarding Agent receives securities during a tender and forwards them to the depository agent.

Tender, Depository Agent

Fourth Market

The Fourth Market includes the direct trading of large blocks of securities between institutional investors through a crossing network. This allows large money managers to minimize brokerage fees.

Crossing Network, Primary Market, Secondary Market, Third Market

Fractional Shares

Fractional Shares represent less than one share of a security and are frequently paid out as dividends. Except in DRIP programs, fractional positions are not accommodated in most systems, and the shareholder must decide whether they want to buy an additional fraction of a share in order to have a complete single share, or if they wish to sell the fraction for cash.

DRIP

Franc

Franc is the currency unit of France.

FF

Frank Russell Trust Company

FRTC is a wholly owned subsidiary of Frank Russell Company which offers investment expertise for defined contribution and defined benefit retirement plans in the US.

Fraud

See *Misrepresentation*

Freddie Mac

See *Federal Home Loan Mortgage Corporation*

Free and Clear

Free and Clear refers to property that is owned without debt.

Free Deliver

See *Deliver Free*

Free Receive

See *Receive Free*

Free Riding

Free Riding is:

- When a broker or a trader buys shares of a new issue that trades at a premium in the immediate aftermarket
- A term that refers to the practice of one firm or individual capitalizing on the perceived expertise of another firm or individual by allowing the actions of the "expert" to dictate their own

Free Stock

Free Stock are those shares that are owned by the firm or which are in a margin account and are available for loans or hypothecation.

Hypothecation

French Trésor

French Trésor is the French Treasury, with is the issuer of Treasury debt in the form of BTANs and OATs which are fully guaranteed by the French Government.

Maturities on BTANs and OATs can vary from three months to 30 years.

FRN

See *Floating Rate Note*

Front End Load

A Front End Load is a sales fee that is charged to a customer when an investment fund is purchased. The maximum front end load stipulated by law is 8.5%; however, most loads do not exceed 6%.

Load

Front Office

See *Middle Office*

Front Running

Front Running is when a broker or a trader buys or sells a security for their own benefit when they have existing orders from customers that they hold until after their trades are completed. Front running is done with the hope that the customers' orders will move the market favorably.

FTC

Abbreviation for Federal Trade Commission

FTP

See *File Transfer Protocol*

FTSE All Share Index

The FTSE All Share Index is a stock index derived from equities listed on the London Stock Exchange.

Full Coupon Bond

A Full Coupon Bond is one whose coupon is at or above current interest rates.

Full Power of Attorney

See *Power of Attorney*

Full Service Broker

A Full Service Broker executes trades, offers investment advice, tax shelters, asset management, financial planning and other services.

Discount Broker

Fully Registered

A security is Fully Registered when the registrar or transfer agent has the complete name and address of an investor recorded on their books.

Fully Valued

A Fully Valued stock is trading at a price which analysts believe matches the company's fundamental earnings power.

Fully-Paid-For Account

The Fully-Paid-For Account is a sub-account within NSCC's CNS system that is used by participants to maintain compliance with the requirements of Rule 15c3-3.

Continuous Net Settlement, Rule 15c3-3

Fund of Funds

A Fund of Funds is a mutual fund that invests in other mutual funds, rather than directly into specific stocks or bonds.

Mutual Fund

Fund/SERV

Fund/SERV is a service offered by the NSCC to assist brokers in settling purchases and sales of mutual funds by automating and standardizing the processing of mutual fund purchase and redemption orders, settlement, and account registration. The system works with CNS to calculate a daily net money settlement amount.

The Underwriting & Tender Offers feature of NSCC's Fund/SERV System automates the process for investment companies to offer new funds in the form of an initial public offering (IPO) or underwriting.

Fund/SERV also streamlines the tender offer process for mutual funds to redeem shares within the redemption period.

Fundamental Analysis

When analysts engage in Fundamental Analysis, they focus on the basic worth of an individual security, and use ratios to compare a security to the industry, its sector or its peers.

Sector, Technical Analysis

Funds Only Settlement Service

With Funds Only Settlement Service (FOSS), NSCC has simplified the routing of envelopes that contain money-only charges to full-service participants located in New York City and Jersey City.

Envelope Settlement Service

Fungible

An instrument is Fungible when it is exactly the same as and can be exchanged for all other instruments of its class. For example, a US twenty-dollar bill is fungible since it is exactly equal to any other US twenty-dollar bill.

Futures

See *Futures Contract*

Futures Contract

A Futures Contract is standardized and is traded on an exchange. It is not an option to buy or sell; it is an agreement to buy or sell at a predetermined price at a predetermined time in the future.

The contract specifies the amount, commodity (or security) and month. A contract typically requires a fraction of the total amount to be placed as margin.

If a Futures Contract is held through the last day of the month in which it matures, the buyer must accept delivery and the seller must deliver. Less than 5% of contracts actually involve delivery.

FX

See *Foreign Exchange*

FX Instructions

FX Instructions are the delivery instructions for a foreign exchange transaction which usually include a bank name and account number.

FY

See *Fiscal Year*

FYI

Abbreviation for For Your Information

GAAP

See *Generally Accepted Accounting Principles*

Gamma

Gamma is the measure of change in the delta of an option compared with the price change in the underlying security.

See Delta

Gateway

A Gateway is a point of access to a network.

GCN

See *Global Clearing Network*

GDP

GDP is the abbreviation for Gross Domestic Product.

General Ledger

A General Ledger is an accounting process that, along with its sub-ledgers, is used to record transactions and to develop a firm's Balance Sheet and Profit & Loss Statement.

Balance Sheet, P&L Statement

General Mortgage Bonds

General Mortgage Bonds are bonds that have been secured by a blanket mortgage on the issuer's property but which may be subordinate to other mortgages.

General Obligation Bond

A General Obligation Bond (GO, pronounced G - O) is a bond issued by a municipality that promises only to use its general taxing authority as the basis for repayment. General Obligation Bonds are backed by the full faith, credit and taxing power of the municipality, but not by any collateral.

General Partner

See *Limited Partnership*

General Services Administration

The General Services Administration was established in 1949 to manage government property and records, and with the authority to issue participation certificates.

Participation certificates are official obligations of the United States government.

General Stock Market Index

The General Stock Market Index (IGBVL) is a stock index derived from equities listed on the Bolsa de Valores de Lima.

General Stock Price Index

The General Stock Price Index (IGPA) is a stock index derived from equities listed on the Bolsa de Comercio de Santiago.

Generally Accepted Accounting Principles

The Generally Accepted Accounting Principles (GAAP) are the rules, conventions, standards, and procedures that are generally accepted as correct by accountants. GAAP rules are established by the Financial Accounting Standards Board.

Financial Accounting Standards Board

Ghana Stock Exchange

The Ghana Stock Exchange is the primary stock exchange of Ghana.

www.ghana.com/stockex/index.html

GIC

See *Guaranteed Investment Contract*

GIF

GIF, which stands for Graphics Interchange Format, is a standard for storing still pictures with up to 256 colors.

JPEG

Gigabyte

A Gigabyte is a billion bytes. Gigabytes are a unit of measurement used to denominate a computer's storage capacity.

Byte

Gilt

See *Gilt-Edged Bond*

Gilt-Edged Bond

A Gilt-Edged Bond is:

- A high-grade bond that has been issued by a blue-chip company in which investors can have confidence that their interest payments will not be interrupted
- A government security issued and guaranteed by the United Kingdom

Ginnie Mae

See *Government National Mortgage Association*

Give-Up

A Give-Up occurs when a member of an exchange who is trading on behalf of a second member gives up the second member's name rather than his own to the trade counterparty.

Glass House

A Glass House is a term that is used to describe a large data center. It has two meanings:

- A data center is a Glass House in that it is considered to be fragile and needs to be protected from outside factors.
- The activities of the data center affect everyone throughout an organization and everything that goes on inside the data center becomes immediately visible to its users.

Glass-Steagall Act

Glass-Steagall is a portion of the Banking Act of 1933 that requires the separation of commercial and investment banking.

Banking Act of 1933

Global Clearing Network

The Global Clearing Network (GCN), developed by the International Securities Clearing Corporation, clears and settles cross-border trades going out of the US. The network clears for more than 40 member firms through a central data transmission facility.

International Securities Clearing Corporation

Global Compass

Global Compass is a PC data-entry and communications software package that features a standard, menu-driven format to facilitate user input and access to overseas markets and clearance and settlement services.

Global Custodian

A Global Custodian provides its customers with worldwide custody services, usually by acting through a network of sub-custodians, which may be subsidiaries, branches or other non-affiliated firms.

In the current environment, a global custodian re-processes each transaction that settles in markets around the world in order to normalize the accounting and create a single consolidated statement.

Branch Office, Sub-Custodian

Global Fund

A Global Fund is a mutual fund that includes at least 25% foreign securities in its portfolio.

GNMA

See *Government National Mortgage Association*

GNP

See Gross National Product

GO

See *General Obligation Bond*

Go Long

When an investor decides to Go Long, they purchase a security hoping that its price will rise.

Go Short

When an investor decides to Go Short, they borrow and sell a security they do not own, hoping its price will fall.

Goal

A Goal is a point where a manager or a firm wishes to be at a certain time in the future.

Standard

Gold Fix

The Gold Fix is the official setting of the price of gold by dealers in a twice-daily meeting in London at the central bank. The fix is the fundamental worldwide price for deriving the prices of gold bullion and other gold-related contracts and products.

Goldman, Sachs & Co.

Goldman, Sachs & Co. is a US-based broker/dealer.

www.gs.com

Good Delivery

In order to settle a trade, the security must meet certain qualifications for Good Delivery. This means that the security should be in proper form in order to comply with the contract of sale and to transfer the title to the purchaser.

Good Delivery includes:

- Correct type of security
- Issuers
- Quantity
- Denomination of the certificate
- Outstanding interest coupons
- Proper endorsement
- Timeliness of delivery

Good-til-Cancelled Order

GTC is an open order that remains in force until it is executed or cancelled. It does not expire at the end of the trading day as a day order does.

Day Order

Gopher

A Gopher is a software tool that is used for browsing on the Internet.

Government Dealer

A Government Dealer is a dealer in US government securities.

Government National Mortgage Association

The Government National Mortgage Association (GNMA), also known as Ginnie Mae, is a US-based corporation wholly owned by the US government. GNMA buys mortgages at better than market price, and then issues and guarantees mortgage-backed bonds and pass-through certificates. GNMA securities settle at the Participants Trust Company, now a part of the Depository Trust Company.

Under this program, principal and interest payments collected on mortgages in specified pools are "passed through" to holders of GNMA-guaranteed certificates after deducting servicing and guaranty fees. Certificates mature in up to 40 years, but the average life is approximately 12 years because of prepayments. The minimum denomination of certificates is $25,000 and issuance is in registered form only.

Depository Trust Company, Participants Trust Company

Government Securities Broker

A Government Securities Broker is any person or firm that regularly acts as an agent for government securities trades.

Government Securities Clearing Corporation

The Government Securities Clearing Corporation (GSCC) was incorporated in 1986 as an affiliate of the NSCC. It was organized to provide an automated

comparison and netting system for brokerage firms trading US Government securities.
GSCC's automated system is an on-line, real-time comparison system for regular way and when issued securities.

The GSCC is a self-regulated organization that is agency registered with and regulated by the Securities and Exchange Commission.

www.gscc.com

NSCC

Government Securities Dealer

A Government Securities Dealer is one of about forty firms that make a market in US government securities. To maintain their status as a government dealer, firms must participate in every government securities auction.

Government Sponsored Enterprises

Government Sponsored Enterprises are quasi-government agencies that work closely with the Federal Reserve System and the Treasury. GSEs can borrow funds in capital markets and lend them at favorable rates.

Some GSEs have a government guarantee of their debt, and all have a line of credit at the US Treasury. GSEs include the following agencies: Connie Lee, FAC, FMHA, Farmer Mac, FFB, FHLSB, Freddie Mac, Fannie Mae, FAC, FICO, GSA, Ginnie Mae, MA, SBA, Sallie Mae, TVA, USPS.

Governments

Governments are securities that are issued by a national government, such as the US Treasury.

Grace Period

The Grace Period occurs between the time a loan payment is due and the point that it begins to incur a penalty.

Graphical User Interface

Pronounced gooey

A Graphical User Interface (GUI) is an interface between a person and a computer that helps the user input requests and see the data that has been recorded by the computer.
A GUI is based upon a conceptual method of interaction that uses buttons, icons and graphical information rather than the lines of text that are typical of text based interfaces.

Typically, a GUI user will rely on a mouse to move a cursor around a screen.

Mouse, Text Based Interface, Cursor

Green Shoe

A Green Shoe provision is an optional term in an underwriting agreement that says that if there is a public demand for the issue that exceeds the amount initially presented, the issuer will authorize additional shares.

Gridlock

Gridlock is a situation in which some transfer instructions have failed, and because of this failure, additional instructions at other institutions cannot be completed. When experiencing gridlock, information stops moving or moves slowly through the financial system.

Gross Earnings

Gross Earnings are the total amount of pretax earnings before any deductions are made.

Gross Income

Gross Income is the total of all income before taxes and/or expenses are deducted.

Gross National Product

Gross National Product (GNP) is the total monetary value of final goods and services in an economy during a period of time.

Gross Settlement

See *Trade-for-Trade Settlement*

Group of Thirty

In the mid-1980's a group of thirty retired CEO's of worldwide bank and brokerage firms met to discuss how to improve the way that securities were settled across borders. Known as the Group of Thirty, the organization's mission was to reduce the risk associated with cross-border trading and to streamline the overall worldwide settlement process so as to improve efficiency. The Group of Thirty created nine recommendations:

- By 1990, all trade comparisons should be accomplished by T+1
- By 1992, all indirect participants should join a trade comparison system
- By 1992, each country should have a central securities depository
- By 1992, each country should consider and install a netting system
- By 1992, all settlements should be DVP
- All settlements should be made with Same Day Funds
- By 1992, all settlements should be finalized by T + 3
- By 1990, all barriers to Securities Lending should be removed
- By 1990, each country should adopt ISO standards

Growth and Income Funds

Growth and Income Funds have the dual objective of investing in securities by growing through income as well as capital gains. These funds generally hold securities issued by established firms that have historically paid attractive and/or rising dividends.

Growth Funds

Growth Funds have the objective of increasing their value by investing in the stocks of growing companies that often pay little or no dividends.

Growth Objective

An investor has a Growth Objective when they have a preference for assuming risk that is consistent with seeking an appreciation ion the value of their portfolio.

Growth Stock

Growth Stock is the stock of a company in a new, rapidly expanding or emerging industry. Growth Stocks are usually purchased for their capital gain potential and not for income.

Capital Gain

GSA

See *General Services Administration*

GSCC

See *Government Securities Clearing Corporation*

GSE All-Share Index.

The GSE All-Share Index is a stock index derived from equities listed on the Ghana Stock Exchange.

GTC

See *Good-til-Cancelled Order*

GTX

GTX is a New York Stock Exchange abbreviation for Good Until Cancelled.

Good-til-Cancelled Order

Guaranteed Bonds

Guaranteed Bonds are used when the interest or principal or both, has been guaranteed by a company other than the issuer. The third party firm could be affiliated with the issuer.

Guaranteed Certificate of Deposit

A Guaranteed Certificate of Deposit is issued by a bank. These certificates characteristically have flexible terms, guaranteed principal, and reinvestment rates similar to the guaranteed investment contracts that are issued by insurance companies.

Bank Certificate of Deposit, Negotiable Certificate of Deposit

Guaranteed Investment Contract

A Guaranteed Investment Contract (GIC) is issued by an insurance company. These contracts characteristically have fixed rates, flexible terms, guaranteed principal, and reinvestment rates similar to the guaranteed certificates of deposit that are issued by insurance companies.

GUI

See *Graphical User Interface*

Guilder Shares (New York Shares)

Guilder Shares are the Netherlands' substitute for ADRs. Because Dutch regulations do not permit their companies to issue ADRs linked to active home-country shares, even if those shares are held by a depository bank, the appropriate quantity of underlying home-country shares are cancelled and the equivalent amount of Guilder Shares (New York Shares) are issued.

ADR

Haircut

A Haircut is:

- The difference between the calculated collateral value of a security and its actual market value. The amount of this difference is used to protect the lender from a loss.
- A formula used to evaluate a security's value in order to determine a broker-dealers net worth.

Handoff

A Handoff is the transfer of responsibility or the transfer of a transaction from:

- One person to another
- One application to another
- One department to another
- One firm to another

Hang Seng Stock Index

The Hang Seng Stock Index is a stock index derived from equities listed on the Stock Exchange of Hong Kong, Ltd.

Hard Drive

A Hard Drive is a device that is used by a computer to store data which needs to be stored locally and accessed quickly.

Hardware

Hardware consists of the physical parts of a computer.

Software, Vaporware

HEDGE

A conservative strategy used to limit investment loss by effecting a transaction which offsets an existing position.

Hedge Fund

A Hedge Fund consists of a small group of investors (less than 500) who have their money invested in a portfolio managed by a professional. The participants in the fund must meet minimum requirement of net wealth, and the fund is not as constrained as a normal mutual fund by the type of investments it can make. Unlike most funds, hedge fund can borrow, sell short, and use options. Hedge funds generally assume higher risk with the intention of producing higher returns.

Hedged Tender

A Hedged Tender is an investor's tender of securities accompanied by the short sale of a portion of the securities tendered. The short sale hedges the possibility that not all the tendered securities will be accepted by the buyer and that the value of those securities not accepted will be less than the tender price.

Hedging

Hedging is the process of reducing investment risks by taking a contrary action at the same time as the original investment. The goal is to offset a potential loss in the original investment since the price change or interest rate movement in the hedge will offset the change in the original investment.

Held

If a security is Held:

- It is present in a portfolio
- At Nasdaq, it is temporarily not available for trading, and market makers are not allowed to display quotes

Help Desk

There are two types of Help Desks:

- An internal Help Desk is typically involved with assisting the users of a data center, or an application, or a network, including a LAN, when they need some technical support.
- An external Help Desk is normally involved with providing support to customers or with answering customer investigations or complaints.

Investigation, Customer Complaints

Helsinki Stock Exchange

The Helsinki Stock Exchange is the primary stock exchange of Finland.

HEX All Share Index

The HEX All Share Index is a stock index derived from equities listed on the Helsinki Stock Exchange.

Hidden Load

A Hidden Load is a sales charge that is not immediately apparent to the investor.

Hidden Values

Hidden Values include assets such as real estate that are owned by a company but not reflected in the balance sheet.

High Grade Bond

A High Grade Bond is one that is expected to be able to easily pay the principal and interest that is due.

High Grade Stock

A High Grade Stock is a security issued by a leading corporation with a very high rating.

High Net Worth Individuals

High Net Worth Individuals are investors who generally have over $5 million in investable assets, not including a primary residence, and who want highly personalized investment services and are willing to pay for them.

High Yield Bond Funds

High Yield Bond Funds generally invest in high yield bonds.

High Yield Bonds

High Yield Bonds

High Yield Bonds generally:

- Pay higher interest
- Have greater potential to fluctuate in price
- Have a significantly lower credit rating by any of the rating agencies (usually Ba or BB and below)

Most High Yield Bonds are considered low grade investments and are sometimes referred to as junk bonds.

Historical Yield

A Historical Yield is the yield produced by an investment over a period of time.

Yield

HNWI

See *High Net Worth Individuals*

Hold

An investor will Hold a security when they own it for an extended period of time.

HOLDER

The purchaser of an option.

Holding Company

A Holding Company is a corporation that owns a large number of shares or a controlling interest in other companies.

A bank holding company is an organization structure that legally permits the holding company to own a bank as well as other financial firms that the bank otherwise could not own. For example, Citibank is owned by Citigroup, which is a holding company.

Glass-Steagall Act

Hong Kong Securities Clearing Company

The Hong Kong Securities Clearing Company Ltd. is the central depository and securities clearing house of Hong Kong.

Hostile Takeover

See *Tender Offer*

House

See *Broker/Dealer*

House Spread

See *Dealer Spread*

Housing and Urban Development

Housing and Urban Development (HUD), is a US government agency established to implement federal housing and community development programs, oversees the Federal Housing Administration.

Housing Authority Bonds

Housing Authority Bonds are used to finance low-income housing and are backed by the Federal Housing Assistance Agency. FHAA debt is guaranteed by the US government.

HSBC Holdings plc

The HSBC Holdings plc is a Hong Kong-based bank.

www.hsbcgroup.com

HTML

Abbreviation for Hypertext Markup Language

Hypertext

HUD

See *Housing and Urban Development*

HUD-1 Uniform Settlement Statement

The HUD-1 Uniform Settlement Statement is a standard form which itemizes the closing costs associated with purchasing a home or refinancing a mortgage loan.

Housing and Urban Development

Hypertext

Hypertext is a method of organizing data, images and video so that a user can move from one point to another point in a document or on the Internet.

Internet

Hypothecation

Hypothecation is a brokerage firm's process of pledging the securities in a margin account to a bank to obtain a loan that will be used to fund the margin account's activity.

Margin Account

IBB Index

The IBB Index is a stock index derived from equities listed on the Bolsa de Bogota.

ICI

See *Investment Company Institute*

Icon

An Icon is a symbol which is used to identify the available options in a PC computer program. When a user places the cursor on an icon and clicks the mouse, the computer will initiate the action designated by the icon.

Cursor, Mouse

ICSD

See *International Central Securities Depository*

See *International Council of Securities Dealers*

ID

See *Institutional Delivery System*

ID/CNS Interface for Prime Broker Business

The ID/CNS Interface for Prime Broker Business is a settlement option that streamlines the processing of Prime Broker trades. The interface connects NSCC's CNS System to DTC's Institutional Delivery (ID) System. Prime Broker transactions that are affirmed in ID and settle at DTC can net in CNS, simplifying trade processing and reducing risk.

Institutional Delivery System, Continuous Net Settlement

IDC

See *International Depository and Clearing*

IESS

See *Intercity Envelope Settlement Service*

II Message

See *Institutional Instructions*

IID

Abbreviation for Interactive Institutional Delivery

Institutional Delivery System, DTC

Il Sole 24 Ore Index

Il Sole 24 Ore Index is a stock index derived from equities listed on the Bolsa Valori de Milan.

Illiquid

See Illiquid Securities

Illiquid Market

See *Liquid Market*

Illiquid Securities

Illiquid Securities are those that have very few investors and which trade infrequently.

IMAB

Abbreviation for the International Markets Advisory Board.

Image Processing

Image Processing is involved when a scanner processes a piece of paper and stores the document in a digitized form so that it can be archived and viewed.

Imaging

See *Image Processing*

Immediate-or-Cancel

Immediate-or-Cancel is an order instruction type that requires the broker/dealer to immediately fill as much of the order as possible, and cancel the rest.

Immobilization

Immobilization is the placement of certificates and financial instruments in a central securities depository to reduce the movement of physical securities in the marketplace and to facilitate book entry transfers. According to modern theory, the next logical step after immobilization is dematerialization, and the final step is complete book entry.

Central Securities Depository, Dematerialization, Book Entry

In Kind

Assets are transferred In Kind when they are transferred into or out of an account free of payment. This usually occurs when a new fund is set up or a new account is created.

In Play

A firm is In Play when it is the target of one or more firms that wish to acquire it.

In The Money

See In-The-Money

Inactive Date

The Inactive Date is the date when a security becomes inactive due to a call, an expiration or maturity.

Income Bonds

An Income Bond is one where the issuer pays interest only when income is earned. Unpaid interest on income bonds accrues until it can be paid.

Income Collection

Income Collection is the process used by banks and brokers to collect interest on bonds and dividend payments on equities.

Income Fund

An Income Fund is a mutual fund with a primary objective to achieve current income for the fund's owners, typically by purchasing bonds, preferred stocks and common stocks that pay high dividends.

Income Portfolio

An Income Portfolio is a portfolio that has been designed to hold securities that are expected to provide a steady stream of income from interest and/or dividends.

Income Stock

An Income Sock is one with a relatively high dividend yield.

Indemnify

To Indemnify is to promise to compensate a person or firm in the event of a loss.

Indenture

The Indenture is usually located on a bond, and lists the terms or covenants of the bond.

Deed of Trust, Covenants

Independent Broker

See *Two-Dollar Broker*

Independent Controls

Independent Controls are guidelines that are imposed from somewhere outside of a business unit or a processing department to ensure accuracy and prevent fraud.

Index

An Index can be:

- An arithmetic (or statistical) summary of the prices of a group of securities that were selected to represent a total universe, e.g., Dow Jones Industrial Average, which can be used to measure changes in the performance of the index
- An option that is priced to relate to an established arithmetic index, and which can be bought and sold
- A published rate that is used to determine interest rate changes on variable rate loans

Dow Jones Industrial Average, Index Fund, ARM

Index Fund

An Index Fund is:

- A fund composed of securities intended to replicate the movement of a specific securities index. The fund may or may not contain all of the securities in the index.
- An account that has been designed to substantially replicate the movement of a specific securities index. The account may or may not contain all of the securities in the index.

Index of the Budapest Stock Exchange

The Index of the Budapest Stock Exchange (BUX) is a stock index derived from equities listed on the Budapest Stock Exchange.

Indication

An Indication is a quote that is sent from a broker to an institutional investor to entice them to buy the security.

Quote

Individual Investor

An Individual Investor is a person who buys or sells securities for their own account. The individual investor, also called a retail investor, generally trades in smaller lots than institutions, and typically doesn't use block trades.

Block Trades, Institutional Investor

Individual Retirement Account

An Individual Retirement Account (IRA) is a tax-deferred retirement custodial account or trust that is available to any individual US taxpayer younger than 70.5 years old.

Roth IRA

Industrial

Industrial is a term that is used for any company that produces goods or services and that is not a utility.

Industrial Bonds

Industrial Bonds are issued by corporations to increase working capital, finance expansion, or refund a previous issue.

Industrial Revenue Bonds

Industrial Revenue Bonds are used to finance the construction of industrial plants, and are repaid by the lease payments that are received as revenue.

Industry Associations

There are several Industry Associations that support the securities industry. Some of the primary ones are:

- American Bankers Association (ABA)
- Bank Depositories User Group (BDUG)
- Futures Industry Association (FIA)
- Securities Industry Association (SIA)
- Industry Standardization for Institutional Trade Communications (ISITC)

Industry Code

See *Standard Industrial Classification*

Industry Standardization for Institutional Trade Communications

The Industry Standardization for Institutional Trade Communications (ISITC) was formed by investment managers, custodian banks and portfolio accounting vendors to enhance S.W.I.F.T. message types that are used to communicate settlement information between banks and advisors.

ISITC standards adhere to S.W.I.F.T. standards (based upon ISO 7775) and ISITC formatted messages can be sent on the S.W.I.F.T. network.

www.isitc.com

ISO 7775, S.W.I.F.T.

Industry Support Groups

The are several Industry Support groups that provide specific services to the securities industry. Some of the primary ones are:

- Financial Advisory Council
- International Business Communications
- Institute for International Research
- New York Institute of Finance
- SEC Institute
- Securities Operations Forum

Industry User Group

The Industry User Group (IUG) was formed in the UK to improve the communication of trade information between brokers and investment advisors. It has subsequently merged with ISITC.

ISITC

Inflation

Inflation occurs when the prices of goods and services rise, thereby reducing the purchasing power of the existing currency.

Deflation

Inflation Indexed Treasury Bonds

In 1997, the US Federal Reserve Board created Inflation Indexed Treasury Bonds that are designed to protect investors against the negative impact of inflation. As inflation increases, so does the yield on the bonds.

Federal Reserve System Board of Governors

Inflation Risk

Inflation Risk is the risk that inflation will eliminate any gains in an investment.

Inflation

Infobahn

See *Information Superhighway*

Information

Information is data that has been organized so that it is useful.

Data

Information Agent

An Information Agent is the agent designated to distribute any written information pertaining to a new offer.

Information Superhighway

The Information Superhighway is a term used by politicians and journalists to identify the internet.

Infrastructure

The Infrastructure consists of regulated institutions that provide services to participants in the securities industry. The Infrastructure consists of:

- Exchanges
- Depositories
- Clearing Houses

Exchange, Depository, Clearing House

ING Bank

ING Bank is a Netherlands-based Universal Bank.

www.ingbank.nl

Initial Public Offering

An Initial Public Offering (IPO) is the initial offering to the public of a new issue of a security. IPOs are distributed in the primary market.

Primary Market

Initial Rate

The Initial Rate is the rate that is charged during the first interval of an Adjusted Rate Mortgage.

Adjustable Rate Mortgage

Input Time

Input Time is the time that it takes to input either a single transaction or a group of transactions.

Inquiry

An inquiry occurs when a customer asks a question regarding their account. If during the resolution of the question, the firm discovers that it has made an error, then the question becomes an investigation.

Investigation

Inside Market

See *Inside Spread*

Inside Quote

See *Inside Spread*

Inside Spread

The Inside Spread is the difference between the best bid and the best ask from all of the Market Makers quoting on a security. Therefore, the Inside Spread is often smaller than the spread offered by any single Market Maker.

Insider Trading

Insider Trading is buying or selling stocks by a company's management, large shareholders, or other individuals based on information that has not yet been made public.

Insider Trading and Securities Fraud Enforcement Act of 1988

The Insider Trading and Securities Fraud Enforcement Act of 1988 is a federal law meant to discourage insider trading. It allows rewards to be given to individuals who provide information about insider trading activity.

Insider Trading

Insider Trading Sanctions Act

The Insider Trading Sanctions Act increased the fines and punishment against those who benefit from insider trading and allows the Securities Exchange Commission to levy fines up to three times the amount gained from insider information.

Securities and Exchange Commission

Institutional Delivery System

The DTC established the Institutional Delivery System (ID) to connect banks, brokers and investment advisors and assist them in the confirmation and affirmation of their transactions.

Confirmation, Affirmation

Institutional Instructions

The DTC has enhanced its Institutional Delivery process to include an automated message type for Institutional Instructions that improves the electronic communication between brokers and investment advisors.

Institutional Investor

An Institutional Investor is an institution that has a large pool of funds that are invested in a range of assets. The assets traded could include securities, real estate, commodities, derivatives, etc. Institutional investors include banks, mutual funds, charitable institutions, universities and employee benefit plans.

Buy Side

Instructing Party

The Instructing Party is the institution that instructs an agent, usually a custodian bank, to settle a transaction.

Insufficient Funds

See *Overdraft*

Insured Account

An Insured Account is one that is opened with a bank, savings and loan or other account that is insured by a federal or private insurance corporation.

Insured Loan

An Insured Loan is one where the lender is assured partial or full payment by a third party if the borrower defaults.

Intangible Assets

Intangible Assets are listed on a firm's balance sheet, and include assets with a value, such as brands, copyrights, goodwill, patents, and trademarks.

Integrated Speech and Data Network

The Integrated Speech and Data Network (ISDN) is a public network, operated by telephone companies, which provides users with a single 256K baud line or two 158K baud lines.

Interactive

Interactive computer programs allow a user to interact and select between alternatives that are offered by the program. This is opposed to a more sequential approach which requires the user to move from one step to the next with little opportunity to change the pattern.

Interactive ID System

The Interactive ID system was created in 1995 to meet the requirements of the move to a three day settlement system in the US.

This system combined the existing ID and International ID systems of the Depository Trust Company, in which batches are processed throughout the day and are therefore made more interactive than the previous overnight-only ID system. This encourages batch users to deal with the DTC in multiple batches throughout the day, rather than in a single end of day batch.

Depository Trust Company, Institutional Delivery System

Intercity Envelope Settlement Service

See *Envelope Settlement Service*

Interest

Interest is the amount a borrower pays to a lender for the use of money (often established as a load). Interest can be calculated as a percentage of the current balance of the amount borrowed or at a pre-determined amount.

Interest Calculation Methods

Various Interest Calculation Methods are used to calculate interest, such as:

- Discount
- CP Discount
- 30/360
- 30/365
- Actual/360
- Actual/365
- Actual/Actual (which could be 365/365 or 366/366)

Interest Coverage

Interest Coverage is the number of times that interest charges are earned. It is calculated by dividing the total of the fixed charges into the earnings available.

Interest Only Strip

An Interest Only Strip consists of the interest rate component of a security that has been removed from its principal repayment obligation.

Strip, Principal-Only Strip

Interest Rate

An Interest Rate is expressed as a percentage of the principal, and is the amount paid by a borrower in order to use a lender's money. Interest rates are generally calculated on an annual basis.

Interest

Interest Rate Future

An Interest Rate Future is a formal futures contract that carries an obligation to make a delivery or receive a fixed-income security under certain conditions and at a specific time.

Futures Contract

Interest Rate Risk

Interest Rate Risk is:

- The risk that rising interest rates will lead to the declining market value of fixed-income securities
- The risk that interest rates will change over time, making a fixed investment that is attractive today, less attractive in the future

Interest Rate Swap

See *Swap*

Interest Rate Types

Interest Rate Types refer to the variety of interest rate instruments, and include instruments such as:

- Fixed Rate Instruments
- Variable Rate Instruments
- Floating Rate Instruments
- Zero Coupon Bonds
- CATS
- Capital Appreciation Instruments
- Capital Accumulation Instruments
- TIGR
- Coupon Instruments
- MBS

- ABS, etc.

Interest Re-Investment Plan

An Interest Re-Investment Plan is one that is provided by an issuer that allows an investor to purchase additional bonds or equity using the interest that is paid by the issuer on one of their bonds.

Interested Party

An Interested Party is one who has been identified by an investor as someone who should also be informed about transactions in their account.

Interface

An Interface is the point of interaction between:

- People
- Organizations
- Departments
- Computers
- People and Computers

For an interface to work properly, both sides must agree on the definitions of the data that is being passed from one side to the other, and the construction of the interface has to establish common denominators (protocols) for moving the data.

Graphical User Interface, Terminal Based Interface, Baud, Protocol

Intermarket Surveillance Group

The Intermarket Surveillance Group (ISG) is an international group that coordinates surveillance and investigations among US and foreign exchanges that trade in securities, options, futures and foreign securities.

Market Surveillance

Intermarket Trading System

The Intermarket Trading System (ITS) is a computer system, operated by SIAC, that links the communications systems of exchanges throughout the US in order to find the best market for investors and prevent arbitrage, including:

- New York (NYSE)
- American (AMEX)
- Boston (BSE)
- Chicago (MSE)
- Cincinnati (CSE)
- Pacific (PSE)
- Philadelphia (PHLX)
- Chicago Board Options Exchange (CBOE)
- Nasdaq

The system enables market professionals to interact with counterparties in other markets whenever the nationwide Consolidated Quotation System (CQS) shows a better price.

Securities Industry Automation Corporation, Consolidated Quotation System

Intermediate Term Bond Funds

Intermediate Term Bond Funds normally hold securities that will mature in the near term, usually, 3 to 10 years.

Short Term Investment Fund, Long Term Bond Fund

Internal Audit

An Internal Audit is performed by a firm's in-house auditors. This audit is designed to ensure that a firm's basic accounting and processing controls are functioning properly.

External Audit

Internal Complaints

Internal Complaints are those that are received from other internal processing areas when a department supports the activities of other departments within its own firm.

Internal Controls

Internal Controls are established within a business unit or a firm to ensure that the unit is accurate and operates without fraud.

External Controls

Internal Rate of Return

An Internal Rate of Return is the discount rate which makes the net present value of an investment equal to zero.

Discount Rate, Net Present Value

Internal Settlement

An Internal Settlement occurs when both parties to a transaction have their securities and cash accounts with the same intermediary, allowing the intermediary to move the involved cash and securities within its own system.

International Central Securities Depository

An International Central Securities Depository (ICSD) is a central securities depository that clears and settles international securities or cross-border transactions in domestic securities, either directly or indirectly to local CSDs.

CSD, Euroclear, Cedel

International Council of Securities Dealers

The International Council of Securities Dealers is an international organization of self-regulatory and industry organizations. The Council's goal is to promote stable and efficient securities markets.

International Depository and Clearing

The International Depository and Clearing (IDC) is a joint venture between the Depository Trust Company and the International Securities Clearing Corporation that focuses on supporting the international users of the ID system and facilitating global Straight Through Processing.

www.idc-llc.com

International Fund

An International Fund is a mutual fund that invests only outside the country in which it is located, i.e. an international mutual fund based in the U.S. would only invest in stocks outside of the U.S.

Global Fund

International Organization of Securities Commissions

International Organization of Securities Commissions' (IOSCO) goal is to harmonize international securities regulation. It supports the development of securities markets worldwide.

International Securities Clearing Corporation

The International Securities Clearing Corporation (ISCC), a subsidiary of NSCC, assisted participants who wished to invest outside of the US. Formed in 1985, ISCC supported trading, clearing and settlement through its primary service, the Global Clearing Network.

It has been replaced by the International Depository and Clearing.

Global Clearing Network, International Depository and Clearing, NSCC

International Securities Identification Number

The International Securities Identification Number (ISIN) is a numbering system, designed by the United Nation's International Organization for Standardization (ISO) and widely accepted by worldwide securities markets as the international industry standard. ISIN is made up of a 2 character prefix representing the country of issue, the national security number if one exists, and a check digit.

International Securities Market Association

The International Securities Market Association (ISMA) is a European organization that supports the global bond market. ISMA offers a processing system called TRAX, which is an ETC product.

ETC

International Standards Organization

The International Standards Organization (ISO) sets worldwide standards on various topics, including securities message types. SWIFT is the secretariat for the ISO for the 7775 series of messages, which are used by the securities industry.

S.W.I.F.T., ISO 7775

International Stock Exchange

The International Stock Exchange is the primary stock exchange in England for trading non-UK securities.

Internet

The Internet is a worldwide network of computers that has a set of basic standards for communication. Originally used exclusively by universities and researchers, it has become a ubiquitous way of sending electronic mail and forms a base for electronic commerce.

Internet Service Provider

An Internet Service Provider (ISP) is a firm that has established an Internet access point. This access point must have:

- A large number of incoming phone lines
- A large number of modems
- A high speed connection to the Internet Backbone
- Software that will manage the interface and the error-free transmission of data

ISPs sell their services to firms and individuals who wish to access the internet at less expense than would be required to connect directly to the Internet Backbone.

Intersettle

Intersettle is an International Central Securities Depository, and is part of SEGA, which is the Swiss depository. It is connected to Easdaq, which is also connected to TRAX. Intersettle is also connected to Cedel and Euroclear so that firms can use these ICSD's for custody after they use Intersettle for clearing.

Cedel, Euroclear, SEGA, International Central Securities Depository

In-the-Money

In-the-Money is the intrinsic value of an option.

A call option is In-the-Money if the strike price is below the current market price of the underlying security.

A put option is In-the-Money if the strike price is above the current market price of the underlying security.

Intrinsic Value, Call, Put, Strike Price

Intraday Credit

See *Daylight Overdraft*

Intranet

An Intranet is an internet that is run by a single firm or a closed group of firms for use by its own members and customers.

Internet, Extranet

Intrinsic Value

Intrinsic Value can be:

- The actual monetary value of an object
- The value of something as an investment
- The basic worth of a corporation
- The amount by which an option contract's (call or put) strike price is above or below the market value of the underlying security

Call, In-the-Money, Put, Strike Price

Inventory

A firm's Inventory contains all of the securities it owns for trading purposes.

Inverse Floater

An Inverse Floater is a bond or derivative that has a variable coupon rate that is designed to move in the opposite direction of regular interest rates.

Variable Rate

Investigation

An Investigation occurs when a customer contacts their financial firm and claims that the firm has made an error. The investigation will determine whether the firm was in error, or not.

Proper procedure suggests that investigations that are resolved in the firm's favor should still be tracked since they reflect a customer's perception of error and can be used to improve customer communications and satisfaction.

Investigations where the firm was in error should also be tracked in order to identify potential process improvements.

Inquiry

Investment

Investment is the process of using available capital in order to receive an acceptable return, which could include income and/or capital gains.

Investment Advisor

See *Investment Manager*

Investment Advisors Act of 1940

The Investment Advisors Act of 1940, which was amended in 1960, was passed to establish rules for the registration of Investment Advisors, and to create laws to prohibit fraud.

People and firms engaged in investment advice were brought under the jurisdiction of the Securities Exchange Commission by this act. The Act specifically prohibits contracts that compensate an advisor for a client's capital gains and aims to prevent the defrauding of clients. Advisers who have more than 15 clients fall under the jurisdiction of the act and must register with the SEC.

Securities and Exchange Commission

Investment Bank

An Investment Bank has a number of specific roles that distinguish it from a commercial, wholesale or retail bank, including:

- Underwriting
- Research
- Portfolio Management
- Trading and Sales
- Broker and / or Dealer

Investment banks can be very profitable and earn their income in a variety of ways:

- Underwriting fees
- Fees per portfolio
- Commissions
- Spreads

Commission, Portfolio Management System, Research, Spread, Underwriter

Investment Banker

See *Underwriter*

Investment Banking

See *Investment Bank*

Investment Company

See *Mutual Fund*

Investment Company Act of 1940

The Investment Company Act of 1940 requires that investment companies (Mutual Funds) register with the SEC, provide a prospectus to investors and formally disclose how the investments are being managed.

Investment Company Institute

The Investment Company Institute (ICI) is the US trade association for the mutual fund industry.

Investment Manager

An Investment Manager has a number of specific roles that distinguish it from banks and brokers:

- Research
- Portfolio Management
- Discretionary and Non-discretionary "Trading"
- Record keeping and Accounting.
- Performance Measurement

Investment Managers can be very profitable and earn their income in a variety of ways:

- Basis points based on asset size
- Fees per portfolio
- Pay for performance
- Fixed costs with unlimited upside revenues
- Combining portfolios for processing economy
- Competition with Index Funds

Investment Management firms have a need for a variety of complex processing functions, which include:

- Shadow record keeping
- Strong accounting skills
- Multiple systems

Portfolio Management System, Performance Measurement, Research

Investment Objective

The Investment Objective is an investor's financial goal. These goals can be:

- Growth
- Current Income
- Tax Deferral
- Liquidity
- Speculation

Growth Objective, Current Income Objective, Tax Deferral Objective, Liquidity Objective, Speculation Objectives

Investment Portfolio

See *Portfolio*

Investment Program

An Investment Program is an individual's or an institution's investment strategy.

Investment Tolerance

See *Risk Tolerance*

Investment Trust

See *Mutual Fund*

Investor

An Investor is a person or a firm with an objective to invest money carefully and profitably over a long period of time.

Individual Investor, Institutional Investor

Investor Profile

An Investor Profile identifies the investor's propensity for risk and their investment objectives.

Investor Registration Option

The Investor Registration Option (IRO) is a new form of registration. A retail investor can establish a book entry position in their own name directly with the Transfer Agent, rather than use a physical certificate, or a broker or a bank for book entry ownership.

Book Entry, Transfer Agent

IO

See *Interest Only Strip*

IOC

See *Immediate-or-Cancel*

IOSCO

See *International Organization of Securities Commissions*

IP

Abbreviation for Internet Protocol.

IPO

The abbreviation IPO can be used in two ways:

- Abbreviation for Input/Process/Output
- See Initial Public Offering

IRA

See *Individual Retirement Account*

IRA Rollover

An IRA Rollover involves the reinvestment of a lump-sum distribution from an IRA or 401(k) plan when the investor takes physical receipt of the funds.

IRIP

See *Interest Re-Investment Plan*

DRIP

Irish Stock Exchange

The Irish Stock Exchange is the primary stock exchange of Ireland.

Irish Stock Exchange Overall Index

The Irish Stock Exchange Overall Index is a stock index derived from equities listed on the Irish Stock Exchange.

IRO

See *Investor Registration Option*

Iron Mountain

Iron Mountain is a for-profit business that stores archival records for many firms. It will pick up and transport a firm's critical records to Iron Mountain's underground storage facility in the mountains of New York state.

IRR

See *Internal Rate of Return*

Irrevocable Transfer

An Irrevocable Transfer is a transfer which cannot be revoked by either party.

IRS Form 1099

IRS Form 1099 is an IRS form that identifies the amount of interest or dividends paid to a taxable entity in a calendar year.

IRS FormW-2

An IRS Form W-2 is used by US firms to report the amount paid to an individual in a given year.

IRS FormW-4

An IRS Form W-4 is used to record the number of deductions claimed by a US taxpayer.

IRS FormW-9

An IRS Form W-9 is used to record that the account holder is a non-resident alien for US tax purposes, and is not subject to withholding tax.

IRS Income Type

IRS Income Type is the IRS code that has been assigned to the specific type of income collected.

IRS Section 401(h)

IRS Section 401(h) pertains to retirement plans.

IRS Section 401(k) Plan

An IRS Section 401(k) Plan is a plan where an employee may elect to contribute up to a specific amount of pretax dollars to a qualified tax-deferred retirement plan rather than receive taxable cash as compensation or bonus.

IRS Section 403(b) Plan

An IRS Section 403(b) Plan is a plan for the employees of non-profit organizations, schools, etc. which offers a tax-sheltered retirement option.

IRS Section 501(c)(9)

IRS Section 501(c)(9) is a portion of the IRS code that pertains to retirement plans.

IS

The abbreviation IS can be used in two ways:

- IS is the abbreviation for Information Systems.
- See Management Information System

ISCC's London Link

ISCC's London Link is a high-speed data communications link between the International Securities Clearing Corporation and the London Stock Exchange. The link allows US broker/dealers to compare and settle transactions in UK equities with LSE members and other ISCC members. The link also allows participating US firms to access the LSE's comparison, settlement and redelivery services.

International Securities Clearing Corporation, International Depository and Clearing, London Stock Exchange

ISE

See *International Stock Exchange*

ISG

See *Intermarket Surveillance Group*

ISIN

Pronounced Eye sin

See *International Securities Identification Number*

ISITC

Pronounced either as iz-it-see or as the five letters I-S-I-T-C.

See *Industry Standardization for Institutional Trade Communications*

ISITC Hub

The ISITC Hub is a service offered by Depository Trust Company that allows investment managers to send a file of ISITC formatted messages that are destined for multiple custodians to DTC. DTC sorts the files and stores them for retrieval by the appropriate custodian.

Depository Trust Company, Industry Standardization for Institutional Trade Communications

ISMA

Pronounced Iss Ma

See *International Securities Market Association*

ISND

Pronounced I-S-D-N

See *Integrated Speech and Data Network*

ISO

Pronounced Eye sew

See *International Standards Organization*

ISO 7775

ISO 7775 is the International Standards Organization's securities message standard. S.W.I.F.T. is the registered secretariat for the standard.

International Standards Organization, S.W.I.F.T.

ISO 9000

ISO 9000 is the International Standards Organization's standard for determining whether a firm is operating in a quality manner.

International Standards Organization

ISP

Pronounced I-S-P

See *Internet Service Provider*

Issuance

Issuance is the creation of a new security, and is the first step in the Trade Life Cycle.

Trade Life Cycle

Issue

The term Issue can be used in two ways:

- As a verb, to Issue is the process by which a new security is created and offered to the marketplace.
- As a noun, an Issue can be any unique security.

Issue Alias

The Issue Alias is another CUSIP number that is used to describe an instrument.

CUSIP

Issue Date

The Issue Date is the date that an instrument was issued.

Issue

Issue Servicing

Issue Servicing functions begin after the trade has settled, and are performed for as long as an investor owns a security. The functions include activities such as:

- Income Collection
- Corporate Actions
- Pricing
- Reporting
- Performance Measurement
- Accounting

Issuer

The Issuer of a security is the municipality or corporation that establishes a formal debt or equity obligation. The issuer receives cash from the underwriter, which distributes the issue to the investors. The issuer has several obligations:

- To record the debt or ownership
- To repay the debt under the terms of the bond covenants
- To pay interest or dividends as applicable

- To update the bondholder or stockholder regarding material events that affect the issuer

Covenants

Issuing Agent

The Issuing Agent is an institution that acts on behalf of the issuer of securities to distribute the securities, collect the funds received from the distribution for, and deliver the funds to the issuer.

Istanbul Stock Exchange

The Istanbul Stock Exchange is the primary stock exchange of Turkey.

www.ise.org

Istanbul Stock Exchange Composite Index

The Istanbul Stock Exchange Composite Index is a stock index derived from equities listed on the Istanbul Stock Exchange.

IT

IT is the abbreviation for Information Technology.

ITS

See *Intermarket Trading System*

ITS/CAES

See *Intermarket Trading System, Computer Assisted Execution System*

Jakarta Composite Share Price Index

The Jakarta Composite Share Price Index is a stock index derived from equities listed on the Jakarta Stock Exchange.

Jakarta Stock Exchange

The Jakarta Stock Exchange is the primary stock exchange of Indonesia.

www.indobiz.com/news/jsx.htm

Jamaica Stock Exchange

The Jamaica Stock Exchange is the primary stock exchange of Jamaica.

www.jamstockex.com

Japan Securities Clearing Corporation

Japan Securities Clearing Corporation is the clearing division of the Tokyo Stock Exchange (TSE).

Japan Securities Depository Center

Japan Securities Depository Center (JASDEC) is the central depository of Japan.

Japanese Government Bond Future

He Japanese Government Bond Future contract is based on the notional Japanese Government Bond with a 6% coupon and a ten year maturity.

JASDEC

Pronounced Jazz Dak

See *Japan Securities Depository Center*

Central Securities Depository

Jefferies & Company, Inc.

Jefferies & Company, Inc. is a US-based broker/dealer.

www.jefco.com

JGB

Abbreviation for Japanese Government Bond

Johannesburg Stock Exchange

The Johannesburg Stock Exchange is the primary stock exchange of South Africa.

www.jse.co.za

Joint Account - Tenants in Common

In a Joint Account - Tenants in Common, the death of one of the account owners has no effect on the survivor's percentage of ownership in the account. For example, the securities owned by the deceased become the property of the deceased's estate and not the surviving account holder.

Joint Account With the Right of Survivorship

Joint Account With the Right of Survivorship

A Joint Account With the Right of Survivorship (or Tenant by the entity) is usually established between husband and wife, and upon death of one partner, the entire account reverts to the survivor.

Joint Account - Tenants in Common

Joint Liability

Joint Liability occurs when liability is shared equally between two or more people or firms.

Joint Tenancy

Joint Tenancy is a form of legal property ownership that gives each person an equal interest in the property, including rights of survivorship.

JP Morgan & Co.

JP Morgan & Co. is a US-based broker/dealer.

www.jpmorgan.com

JPEG

JPEG, which stands for Joint Photographic Experts Group, is a standard for compressing still pictures that replaces the GIF standard. With a file extension of .JPG, a file can have individual pictures that include up to 16 million colors.

GIF

JSE Daily Index

The JSE Daily Index is a stock index derived from equities listed on the Jamaica Stock Exchange.

JSE-Actuaries All Share Index

The JSE-Actuaries All Share Index is a stock index derived from equities listed on the Johannesburg Stock Exchange.

Jumbo Loan

A Jumbo Loan is a mortgage loan that is larger than the $227,150 limit set by the Federal National Mortgage Association and the Federal Home Loan Mortgage Corporation.

FHLMC, FNMA

Junior Mortgage

A Junior Mortgage is one that is subordinate in bankruptcy to the claim of a prior lien or another mortgage.

Junior Security

A Junior Security is a security with a lower claim to assets and income than a senior security during a bankruptcy.

Junk Bonds

See *High Yield Bonds*

Kaisen

Pronounced Kye Zen

Kaisen is a Japanese word that means making small incremental improvements.

Continuous Improvement

Kansas City Board of Trade

Kansas City Board of Trade issues futures contracts on wheat and Value Line Stock Index futures contracts.

Kappa

See Vega

Kassenverein

See Deutscher Kassenverein

Kassenverein

The Kassenverein are several interconnected depositories in Germany that clear and settle German securities.

Ausland Kassenverein

KATI-system

The KATI-system is the clearing and settlement system of the Helsinki Stock Exchange.

KCBT

See *Kansas City Board of Trade*

KELER Ltd.

KELER Ltd. is the central depository and securities clearing house of Hungary.

Keogh Plan

Pronounced Key Oh

A Keogh Plan is a federally approved, tax-deferred individual retirement program that can be established by a self-employed person, and which allows the person to invest up to $30,000 or 25% of the person's income, whichever is lower.

Key

A Key is used to encrypt and decrypt messages.

Encryption

Keynesian Economics

Keynesian Economics is the economic philosophy that was defined by John Maynard Keynes, which advocates an active government role in maintaining the economy.

KFX Share Index

The KFX Share Index is a stock index derived from equities listed on the Copenhagen Stock Exchange.

Kilobyte

A Kilobyte is a thousand bytes. Kilobytes are a unit of measurement used to denominate a computer's storage capacity.

Byte

KISS

KISS is:

- An abbreviation for Keep It Simple Stupid
- The Frankfurt Borse's price reporting and quote dissemination system

Kitchen Sink Instrument

A Kitchen Sink Instrument is one that has been assembled from the parts that have been left over after other derivative transactions have been created.

Derivative

Kiting

Kiting involves either:

- Collusion between a buyer and a seller with the intent of driving up a stock's price through trading.
- Any manipulative trading practice designed to inflate stock prices.

- Writing checks against accounts that do not have enough funds to cover the checks and depositing them in other accounts with the hope of withdrawing the funds before the original check is rejected.

Know Your Customer

Brokers are required to Know Your (their) Customer's propensity for risk, their investment objectives, and their ability to invest in complex securities instruments. Broker's demonstrate that they have fulfilled this requirement by collecting information from a customer at the time an account is opened.

Korea Composite Stock Price Index

The Korea Composite Stock Price Index (KOSPI) is a stock index derived from equities listed on the Korea Stock Exchange.

Korea Securities Depository

Korea Securities Depository (KSD) is the central depository and securities clearing house of South Korea.

Korea Stock Exchange

The Korea Stock Exchange is the primary stock exchange of South Korea.

Kuala Lumpur Stock Exchange

The Kuala Lumpur Stock Exchange is the primary stock exchange of Malaysia.

Kuala Lumpur Stock Exchange Composite Index

The Kuala Lumpur Stock Exchange Composite Index is a stock index derived from equities listed on the Kuala Lumpur Stock Exchange.

La Caja

La Caja is the central securities depository of Peru.

Laddering

Laddering is the process of building a bond portfolio that will mature in a series of steps, thereby providing income over a period of time which can be used by the investor or reinvested at current rates.

Lagging Economic Indicator

A Lagging Economic Indicator is an economic or financial variable that tends to follow the movement of overall economic activity.

Leading Economic Indicator

LAN

See *Local Area Network*

Laptop Computer

A Laptop Computer is a Personal Computer that is portable.

Large Cap

See Large Capitalization Stock

Large Capitalization Stock

A Large Capitalization Stock is the stock of a big company that has a large amount of common stock outstanding, typically with a market capitalization of over $3 billion.

Last Call Year

The Last Call Year is the year of the last eligible call for an issue.

Call

Last Coupon Date

The Last Coupon Date is the final day that an interest payment will be paid by the issuer to the holders of a fixed income security.

The Last Coupon Date is used for interest accrual and cash flow purposes. For example, for a U.S. corporate bond issued on 6/15/99, maturing 6/15/09, the Last Coupon Date could be 6/15/09.

First Coupon Date

Last Ex-Dividend Date

The Last Ex-Dividend Date is the date of the last time an issue traded Ex-dividend.

Ex-Dividend

Last In-First Out

Last In, First Out (LIFO) is an accounting standard that says that the last available transaction will be used first when any portion of a position is sold. In a rising market, this means that the lots purchased later, and presumably at a higher price, will be sold first, thereby minimizing the amount of gain that would be subject to tax.

First In-First Out

Last Sale

The Last Sale is the last price for a security on a specific day or at a particular time during a trading session.

Last Sale Reporting

Last Sale Reporting is required by Nasdaq and the exchanges. Executions must be reported within a predefined period of time. For Nasdaq, a Market Maker must electronically submit the price and the number of shares of a transaction within 90 seconds of the execution of an order.

Last Sale Service

Last Sale Service

The Last Sale Service is a specific service offered by Nasdaq that allows real-time access to the last-sale information that is reported by Market Makers.

Last Sale Reporting

Late Charge

A Late Charge is a penalty that is paid by a borrower when a payment is made after the due date.

Laundering

See *Money Laundering*

LBO

See *Leveraged Buy Out*

LCH

See London Clearing House

Lead Manager

See *Underwriting Manager*

Lead Time

Lead Time is the amount of time a manager has to plan ahead in order to ensure that multiple legs of a project come together properly. For example, the lead time on ordering a telephone line in some countries could be several weeks or months.

Project

Leading Economic Indicator

A Leading Economic Indicator is an economic or financial variable that tends to move ahead of and in the same direction as general economic activity.

Lagging Economic Indicator

LEAPS

See *Long Term Equity Anticipation Securities*

Ledger Balance

A Ledger Balance is the amount of money in an account that has not been used. It includes available funds and uncleared funds that are not yet available for use.

Available Balance, Available Date

Legacy

A Legacy system is an old system that, while probably performing the tasks required adequately, is based upon less efficient technology and is usually difficult to maintain.

Frequently, legacy systems have been coded by many people over many years, and do not have complete documentation and/or all of the source code that would be needed to compile the object code into the machine-readable language that is used by the computer to operate. This means that it is often very difficult to make changes to a legacy system's functionality.

Source Code, Object Code, Compile, Machine Readable Language

Legal Ownership

Legal Ownership is the legal recognition of the owner of a security.

Legal Risk

Legal Risk is the risk of loss because a contract or other right cannot be legally enforced.

Legal Transfer

A Legal Transfer is a security transfer that requires documentation in addition to the normal forms and is required when the security is in the name of a deceased person, a trust or unavailable third party.

Lehman Brothers

Lehman Brothers is a US-based broker/dealer.

www.lehman.com

Lender

A Lender can be:

- A bank, mortgage company, or mortgage broker offering a loan.
- An investor in a debt security.

Letter of Intent

A Letter of Intent is a document letter that formalizes:

- The relationship between an underwriter and an issuer. The letter of intent includes key terms, such as: underwriter fees, ranges for stock prices, and other points.
- Any promise to utilize a firm's services or products. These letters are typically not binding, if properly written, and are used to clarify an emerging relationship between two firms.

Letter Stock

Letter Stock is a special issue of common stock that is made in a Private Placement to a small group of investors without registering the issue with the Securities Exchange Commission. Certificates are not issued, but ownership is defined in a legal letter.

Common Stock, Private Placement

Leverage

Leverage is:

- A way to increase investment power for generating greater returns, value and return by borrowing funds or committing less capital. This is called Financial Leverage.
- A method of using fixed cost equipment to replace variable cost. This is called Operating Leverage.

Leveraged Buy Out

A Leveraged Buy Out occurs when an acquiring firm uses the assets of the target company as collateral for most or all of the debt incurred in the acquisition.

Leveraged Stock

Leveraged Stock is stock that is purchased with credit, typically in a margin account.

Liability

A Liability is any claim against the assets of a corporation, including accounts payable, salaries payable, dividends declared, accrued taxes, and fixed or long term debt such as bonds and bank loans.

Liabilities are listed on the firm's balance sheet.

Balance Sheet

LIBOR

Pronounced Lie Bore

See *London Interbank Offered Rate*

Lien

A Lien is a legal claim against some form of property.

LIFFE

See London International Financial Futures and Options Exchange

LIFFE Membership

LIFFE Membership consists of approximately 200 member firms who each hold an equity stake in the organization.

LIFO

See *Last In-First Out*

FIFO, Tax Lot

Limit Order

A Limit Order is an order where the customer sets the maximum buying price or the minimum selling price they are willing to accept. Buy orders may be executed below the maximum and sell orders above the minimum.

Stop Loss Order

Limit Order File

The Limit Order File is a file that is maintained by Nasdaq's Small Order Execution System that stores customers' unexecuted limit orders.

Small Order Execution System

Limit Order Processing

Nasdaq's Limit Order Processing system electronically files orders up to 99,999 shares which are to be executed when and if the specific limit price is reached. Good-'til-cancelled orders that are not executed on their submission date are retained until executed or cancelled.

Good-til-Cancelled Order, Limit Order

Limited Order

See *Limit Order*

Limited Partnership

A Limited Partnership is a partnership in which there are two categories of partner: Limited and General.

Limited Partners only risk their investment, and do not have any say in how the business is managed.

General Partners usually do not risk as much money, but are responsible for managing the business and could have the risk of being sued.

Limited Power of Attorney

See *Power of Attorney*

Limited Price Order

See *Limit Order*

Line of Code

A Line of Code is written by a programmer to define a specific task that a computer should perform at a certain time or under certain circumstances.

A group of lines of code form a program, while a group of programs form an application.

One application, or a group of applications and their associated hardware and telecommunication form a system.

Application, Code, Program

Line of Credit

A Line of Credit can be established for a firm or an individual. It is based upon their credit history and ability to repay loans, and can include secured, unsecured or margin loans.

Liquid Asset

A Liquid Asset is a security that can easily be sold for cash.

Liquid Market

A Liquid Market is one in which securities can be easily bought and sold.

Liquidation

A Liquidation is:

- The closing of a position by a customer
- The closing of a firm and the subsequent distribution of the remaining assets
- The closing of a position by a margin department when a client has not paid for a purchase or when a margin call has not been filled

Liquidity

Liquidity has many meanings, including:

- A market is considered liquid when investors can buy and sell securities easily.
- A stock is considered liquid when it can absorb a large volume of trades without a serious price change.
- An asset is considered liquid when it can be sold easily for cash for a fair value
- An individual is considered liquid when the person has nearly immediate access to cash in place of their securities.
- A mutual fund is considered liquid since an investor can readily sell their shares in a fund and get cash.

Liquidity Objective

An investor has a Liquidity Objective when they have a preference for holding cash and/or cash equivalents in their portfolio.

Liquidity Ratio

A Liquidity Ratio is the relationship between the trading volume of a security and a change in its price. The higher the ratio, the more the security can be traded with a minimum impact on price.

Liquidity Risk

Liquidity Risk is the risk that:

- A counterparty will not have the necessary funds to settle on settlement date and that the seller will have to wait for their cash
- There is no market for a security when the investor wants to sell it

Listed Option

A Listed Option is an option that has met the requirements to be listed and traded on an established exchange.

Listed Security

A Listed Security is a stock or bond that is accepted for public trading on one of the major exchanges or marketplaces.

Listed Stock

A Listed Stock is an equity that has met the requirements to be listed and traded on an established exchange or Nasdaq.

Listing

See *Listed Stock*

Stock Exchange

Listing and Maintenance Agreement

A Listing and Maintenance Agreement is a written contract between an exchange and an issuer, wherein the issuer agrees to meet and adhere to the market's listing standards.

Listing Requirements

Listing Requirements are the criteria that a security must meet in order to be listed on an exchange.

Litigation

Litigation is a legal proceeding whereby one party sues another party.

Arbitration, Mediation

Ljubljanska Stock Exchange

The Ljubljanska Stock Exchange is the primary stock exchange of Slovenia.

Lloyds Bank

Lloyds Bank is a UK-based Universal Bank.

www.lloydsbank-corporate.co.uk

LME

See London Metal Exchange

Load

A Load is a sales charge on an investment, typically a mutual fund, that is imposed on the purchase of the shares to cover the cost of sales, distribution, management and administration of the fund.

Front End Load, Back End Load

Load Fund

See Load

Loan

A Loan is a formal agreement between a borrower and a lender. Loans usually have specific terms, such as:

- Interest rate and periodicity
- Repayment period
- Other terms

Interest Rate

Loan Value

The Loan Value is the total amount of money that a brokerage customer may borrow from a firm if they have established a margin account, based upon the market value of the customer's available collateral.

Credit Balance, Margin Account

Loans Types

Loan Types refer to the variety of possible loans, including:

- Purpose Loan
- Non-purpose Loan
- Margin Loan

- Unsecured Loan
- Margin Account

Local Area Network

A Local Area Network (LAN) is a way to group independent personal computers or workstations so that they can share programs, applications and data. A LAN typically has at least one computer that acts as a server, or controller.

Server

Local Currency

Local Currency is the currency of the local settlement country.

Local Custodian

A Local Custodian is a bank that provides custody for securities that are traded and settled in the country in which the custodian is located.

Sub-Custodian, Global Custodian

Lockbox

A Lockbox is a service provided by one firm, usually a bank, that receives and processes checks and ACH transfers that are sent as payments. The Lockbox processes the checks and records some essential data about the sender so that the firm buying the service can electronically update their accounts receivable records.

Locked In

Locked In refers to:

- An executed trade that has been agreed upon by both parties. A locked-in trade is guaranteed to settle through the clearing corporation unless the parties mutually agree to cancel the transaction.
- A lender's guarantee of a specific interest rate for a set period of time, usually between loan application approval and loan closing
- The condition when an investor owns a security that is trading at a price higher than what they paid, and therefore decides to hold the security to avoid realizing the gain and having it subject to tax

Locked Quotation

A Locked Quotation is a short term condition where one market maker's asked price is the same or lower than another market bid.

Market Maker

London Clearing House

The London Clearing House (LCH) is a Recognized Clearing House under the Financial Services Act (1986) in the UK. LCH's primary role is to act as the central counterparty for contracts traded on LIFFE, the IPE and the LME.

When LCH has registered a trade, it becomes the buyer to every LCH member who sells and the seller to every LCH member who buys, ensuring the financial performance of trades. To protect itself against the risks assumed as central counterparty, LCH has established margin requirements.

London Interbank Offered Rate

The London Interbank Offered Rate (LIBOR) is the interest rate for short term loans between banks in London. LIBOR is based upon the rate for 3 month Eurodollar Time Deposits and is derived from the average rates offered by a predetermined group of banks.

London International Financial Futures and Options Exchange

The London International Financial Futures and Options Exchange (LIFFE) was established in 1982 as a physical exchange using open outcry and has more recently established the automated trading of financial futures and options contracts.

LIFFE merged with the London Commodity Exchange (LCE) on 16 September 1996, and is a physical exchange trading soft commodity futures and options contracts on Cocoa, Robusta Coffee, Sugar, Wheat, Barley, Potatoes and BIFFEX (dry cargo freight).

Trading is by open outcry except for White Sugar which is traded on the Exchange's automated trading system (FAST).

London Link

See *ISCC's London Link*

London Metal Exchange

The London Metal Exchange (LME) is a physical exchange using open outcry and with automated trading of non-ferrous metals (namely copper, primary aluminum, aluminum alloy, lead, nickel, tin and zinc), futures and options contracts.

London Stock Exchange

The London Stock Exchange is the primary stock exchange in England for trading British securities. It is a physical exchange using an order driven system for the trading of quoted UK and international equity securities.

www.stockex.co.uk

London Stock Exchange Sequence Program

The London Stock Exchange *Sequence* Program is the technological infrastructure on which the London Stock Exchange's electronic trading services are built and linked.

London Traded Options Market (LTOM)

The London Traded Options Market (LTOM) formerly offered exchange-traded options only. It merged with LIFFE in 1992 to form a physical exchange for open outcry and the automated trading of financial futures and options.

Long

See *Long Position*

Long Bond

The Long Bond is the US Government thirty year bond.

Long Gilt Future

The Long Gilt Futures contract is based on a notional UK Gilt of £50,000 nominal value with a 7% coupon and 10 - 15 year maturity.

Long Position

A Long Position is:

- When a customer has securities that are either fully paid for in a cash account, or partially paid for in a margin account
- A debit balance for any position on a firm's books
- A position where an investor is a net holder in a specific series of options

Margin Account

Long Term Assets

Long Term Assets include processing plants, equipment, real estate and other capital assets, net of depreciation.

Long Term Bond

A Long Term Bond is a debt security with a holding period ranging greater than 15 years to maturity and a duration of over 6 years.

Long Term Bond Fund

A Long Term Bond Fund holds bonds with long term maturities and generally pays higher interest than intermediate-term bond funds.

Long Term Equity Anticipation Securities

Long Term Equity Anticipation Securities (LEAPS) are American Style long term stock or index options, which are available as calls and puts, and which have expiration dates that can be up to three years in the future.

Option, American Style Option

Long Term Goals

Long Term Goals are financial goals that are set by an investor for a period of five years or more.

Long Term Investor

A Long Term Investor is one who sets investment goals of five years or more.

Long Term Yield

Long Term Yield is the estimated amount of income for a portfolio over the long term. It includes the coupon rate and the current price, relative to the redemption price.

Loss Leader

A Loss Leader is something that is sold at less than its real value in order to attract business.

Loss Sharing Agreement

A Loss Sharing Agreement is an agreement among the participants in a clearing or settlement system that defines the allocation of any losses by the system.

Loss Sharing Pools

Loss Sharing Pools consist of cash, securities or other assets that are held by a clearing or settlement system to ensure that loss sharing agreements can be funded.

Loss Sharing Agreement

Lottery

A Lottery is a process that allocates the number of debentures or shares to individual accounts when there is a partial call.

Call

LSE

See *London Stock Exchange*

LSE Settlement System

LSE Settlement System is a clearing service offered by the Lima Stock Exchange.

LTOM

See London Traded Options Market

Lump Sum Distribution

A Lump Sum Distribution is the disbursement of an individual's retirement benefits in a single payment.

M1

M1 is a measure of domestic money supply accounting for currency, checking account balances and traveler's checks.

M2

M2 is a measure of domestic money supply accounting for M1 plus savings and time deposits, repurchase agreements and money market accounts.

M3

M3 is a measure of money supply that includes M2 plus large time deposits and money market fund balances held by institutions.

Machine Readable Language

Machine Readable Language is the type of code that can be understood by a computer. A computer does not understand human languages, but it does understand a series of binary bits. An example of a machine readable language is Assembler.

Binary, Bit

Madrid General Index

The Madrid General Index is a stock index derived from equities listed on the Bolsa de Madrid.

Mailbox

See *DTC Hub*

Mainframe

A Mainframe is a large, centrally run computer. A mainframe is normally operated in a data center, with a controlled environment and access. A mainframe has much higher operating speeds than a PC, significant data storage, and can operate with many simultaneous users.

Personal Computer, Client/Server

Mainframe Dual Host

Mainframe Dual Host (MDH) is the DTC's message-based communications system that is used to connect DTC participants' mainframe computers directly to the DTC.

Maintenance

Maintenance is the term used for the activities that are performed to keep an existing computer application running properly. Maintenance includes fixing errors and updates that are required to keep the system functioning properly. It does not include the addition of new functionality, which is called an enhancement.

Enhancement

Majority Shareholder

The Majority Shareholder is one person or a group of shareholders who together control more than half of the shares of a corporation

Making a Market

See *Market Maker*

Over-the-Counter Market

Maloney Act of 1938

The Maloney Act of 1938 established Self Regulating Organizations.

Managed Account

A Managed Account is an investment account that consists of money that one or more clients entrust to a manager, who decides when and where to invest it. Clients are charged a management fee, which is usually a fixed percentage of the fund's asset value.

Management Company

A Management Company is responsible for managing a mutual fund's portfolio.

Management Fee

A Management Fee is the fee that is paid by a mutual fund to an investment adviser for its services. Management Fees currently average about 0.5% of a fund's assets, and since they are deduced from the fund's profits, they reduce the overall yield to the investor.

SEC Rule 12b-1

Management Information System

A Management Information System (MIS) is:

- The firm's department that manages data processing, development and application maintenance. It can also be called IT or IS.
- A category of internal reporting that is designed to provide managers with the information necessary to do their job. MIS reporting can be automated or manual.

Management Letter

The Management Letter is required annually by FDICIA, and is used to report management's compliance with FDICIA's requirements.

FDICIA

Manager

See *Syndicate Manager*

See *Investment Manager*

Managing Underwriter

See *Syndicate Manager*

Mandatory Corporate Action

A Mandatory Corporate Action is one where the issuer has the right to insist that the corporate action take place. This is different from a voluntary corporate action where the holder of the security has the right to decide whether they want to accept a proposed corporate action or reject it.

Voluntary Corporate Action

Manual Processing

Manual Processing occurs when people are involved in performing a task. From an operating perspective, manual processing is high cost and high risk since people make errors, and increasingly people are the most expensive component of a process.

Marché à Terme International de France

Marché à Terme International de France (MATIF) is the French International Futures and Options Exchange. It is a physical exchange that has been established for the automated trading of financial and commodity futures and options.

Margin

Margin is:

- The amount of money that is required to carry stocks and/or bonds with the balance being loaned by the brokers at an interest rate that is controlled by Regulation T. The amount of margin required to carry stocks has ranged from 40% to 100% of the purchase price over the last fifty years.
- The Performance Bond that is deposited to support investments in futures contracts and short options
- A specified percentage that is added to a predefined financial index to determine the new interest rate when an Adjustable-Rate Mortgage is recalculated
- The difference between the revenue for a product or a firm and the direct cost of providing the service. This is also called gross margin.

Margin Account, Performance Bond, Regulation T

Margin Account

When a customer establishes a Margin Account with a brokerage firm, they are establishing a secured credit relationship. The broker will open a credit account with a formal margin agreement that defines the terms for the loan. The customer puts up part of the cash that is needed for purchases and the broker lends the rest of the required funds by using securities that are already in the customer's account as collateral for the loan.

Collateral

Margin Call

A Margin Call is:

- A notification from a broker to their customer to increase the amount of equity in the account to bring the balance up to a required minimum level
- The amount of the call

Margin Department

The Margin Department is the operations area that is responsible for ensuring that customers' accounts are maintained in accordance with the firm's policies and the regulators' margin rules and regulations.

Maritime Administration

The Maritime Administration is authorized to issue Merchant Marine obligations for ship financing, which are issued and guaranteed by the US Department of Transportation.

Mark to Market

When a security or portfolio undergoes a Mark to Market, it is fully priced by multiplying the number of shares (or bonds) held by the current market prices per share (or bond).

The result of a mark to market can be any one of the following:

- An unrealized gain or loss
- An identification of a credit balance in a margin account

- An identification that additional collateral may be required to fully collateralize a loan

Uniform Practice Code

Markdown

A Markdown is a charge that is subtracted from the price of a security that a customer is selling to a broker/dealer for the broker/dealer's own account. The markdown is the equivalent of a commission on the sale.

Markup

Market

A Market is a place, either physical or electronic, that is used to bring together buyers and sellers of securities.

There are currently four different types of securities markets in the US:

- Primary Market
- Secondary Market
- Third Market
- Fourth Market

A Market can also be related to any of the following dimensions:

- Financial Market
- Exchanges
- Security Types
- Geographic

Primary Market, Secondary Market, Third Market, Fourth Market

Market Action

Market Action is the change in the value of a portfolio that can be attributed to changes in the underlying market value of the securities in the portfolio.

In addition to Market Action, the other major factor to consider when evaluating the performance of cross-border portfolios is the change in the relative value of the currencies in the portfolio as compared to the investor's base currency.

Base Currency

Market Cap

See *Capitalization*

Market Capitalization

An equity's Market Capitalization is its current market price multiplied by the total number of shares outstanding.

Market Data

Market Data is available via real-time access and batch transmissions. This category of data includes prices, quotes, corporate action information and trading activity.

Market Data Vendors

Market Data Vendors

Market Data Vendors provide data such as pricing, income and corporate action information, usually in electronic for, to investors and firms in the securities industry.

Market Data Vendors

Market Data Vendors' systems are used to send prices, quotes and trading activity to market participants. Much consolidation has occurred in this market area and the major participants are well entrenched.

The sources of the market data provided by the vendors are widespread and the successful vendors are able to integrate data, disseminate it in real-time and present it elegantly.

The vendor is a key link in Market Data systems.

Market Data

Market Depth

See *Depth of Market*

Market Information Data Access System

The Market Information Data Access System (MIDAS) is a NASD computer system that supports market regulation and examination programs by providing historical data on Nasdaq quotes and volume.

Market Maker

A Market Maker is a dealer or specialist that is trading for their own account in the OTC market. Generally, they have an inventory, but could be long or short in the security.

In order to be a market maker, the firm must continuously post a bid and asked price (two-sided quotation) without knowing if the person asking for the quote is a potential buyer or seller.

Market Makers are expected to maintain an orderly market by being available to buy or sell. Market Makers attempt to profit by the spread between the bid and asked price and through buying or selling along with market moves.

About 10 percent of NASD firms are Market Makers. To become a Market Maker a broker/dealer must meet the capitalization standards of the NASD.

Asked, Bid, NASD, Market Maker Spread

Market Maker Spread

The Market Maker's Spread is the difference between their bid and offer price.

Bid, Offering Price, Market Maker

Market Order

A Market Order is an order to buy or sell a specific amount of a security immediately at the best price available at the time the order is executed.

Market Order Processing

See *SuperDot*

Market Price

A Market Price is the last reported price at which a stock or bond was sold. In principle, a Market Price is simultaneously the highest price which a buyer would pay and the lowest a seller would accept.

Market Risk

Market Risk is the risk that the value of an investment will rise and fall as a result of changes in:

- Interest rates
- The economy
- Expectations for the markets' future
- The prospects for the firm which issued the security

Market Sentiment

Market Sentiment is the market's trend that is shown by the activity and general price movement of the securities. A bullish market sentiment results from rising prices while a bearish sentiment results from falling prices.

Market Surveillance

Market Surveillance is the automated process of investigating illegal, abusive or manipulative trading practices. The existence of Market Surveillance tends to prevent most people from breaking the market's rules and regulations.

Market Timing

Traders or investors who engage in Market Timing are trying to predict the exact moment to buy before an advance gets underway or to sell before a decline.

Market Value

See *Market Price*

Book Value

Marketable Securities

Marketable Securities are those where there is always a ready market where the security can be bought or sold.

Market-On-Close Order

A Market-On-Close Order is one that is to be executed at the close of the exchange's trading day with an anticipation of an execution price that is as close as possible to the closing market price.

At the Close

Markup

A Markup is a charge that is added to the price of a security that a customer is buying from a broker/dealer. The broker/dealer adds a Markup to the price when it sells a security to a customer from its own account. The Markup is the equivalent of a commission on the sale.

Markdown

Master Custody

Master Custody is a service similar to Master Trust, without a legal requirement to be a trustee.

Master Custody is targeted at:

- Public Employee Plans
- Endowments
- Foundations
- Master Trust

Master Trust

A Master Trust is a trust in which a plan sponsor's assets are distributed over multiple investment managers and are maintained by a central custodian under a single trust agreement. The portfolios are used to support multiple retirement plans.

The opportunity for Master Trust was created by the 1974 Employee's Retirement Income Security Act (ERISA), which defined the role of the trustee, the Pension Funds' record keeping requirements, and the requirement to monitor the investments by internal and external Portfolio Managers.

A Master Trust arrangement is a legal relationship that establishes the Master Trustee in a fiduciary role.

Fiduciary, Master Trustee

Master Trustee

A Master Trustee is an institution with fiduciary authority to administer to a portfolio under the terms of a Master Trust arrangement. Master Trustee services include:

- Custody
- Reporting
- Securities Processing
- Securities Lending
- Accounting
- Collect periodic investment funds
- Monitor investment decisions
- Administrate the investment process
- Distribute funds to beneficiaries

There are two major categories of Master Trust Account:

- Defined Benefit
- Defined Contribution

Master Trust, Defined Benefit Program, Defined Contribution Program

Matching

Matching is the process by which two brokerage firms that have engaged in a trade compare the settlement details of the trade provided by both counterparties.

Matching is done to verify all aspects of a trade and ensure that all parties agree on the terms of the transaction.

This comparison can be either through a clearing corporation which will net the trades or on a trade-by-trade basis.

Clearing Corporation

Matching Networks

See *Crossing Network*

Material News

Material News is information released by a company that, according to the SEC, "might reasonably be expected to affect the value of a company's securities or influence investors' decisions."

MATIF

See Marché à Terme International de France

Maturity

The Maturity of a bond defines a bond's life span. The life of a bond is the period of time between issuance and redemption.

Issuance, Redemption

Maturity Date

The Maturity Date is the date upon which an issue or loan matures and when the principal is to be redeemed.

Maturity

May Day Revolution

The May Day Revolution marked the end of fixed brokerage fees on May 1, 1975.

MBARS

See *Municipal Bond Acceptance and Reconciliation Service*

MBSCC

See *Mortgage Backed Securities Clearing Corporation*

MCC

See *Midwest Clearing Corporation*

Mean

The arithmetic Mean is an average measure of central tendency. The mean is calculated by adding all of the data elements and dividing by the number of data elements.

Mode, Median

Media

Media is the physical entity that is used to store information. Some type of media include:

- Microfiche

- Tape
- Floppy Disk
- Hard Drive
- CD ROM

Median

The Median is the arithmetic value derived by determining the middle value in a list of data. One half of all values in a data selection is either above or below the median. When a data selection has an even number of values, the median is derived by taking the average of the two middle values.

Mean, Mode

Mediation

Mediation is a voluntary process that is used to settle disputes. The process involves a mediator who helps the disputing parties negotiate a mutually-acceptable resolution.

Arbitration, Litigation

Megabyte

A megabyte is a million bytes. Megabytes are a unit of measurement used to denominate a computer's memory storage capacity.

Byte, Memory

Mellon Bank

Mellon Bank is a US-based bank.

www.mellon.com

Member

A Member, with regard to an exchange, is an individual or institution that holds special rights to interact on the exchange, including but not limited to the right to trade listed securities.

Seat

Member Firm

A Member Firm is a sole proprietorship, partnership or corporation that owns a membership on an organized exchange or that is a member of the NASD, and which is engaged in the basic business of buying or selling securities.

Broker, NASD, Seat

Memorandum Order

A Memorandum Order is a limit order that is held by the broker until the market moves to the pre-determined price, at which point the order becomes a market order.

Sell Stop, Buy Stop, Limit Order

Memory

There are two primary categories of Memory that are used by computers:

- Read Only Memory (ROM)
- Random Access Memory (RAM)
- Read Only Memory, Random Access Memory

Merchant Bank

Merchant Banks were established in Europe in the fifteenth century to finance goods that were being sold across borders and to provide the venture capital that was necessary to establish new companies. They were the forerunners of the modern investment bank.

Investment Bank

Merger

A Merger is a combination of the assets and liabilities of two or more companies into one legal entity through the exchange of equity.

Merrill Lynch

Merrill Lynch is a US-based broker/dealer.

www.ml.com

Merval Index

The Merval Index is a stock index derived from equities listed on the Bolsa de Comercio de Buenos Aires.

Message

A Message is a group of related data elements that may be a complete transaction, an information record, a confirmation of a transaction, etc.

Messaging

See *Message*

Messenger

A Messenger on Wall Street is a person who delivers physical instruments to the buying firm.

MIDAS

See *Market Information Data Access System*

MidCap SPDR

Standard & Poor's MidCap 400 Depository Receipts represent ownership in the MidCap SPDR Trust, a unit investment trust which holds a portfolio of common stocks that closely tracks the price performance and dividend yield of the S&P MidCap 400 Index.

Depository Receipt, Index, Standard & Poor's Depositary Receipts

Middle Office

The Middle Office, which typically combines some of the functions that have historically been conducted by the Front Office and/or the Back Office, usually consists of functions such as:

- Investment Accounting
- Risk Management
- Decision Sup

Middleware

Middleware is the layer of code that sits between the processing applications and the network and performs three basic functions:

- Routing
- Reformatting
- Protocol conversions

In the past, each programmer wrote specific code that generated its output format and told the network where to send it. Middleware automates many of these functions.

The Middleware market, according to IDC, is expected to grow to a $5.9 billion market in 2000.

MIDI

Musical Instrument Digital Interface

Midwest Clearing Corporation

The Midwest Clearing Corporation (MCC) offered services similar to the NSCC, but to a smaller, regional set of users. In 1997 it was consolidated into the NSCC.

Midwest Securities Trust Company

The Midwest Securities Trust Company (MSTC) was a regional depository that was consolidated into the Depository Trust Company in 1997.

Milestone

A Milestone is a measurable task or a check point in a plan.

Checkpoint

Minicomputer

The Minicomputer was a class of computers that was used widely starting in the 1970s. Smaller than a mainframe and not dependent upon a data center's protected environment, minicomputers took over many of the processing tasks that were required by banks and brokers.

Minicomputer platforms today include IBM's AS/400, HP, Digital, etc.

Minimum Maintenance

Minimum Maintenance is the funding level to which the cash plus equity in an account may fall before the client is required to add additional cash.

Margin

MIS

See *Management Information System*

Misery Index

The Misery Index is the index that consists of both inflation and unemployment rates.

Misrepresentation

A Misrepresentation is a false statement of a matter of fact which deceives another person.

Mode

The Mode is the arithmetic average that describes the most frequently occurring category of data. If more than one category shares the greatest frequency, the distribution is bi-modal or multi-modal.

Mean, Median

Modem

A Modem is the commonly used term for a Modulator-demodulator. A Modem is used to convert digital signals that are being sent by a computer into an analog signal that can be transmitted over normal telephone lines. A Modem at the other end of the telephone line converts the analog signal back into digital form so that the information can be understood by another computer.

Moderate Investor

An investor's risk tolerance is Moderate when they have one portion of their portfolio in low risk investments, and are willing to subject a portion of their portfolio to a higher risk in order to obtain a greater return.

Risk Tolerance

Monetary Policy

Monetary Policy refers to any policy dealing with the supply or use of money in an economy. Monetary Policy is usually established and managed by a country's central bank.

Money Laundering

Money Laundering is the process whereby banks or other firms take in money from questionable or illegal sources and either move it to another account or exchange it for other assets that can be sold legally.

Money Manager

See *Investment Manager*

Money Market

The Money Market is the over-the-counter, telephone-based process of trading short term (less than one year) instruments. There are several different types of Money Market instruments, all of which are considered short term instruments:

- Banker's Acceptances
- Certificates of Deposit
- Commercial Paper
- Repurchase Agreements

- Reverse Repos
- Fed Funds
- U.S. Treasury Bills

Bankers' Acceptance, Certificate of Deposit, Commercial Paper, Repurchase Agreement, Fed Funds

Money Market Funds

Money Market Funds are mutual funds that invest in short term money market instruments such as treasury bills, repos and bank certificates of deposit. MMFs in the US have been designed to maintain principal and have a share value always equal to one dollar. Interest income is automatically used to buy additional shares of the fund.

Money Market

Money Market Instruments

See *Money Market*

Money Settlement

The Money Settlement process is used by participants in the NSCC's trade clearance and settlement system as a way to net their cash obligations into a single debit or credit amount. This amount is paid on settlement date through one of the money settlement banks.

Money Supply

The Money Supply is the amount of money in the economy.

M1, M2, M3

Montreal Stock Exchange

The Montreal Stock Exchange is a Canadian stock exchange located in the province of Quebec.

www.me.org

Moodys

Moodys is a rating service that issues ratings that report the relative investment quality of corporate and municipal bonds.

Morgan Stanley Dean Witter & Co.

Morgan Stanley Dean Witter & Co. is a US-based broker/dealer.

www.msdw.com

Mortgage

A Mortgage is a contract between a lender, usually a savings and loan association, bank, etc., and a property owner, that provides a loan that defines the property as collateral. Most mortgages are paid off through fixed monthly payments of principal and interest for a specified period of time.

Mortgage Backed Securities

Mortgage Backed Securities

Mortgage Backed Securities (MBS) are bonds which are a general obligation of the issuing institution and are also collateralized by a pool of individual mortgages.

MBS are also called pass-through securities since the principal and interest collected by intermediaries is passed on to the investor.

Mortgage

Mortgage Backed Securities Clearing Corporation

The Mortgage Backed Securities Clearing Corporation (MBSCC) was established in 1979 as an affiliate of the NSCC to reduce the costs and risks of trading forward and TBA mortgage-backed securities.

MBSCC provides services that are required by their members, including:

- Automated trade comparison/confirmation
- Net settlement and pool notification services
- Managing financial risk
- Improving the market systems and technologies that are used in the mortgage-backed securities market
- Enhancing communication throughout the mortgage-backed securities market

www.mbscc.com

Electronic Pool Notification, NSCC, TBA

Mortgage Banker

A Mortgage Banker is an individual or a firm that originates and/or services mortgage loans, and packages these loans for resale into the marketplace.

Mortgage Broker

Mortgage Bonds

A Mortgage Bond is a bond that is issued by a corporation and which is secured by a mortgage on some real property.

Mortgage

Mortgage Broker

A Mortgage Broker is an individual or firm that arranges financing for borrowers.

Mortgage Banker

Mortgage Loan

See *Mortgage*

Mortgage Note

The Mortgage Note is the legal document that identifies the borrower's obligation to repay the loan. It identifies the principal, interest rate, maturity date of the loan and describes the property that is pledged as collateral for the loan.

Mortgagee

The Mortgagee is the lender of a mortgage loan.

Mortgagor

A Mortgagor is the borrower of a mortgage loan and the owner of the property pledged as collateral.

Borrower

Mosaic

Mosaic is a graphical user interface for the Internet which replaces standard Internet commands and file names with Windows-like functionality.

Graphical User Interface

Moscow Central Depository

Moscow Central Depository (MCD) is a central securities depository in Russia.

Moscow Central Stock Exchange

The Moscow Central Stock Exchange is the primary stock exchange of Russia.

www.fe.msk.ru/infomarket/rinacoplus/overview/overview.html

Moscow Times Index

The Moscow Times Index is a stock index derived from equities listed on the Moscow Central Stock Exchange.

Most Active

The term Most Active is used to identify the securities with the highest trading volume on an exchange over a defined period of time.

Mother Board

The Mother Board is the main component of a PC to which almost everything else connects. It has the primary circuitry for the computer.

Mouse

A Mouse is a handheld device that is manipulated by a user in order to control the movement of the cursor on the screen of a graphical user interface application.

Cursor, Graphical User Interface

MPEG

MPEG (Motion Pictures Experts Group) is a compression standard for digital video.

JPEG

MSCI EAFE Index

The MSCI EAFE Index is the Morgan Stanley Capital International index for Europe, Australia, and Far East Index.

MSRB

See *Municipal Securities Rulemaking Board*

MSTC

See *Midwest Securities Trust Company*

Multi-Currency

A Multi-Currency environment is one where securities that are denominated in various currencies can be bought, sold and recorded.

Multilateral Netting

Multilateral netting occurs when more than two parties are involved in the overall netting process.

Netting

Multi-Management System

In a Multi-Management System, the plan sponsor uses more than one investment manager to diversify the styles and classes of investments used in the plan.

Plan Sponsor, Investment Manager

Muni

See *Municipal Bond*

Municipal Bond

A Municipal Bond is a debt instrument that is issued by a US state or local government to fund projects such as building roads, bridges and schools, and to fund operating budgets. Muni bonds, as they are also called, are exempt from federal tax and are also exempt from state and local taxes for the investors who reside in the state where the bond is issued. A Muni bond usually carries a fixed rate of interest, which is paid semiannually. Municipal Bonds may be general, secured or insured.

Direct and general obligations are covered by the "full faith and credit" of the municipality, which means that the interest and redemption of the bond is covered by the municipality's ability to tax within its jurisdiction.

Revenue Bonds, Special Assessment Bonds

Municipal Bond Acceptance and Reconciliation Service

The Municipal Bond Acceptance and Reconciliation Service (MBARS) was designed to automate the submission of municipal bond trade data to the clearing corporation and to assist in the comparison and clearing of municipal bonds, OTC corporate bonds, and UIT trades.

OTC, UIT

Municipal Bond Fund

A Municipal Bond Fund is a mutual fund that invests in tax-exempt securities and passes through tax-free current income to its shareholders.

Municipal Note

A Municipal Note is a debt instrument issued by a US state or local government. Typical municipal notes are short term revenue notes and tax anticipation notes which have a first claim on taxes that are collected.

Municipal Securities Broker

A Municipal Securities Broker is a broker that trades municipal securities for their customers' accounts.

Municipal Securities Dealer

Municipal Securities Dealer

A Municipal Securities Dealer can be a person or any firm, except a bank, that buys and sells municipal securities for their own account.

Municipal Securities Broker

Municipal Securities Rulemaking Board

The Municipal Securities Rulemaking Board (MSRB) establishes rules that govern the trading and settlement of Municipal Securities in the US.

Musical Instrument Digital Interface

Musical Instrument Digital Interface (MIDI) is an industry standard for recording and recovering digital sound with multimedia programs.

Mutual Fund

A Mutual Fund is an investment company that pools many investors' money for specific investment purposes by selling shares in a goal oriented portfolio.

A Mutual Fund may be open end or closed end and charge either a front end load, back end load or no load on the purchase of shares.

Although originally designed to simplify investment decisions, there are now more mutual funds than equities listed on the New York Stock Exchange.

Mutual Funds provide the investor with several benefits:

- Professional management
- "Commingling" of funds and reduction of processing costs
- Distribution of risk through diversification

Because of the demand for funds, there are an increasing number of distribution methods, including:

- Direct distribution from the mutual fund
- Distribution via investment management firms
- Distribution via broker/dealers
- Distribution via banks

Mutual Funds have processing requirements that are different from those of banks, brokers and investment managers, including:

- Transfer agent service
- Shareholder servicing
- Fund accounting
- Custody

Open End Mutual Fund, Closed End Fund, Front End Load, Back End Load, No Load Fund

NACK

See *NCK*

Nagoya Stock Exchange

The Nagoya Stock Exchange is a stock exchange located in Japan.

www.iijnet.or.jp/nse-jp/e-home

Nairobi Stock Exchange

The Nairobi Stock Exchange is the primary stock exchange of Kenya.

Naked Option

A Naked Option is usually written by a speculator who does not own the underlying security or any off-setting option on the same security, and who believes that the market is about to move up or down and therefore sells a put or a call.

Option, Covered Option

NASAA

See *North American Securities Administrators Association*

NASD

See *National Association of Securities Dealers*

NASD By-Laws

The NASD By-Laws are the basic marketplace rules and regulations that govern the National Association of Securities Dealers, Inc.

Attached to the By-Laws are several schedules:

- Schedule A - NASD assessments and fees
- Schedule B - NASD district boundaries
- Schedule C - Registration and examination qualification requirements
- Schedule D - Participation in the Nasdaq market by issuers and members
- Schedule E - Requirements for distributing a public offering
- Schedule G - Procedures for reporting over-the-counter transactions
- Schedule H - Procedures for reporting and trading non-Nasdaq over-the-counter securities
- Schedule I - Rules governing all aspects of the PORTAL Market

PORTAL

NASD Form U-4

Form U-4 is NASD's uniform application for security registration or transfer.

NASD

NASD Form U-5

Form U-5 is NASD's uniform termination notice for security registration.

NASD

NASD Information Request Form

The NASD Information Request Form can be used by the public to obtain certain types of disciplinary and registration information regarding member firms and associated persons.

NASD

NASD Rules

NASD Rules include:

- Certificate of Incorporation
- By-Laws
- Rules of Fair Practice
- Government Securities Rules
- Code of Procedure
- Uniform Practice Code

National Association of Securities Dealers

NASD Rules of Fair Practice

See *Fair Practice Rules*

NASD

Nasdaq

See *National Association of Securities Dealers Automated Quotation*

Nasdaq Composite Index

The Nasdaq Composite Index is a statistical measure that indicates changes in the domestic and foreign securities that are traded on Nasdaq. The index is market-value weighted, since each company's security affects the index in proportion to its market value.

Nasdaq International Service

The Nasdaq International Service is an extension of Nasdaq to the United Kingdom and supports a trading session from 3:30 AM to 9 AM EST.

Nasdaq Level 1 Service

Nasdaq Level 1 Service is a vendor-distributed service that consists of real-time inside bid/ask quotations. Data is available for securities that are quoted on Nasdaq and through the OTC Bulletin Board Service.

Nasdaq Level 2 Service

Nasdaq Level 2 Service is a component of Nasdaq's Workstation II. This includes real-time access to Market Makers' quotes on Nasdaq and the OTC Bulletin Board Service.

Nasdaq Level 3 Service

Nasdaq Level 3 Service is Level 2 Service plus the ability to enter quotations, direct/execute orders, and send information. This service is only provided to

Market Makers of either Nasdaq, exchange-listed, or OTC Bulletin Board securities.

Nasdaq Quotation Dissemination Service

The Nasdaq Quotation Dissemination Service delivers real-time Nasdaq quotation information for Market Makers and electronic communication.

Nasdaq Stock Market

The Nasdaq Stock Market is a US-based electronic method of trading Nasdaq-listed securities. There is no central floor where members meet to trade.

www.nasdaq.com

National Association of Securities Dealers Automated Quotation

Nasdaq Trade Dissemination Service

The Nasdaq Trade Dissemination Service delivers Nasdaq real-time trade price and volume data to market data vendors and other data feed recipients. This includes the price and size for all trades submitted to the Automated Confirmation Transaction Service.

Automated Confirmation Transaction Service

Nasdaq Workstation II

Nasdaq Workstation II is a PC-based trading tool that provides market makers, brokers, and institutions access to Nasdaq markets.

National Association of Automated Clearing Agencies

The National Association of Automated Clearing Agencies (NACHA) has been established as the clearing agency for all of the Automated Clearing Houses in the US.

Automated Clearing House

National Association of Real Estate Investment Trusts

The National Association of Real Estate Investment Trusts (NAREIT) is an organization for individuals and organizations conducting business in the Real Estate Investment Trust (REIT) industry.

National Association of Securities Dealers

The National Association of Securities Dealers (NASD), regulated by the SEC, is the rule making body that governs the over-the-counter brokerage industry. The NASD, a self regulating organization, is organized to "adopt, administer, and enforce rules of fair practice and rules to prevent fraudulent and manipulative acts and practices, and in general to promote just and equitable principles of the trade for the protection of investors."

NASD is responsible for the operation and regulation of Nasdaq and the over-the-counter securities markets.

www.nasd.com

Self Regulating Organization

National Association of Securities Dealers Automated Quotation

Nasdaq is an electronic network that is used to store quotes, access quotations, and trade selected over-the-counter securities.

- Level I service provides the best bid and offer for a security without identifying the market maker.
- Level II service provides the best bid and offer and identifies the market maker.
- Level III service allows registered market makers to compete and trade by entering their own bids and offers.

Many stocks traded on the Nasdaq are technology stocks or new small to medium sized companies.

Nasdaq Level 1 Service, Nasdaq Level 2 Service, Nasdaq Level 3 Service

National Depository for Securities

The National Depository for Securities is the central depository and securities clearing house of Poland.

National Investment Company Service Association

The National Investment Company Service Association is the industry organization that supports Investment Companies.

www.nicsa.org

National Market System

The National Market System (NMS) was required by the Securities Act Amendments of 1975. The NMS consists of three major systems:

- The Consolidated Tape System (CTS) collects trade data from the NYSE, Amex and regional exchanges and distributes this information to vendors and news media for commercial distribution.
- The Consolidated Quote System (CQS) collects quote data from the NYSE, Amex and regional exchanges and distributes this information to vendors and news media for commercial distribution.
- The Intermarket Trading System (ITS) began operation in 1978 and electronically connects nine markets (American, Boston, Cincinnati, Chicago, New York, Pacific, Philadelphia and NASD). ITS allows traders at any exchange to seek the best available price for a security that is traded on multiple exchanges.

Consolidated Tape, Consolidated Quotation System, Intermarket Trading System, Securities Acts Amendments of 1975

National Securities Clearing Corporation

The National Securities Clearing Corporation (NSCC) is a clearing corporation that is responsible for netting the cash and securities transactions that occur each day between brokers in the US. NSCC, which is owned by the NYSE, Amex and NASD, also provides trade comparison of NYSE, Amex, and over-the-counter transactions.

Through the NSCC, brokers have established an efficient mechanism to settle among themselves called Continuous Net Settlement, and have created other processing services, including:

- Movement of cash and securities among participants
- Trade Recording and Processing
- Clearing and Settlement
- Delivery Systems
- Dividend and Interest Settlement Services

www.nscc.com

Continuous Net Settlement

National Securities Depository Limited

The National Securities Depository Limited (NSDL) is the central securities depository of India.

National Securities Trading System

The National Securities Trading System is used to facilitate round lot trading for equities, where one broker is a Market Maker for each security. The executed trades are locked in and sent to the NSCC and DTC for clearing and for settlement.

Round Lot, Locked In, NSCC, DTC

National Stock Exchange of India

The National Stock Exchange of India is the primary stock exchange of India.

www.nse-india.com

National Transfer Service

National Transfer Service (NTS) was created to facilitate the delivery of physical securities to transfer agents in order to re-register securities that are not DTC eligible. NTS handles items that result in account-closing activities including:

- Trading cycle
- Book-closing items
- Legal transfers and accommodation transfers
- Transfer Agent

NationsBanc Montgomery Securities

NationsBanc Montgomery Securities is the broker/dealer subsidiary of NationsBanc.

www.nationsbancmontgomery.com

NationsBank

NationsBank is a US-based bank.

www.nationsbank.com

NAV

See *Net Asset Value*

Navigation

Navigation is the process whereby an application's user moves from screen to screen, usually by controlling a cursor with a mouse, in search of desired information.

NCK

Pronounced NACK

A NCK is an acknowledgment sent by S.W.I.F.T. to the sender of a message, notifying the sender that an original message has been rejected.

ACK

Negotiable

A financial instrument is considered Negotiable when it is freely transferable from a buyer to a seller.

Fungible

Negotiable Certificate of Deposit

A Negotiable Certificate of Deposit is one that is issued in an amount over $25,000 and which can be bought and sold without the penalties normally associated with a CD.

Certificate of Deposit

Negotiated Underwriting

In a Negotiated Underwriting, the issuing firm's investment banker acts as the underwriting manager.

Underwriting Manager, Competitive Underwriting

Nesbitt Burns

Nesbitt Burns is a US-based broker/dealer.

www.nesbittburns.com

Net Amount

The Net Amount consists of the trade amount, trade price multiplied by quantity, minus applicable commissions, fees and taxes.

Net Asset Value

Net Asset Value (NAV) is a mutual fund's total asset market value, plus accruals, less expenses, divided by the number of shares outstanding. Shares are sold to the public at NAV plus any sales charges, and shares are redeemed at NAV, less any redemption charges.

The NAV is calculated using the previous day's closing prices and is published in newspapers on the evening of the day that it is calculated.

Net Capital Rule

See *SEC Rule 15c3-1*

Net Change

The Net Change is the difference between today's last trade and the previous day's last trade for a specific security.

Net Income

Net Income is the income remaining after all expenses and taxes have been deducted.

Net Position

A participant's Net Position in funds or in a security is the sum of all the incoming transfers minus the outgoing transfers. If positive, the participant is in a net credit position; if negative, the participant is in a net debit position.

The net credit or net debit position at settlement time is the net settlement position.

Net Settlement Position

Net Present Value

See *Present Value*

Net Settlement

Net Settlement is a process where several transactions between counterparties are settled on a net basis.

Netting

Net Settlement Position

The Net Settlement Position is a firm's net credit or net debit position at settlement.

Net Settlement

Net Tangible Assets

Net Tangible Assets is an accounting term that includes stockholders' equity minus goodwill.

Balance Sheet

Net Worth

See *Balance Sheet*

Netting

Netting is the process of bringing together all of the trades or transactions made by a netting system's participants that will be used to offset each other, and creating a single net debit or net credit position for each of the participants in cash and in each security.

Netting can be either bilateral or multilateral.

Net Settlement, Net Position, Net Position

Networking

Networking is:

- A generic term for electronic connectivity between computers

- The NSCC's automated record keeping system that coordinates non-trade-related client information between the records of a brokerage firm and a mutual fund or the fund's transfer agent

New Account Information Form

The New Account Information Form is a document that is completed by a broker describing a new client's financial condition, risk propensity and investment objectives.

New Issue

A New Issue is a stock or bond that is being sold in the market for the first time.

Initial Public Offering

New Straits Times Industrial Index

New Straits Times Industrial Index is a stock index derived from securities listed on the Stock Exchange of Singapore.

SES All Singapore Index

New York Futures Exchange

One of the late entries into the arena of futures trading, the New York Futures Exchange (NYFE), established in 1980 and located in New York at 30 Broad Street, trades futures contracts on foreign currencies, U.S. government securities, and futures contracts on certificates of deposit.

New York Mercantile Exchange

New York Mercantile Exchange (NYMEX) combined with the Gold Exchange. Previous to this, it traded futures contracts on cash and commodities, which included the round white potato and crude oil options.

New York Stock Exchange

The New York Stock Exchange (NYSE) is the primary floor exchange in the US. Located at 11 Wall Street, New York, New York, NYSE is an unincorporated, voluntary association that was founded in 1792 and exists under a written constitution and by-laws.

Seats on the exchange may be bought and sold. Membership and Securities listing requirements are strict, which makes the NYSE the most prestigious exchange in the US.

Liquidity is provided by individual and institutional investors, member firms trading for their own accounts, and assigned specialists.

The NYSE is linked with other markets trading listed securities through the Intermarket Trading System.

Intermarket Trading System, Liquidity, Seat, Specialist

New York Window

The NSCC established the New York Window to receive and deliver physical instruments on behalf of its customers. There is a US securities requirement that firms must have a physical window to receive securities, and that window must be in lower Manhattan below Houston Street and east of Jersey City, NJ. NSCC transferred this function to DTC in 1998.

NSCC, DTC

Next Day Funds

Next Day Funds are funds that are transferred today, but are not available for investment until tomorrow. This category was eliminated in the US in 1996 when the US securities industry adopted universal Same Day Funds.

Same Day Funds

Next Ex-Dividend Date

The Next Ex-Dividend Date is the next date on which an issue will go Ex-dividend.

Ex-Dividend

Next Put Date

The Next Put Date is the date of the next Put on a bond option.

Put

NH

See *Not Held*

NICSA

See *National Investment Company Service Association*

Nikkei 225 Index

Pronounced Nee Kay

The Nikkei Index is a price-weighted index of the performance of 225 large, selected stocks on the Tokyo Stock Exchange.

NIRF

See *NASD Information Request Form*

No Load Fund

A No Load Fund is an open end mutual fund that does not charge a front end or deferred sales change. For this type of fund, the 12b-1 charge must not exceed 0.25% per year. If it does not have a 12b-1 charge, it is called a pure no load.

Open End Mutual Fund, Front End Load,12b-1

No Quote

When a No Quote condition exists, there are no Market Makers currently making an inside market.

Inside Market

NOE

See *Notice of Order Execution*

Nominal Interest Rate

The Nominal Interest Rate on a bond is the ratio of the amount of annual interest promised by the bond divided by the stated value of the bond.

Nominal Return

The Nominal Return on an asset is the rate of return at the current price.

Real Return

Nominee

A Nominee is a person or legal entity that is designated by another person or legal entity to act on his/its behalf. The nominee concept is used in the securities industry to obtain registration and transfer ownership of a security.

Non Callable Securities

Non Callable Securities are those securities which cannot be redeemed by the issuer before maturity.

Callable

Non Market Risk

Non Market Risk refers to that potential for gains and losses in a portfolio that are not related to the movement of the market in general.

Non Qualified Plan

A Non Qualified Plan is a retirement plan that does not meet the requirements of the IRS Code, and are only contractual promises by a company to pay future benefits. These plans are used to give extra benefits to top executives and directors.

Qualified Plan

Non Regular Way

Regular Way settlement for most US securities occurs on the third business day after the trade. If both sides to a trade agree, the trade can be settled with different cash, delivery and settlement conditions. Such a settlement is termed Non Regular Way.

Regular Way

Non Resident Alien

A Non Resident Alien is a person who is not a US citizen and who does not reside in the US.

Resident Alien

North American Securities Administrators Association

The North American Securities Administrators Association (NASAA) is an association of the securities commissioners from each of the 50 states, the District of Columbia, Puerto Rico, and several Canadian provinces.

Northern Trust Bank

Northern Trust Bank is a US-based bank.

www.ntrs.com

Not Held

A notation of Not Held (NH) on an order indicates that the broker or trader has discretion over the time and price, and therefore can take whatever time is needed to get a good execution.

Note

A Note is:

- A medium term debt instrument, such as US Treasury Notes
- A legal document that a borrower signs to signify that they recognize the obligation to repay the loan with a stated interest rate and within a specified period of time

US Treasury Note

Notice of Default

A Notice of Default is a written notice from a lender to a borrower stating that a default has occurred.

Notice of Order Execution

The Depository Trust Company has enhanced its Interactive Delivery process to include an automated Notice of Order Execution that improves the electronic communication between brokers and investment advisors.

Depository Trust Company

NQ

See *No Quote*

NQDS

See *Nasdaq Quotation Dissemination Service*

NSCC

See *National Securities Clearing Corporation*

NSE Index

The NSE Index is a stock index derived from equities listed on the Nairobi Stock Exchange.

NSE Stock Price Index

The NSE Stock Price Index is a stock index derived from equities listed on the Nagoya Stock Exchange.

NSTS

See *National Securities Trading System*

NTDS

See *Nasdaq Trade Dissemination Service*

NYFE

See *New York Futures Exchange*

NYSE

See *New York Stock Exchange*

NYSE Common Stock Index

See *NYSE Composite Index*

NYSE Composite Index

The New York Stock Exchange established the NYSE Composite Index in 1966 as a value of 50.0 to provide a consistent measurement of the changes in the daily market. The indexes consist of all common stocks listed on the NYSE and four subgroup indexes:

- Industrial
- Transportation
- Utility
- Finance

The indices measure the change in the adjusted total market value of NYSE common stocks. Adjustments are made to reflect the effect of capitalization changes, new listings and delistings.

NYSE Listed Securities

NYSE Listed Securities are securities that been approved to trade on the New York Stock Exchange.

OATs

See French Trésor

OATS

See *Order Audit Trail System*

Object Code

A system's Object Code is the code that can be read and understood by a computer.

Source Code, Compile

Obligation

In general, an Obligation is a duty that is imposed by contract or law.

In the securities industry, the term is also used to describe a financial instrument, such as a stock or bond, which identifies the issuer's promises to repay the lender or purchaser.

OBO

See *Order Book Official*

OCC

The abbreviation OCC can be used in two ways:

- See Options Clearing Corporation
- See Office of the Comptroller of the Currency

OCC Regulation 9

OCC Regulation 9 defines the role and responsibilities of bank investment managers who must exercise discretion in investing their clients' assets.

Office of the Comptroller of the Currency

OCR

Pronounced O-C-R

See *Optical Character Recognition*

Odd Lot

An Odd Lot is a number of securities traded at one time that is smaller than the standard round lot of 100 shares or 5 bonds. Inactive shares can be traded in round lots of 10 shares.

Round Lot

Oesterreichische Kontrollbank

Oesterreichische Kontrollbank is the parent company of both the central depository of Austria and the central clearing agency of the Vienna Stock Exchange.

Off Line

The term Off Line can be used in two ways:

- A program runs Off Line when it is not interacting with the user. Batch programs are often run in background mode or off-line.
- Off Line can also refer to a condition where a computer is taken out of service.

Off Site

Something is Off Site when it is not on the firm's premises.

On Site

Off-Board

Off-Board refers to:

- OTC trades in unlisted securities
- A trade of exchange-listed shares which was executed off of a national securities exchange in the third market. Transactions are conducted through negotiation rather than an "auction" system.

Third Market

Offering Price

The Offering Price is:

- The price at which a seller is willing to sell

- The price at which members of an underwriting syndicate for a new issue will offer securities to investors

Off-Hours Trading

Off-Hours Trading is trading that takes place outside of an exchange's regular hours of operation. Off-hours trading can be conducted via the exchange, or over-the-counter.

Office of Supervisory Jurisdiction

The Office of Supervisory Jurisdiction (OSJ) can be any main office or branch office of an NASD member where any one of the following activities occurs:

- Order execution or market making
- Public offerings or private placements are structured
- Customers' funds or securities are held
- New accounts are approved
- Customer orders are reviewed and endorsed
- Advertising or sales literature for use by the member's associated persons is approved

The OSJ is responsible for supervising the activities of associated persons at the member's other branch offices.

Office of the Comptroller of the Currency

The Office of the Comptroller of the Currency (OCC), created by a law passed in 1863, is the federal regulatory body that is responsible for the administration and enforcement of trust and regulatory banking law. It oversees the operations and liquidation of all US national banks and Trust Companies.

The Comptrollers must approve the establishment of new national banks and bank mergers, and the OCC regulates how banks may invest their customers' funds.

Discretion, OCC Regulation 9

OID

See *Original Issue Discount*

OM Stockholm

OM Stockholm is a recognized exchange and clearing house for financial derivatives in Sweden.

Omnibus Account

An Omnibus Account is one in which money or securities for more than one beneficial owner are commingled by a custodian or a sub-custodian.

This is a common practice for global custodian banks because it is less expensive to keep one account at the sub-custodian and do the sub-accounting at the central level.

On Line

The term On Line can be used in two ways:

- A PC is On Line, when it is connected to a computer by a phone line. When using a PC by itself, the term on line is generally not used.
- A person is On Line when they are interacting with a computer through a terminal.

On Line Service Providers

See *Internet Service Provider*

On Site

Something is On Site when it is on the premises of a company.

Off Site

Open End Company

An Open End Company is an investment company, or mutual fund that constantly offers new shares for sale which are redeemable on any business day at their NAV.

Participants can buy and sell shares at any time, and the size of the fund is not limited.

Closed End Fund, NAV

Open End Mutual Fund

See *Open End Company*

Open Interest

Open Interest is the current number of outstanding option or future contracts that have not been exercised or expired.

Open Order

An Open Order is an order to buy or sell a specific security at a stipulated price which remains in effect until it is executed, canceled, or changed to a different price by the customer.

Open Outcry

Open Outcry is the technique used for trading where any bids and offers for a particular contract are made audibly to all other members in the pit.

Open Systems

An Open System is one that has been designed to use an operating system and database that can interact with the products provided by several different vendors. By using an open system design, developers keep their hardware options open to new products as they are developed by other vendors.

Proprietary Systems

Opening Automated Reporting System

Part of the SuperDot system, the Opening Automated Reporting System (OARS) is designed to accept member firms' pre-opening market orders for all stocks up to 30,099 shares for immediate systematic execution and reporting. OARS continuously pairs the appropriate buy and sell orders and presents the imbalance to each specialist before a stock opens to assist the specialist in establishing the opening price.

Opening Price, Specialist, SuperDot

Opening Price

The Opening Price for a security is established by the specialist on an exchange and by the competitive activity of all of the market makers in a specific security.

Market Maker

Operating Expenses

An Operating Expense is one that is incurred in the normal cost of processing transactions and reporting.

Operating Leverage

See *Leverage*

Operating System

The Operating System is the application that runs a computer's hardware and also manages the other applications that run on the computer.

Operations

The Operations area, also called the back office of a financial firm is where all of the clerical functions related to trade processing, clearing, settlement and issue servicing are conducted.

Back Office

Oppenheimer & Co., Inc

Oppenheimer & Co., Inc is a US-based Investment Manager.

www.oppenheimer.com

OPRA

See *Options Prices Reporting Authority*

Optical Character Recognition

Optical Character Recognition is a process that converts the image of text into data. When the computer stores an image, it can only retrieve the exact image and not relate the image to other data. When text is stored as data, it can be manipulated by the user or a program, and can be related to other data in the computer.

For example, an incoming fax arrives as an image. Through OCR, the name, account number, amount, etc. that is shown on the fax can be converted into data that a computer can store in the appropriate record, and can be used to initiate a transaction.
The quality of OCR depends upon the quality of the image, but a clean image can be read with a very high accuracy rate.

Fax

Optimization

The term Optimization can be used in two ways:

- The processes of maximizing profits on the sale of mortgage backed securities is called Optimization. According to PSA rules, the seller of a new mortgage-backed security is allowed to deliver anywhere from 98% to 102% of the sales amount, at the contracted unit price. Deliveries of securities can consist of up to three pieces per million.
- Portfolio Optimization involves selecting a portfolio that maximizes the potential return for any given level of risk.

Mortgage Backed Securities, PSA

Option

An Option is a legal contract that entitles, but does not require, the buyer to buy or sell a specific quantity of an underlying security before a specified date at a specific price.
One Option contract usually represents 100 shares of the underlying security.

Call, Put, Asian Option, American Style Option, European Style Option, Capped Style Option

Option Growth Fund

An Option Growth Fund is a mutual fund that invests at least 5% of its portfolio of securities in options.

Option Premium

An Option Premium is the amount paid to the writer of an option in addition to the intrinsic value of the option. Several factors influence the price of the option, including: supply and demand, the duration of the contract, and the difference between the fluctuations.

Option Principal Members

See *Competitive Trader*

Option Writer

An Option Writer is the person or institution that creates an options contract (either a put or call) by extending to the buyer the right to buy or sell the underlying security at a specified price and before a specified time.

An Option Writer may be trying to increase their yield by writing covered options or may be speculating by writing naked options or complex option strategies such as straddles and spreads.

Yield, Naked Option, Covered Option, Straddle, Spread

Options Clearing Company Ltd.

Options Clearing Company Ltd. (OCC) is a wholly-owned subsidiary of the Stock Exchange of Singapore that provides clearing and settlement facilities for stock options traded on the Exchange.

Options Clearing Corporation

The Options Clearing Corporation (OCC) is the central clearing corporation in the US for listed options, and is owned by the exchanges that deal in listed options.

www.optionsclear.com

Options Contract

See Options

Options Income Fund

An Options Income Fund is a mutual fund that attempts to provide current income by writing covered options on securities held in the fund's portfolio.

Options Notification Date

The Options Notification Date is the "First Window Date" for a put option.

Put

Options Prices Reporting Authority

The Options Prices Reporting Authority (OPRA) is an industry process that distributes inside quotations and the sale price and volume information for the options market.

Options Strike Price

The Options Strike Price is the price of the underlying asset at which a call or put option can be exercised.

Call, Put

Order

An Order is an instruction by a customer to buy or sell a particular security under specific terms, such as:

- At the market
- Good until cancelled
- Limit order, etc.

At the Market, Good-til-Cancelled Order, Limit Order

Order Audit Trail System

The Order Audit Trail System (OATS), which should go live in 1999, will allow regulators to monitor how a dealer handles a customer order from initiation to settlement.

Order Book Official

The Order Book Official is an exchange employee who keeps track of limit orders and executes these orders for the exchange's members.

Order Flow

Order Flow is the total of the orders that are sent from a buy-side firm to a sell-side firm, or from a broker to a dealer.

Buy Side, Sell Side

Order Indication Systems

Order Indication Systems are vendor applications and networks that help investment managers send position information and advertise. The FIX standard has opened up this market area by allowing brokers to send indications directly to investment managers.

FIX

Order Management Systems

Order Management Systems (OMS), which are often called trading systems, provide order, execution and allocation functionality to investment managers and brokers. The vendors of these applications and networks focus their resources on front office functions. Investment Managers have had difficulty beating the indices during this long bull market, so they are very conscious of the fees they receive and therefore need efficiency.

The successful vendors present data elegantly and have robust interfaces to order routing, portfolio management, back office, security master and pricing systems.

The market for Order Management Systems is still open since only 40% of investment management firms with over $1 billion in assets have them. Overall, only 10% to 25% of all investment management firms have an OMS.

Order Management Systems typically cost between $25,000 and $250,000.

Order Routing Systems, Portfolio Management System, Back Office

Order Matching

Order Matching is the process by which market makers pair their buy and sell orders for similar amounts of securities at identical prices.

Market Maker

Order Room

The Order Room is the operations department of a brokerage firm that tracks pending orders, records buys and sells, maintains the firm's open book of customer orders, and reconciles uncompared trades.

Order Routing Systems

Order Routing Systems allow investment managers to route their orders directly to a broker's order system and then to the exchange floor. The vendors in this area are very entrenched since order routing interfaces are complex and real-time.

Order Ticket

The Order Ticket is the form that a registered representative uses to record an order from a customer.

Ordinary Share

See *Equity*

Organization Chart

An Organization Chart is used to identify the various positions that exist in a firm, department or unit and which shows:

- Titles
- Names of incumbents
- Reporting relationships

Original Issue Discount

A security which is issued with an Original Issue Discount (OID) is one that originally sold for less than its face value. An investor buys an OID security with the expectation that the value of the security will steadily increase as the issue approaches maturity and redemption.

For a zero coupon bond, the Original Issue Discount is the par value at maturity minus the price when the bond was originally issued. Zero coupon bonds pay principal in the future, but do not pay interest throughout the life of the security. The Original Issue Discount is used for tax purposes; the IRS taxes the annual appreciation in the bonds value as though it was an interest bearing security.

Face Value, Zero Coupon Bond

Origination Fee

An Origination Fee is an amount that is charged by a lender to a borrower to cover costs of processing a loan or establishing a security.

OSE Total Index

The OSE Total Index is a stock index derived from equities listed on the Oslo Stock Exchange.

OSJ

See *Office of Supervisory Jurisdiction*

Oslo Stock Exchange

The Oslo Stock Exchange is the primary stock exchange of Norway.

nettvik.no/finansen/osloboers

OTC

See *Over-the-Counter Market*

OTC Bulletin Board Service

The OTC Bulletin Board is a regulated quotation service that displays real-time quotes, last-sale prices, and volume information in over-the-counter equity securities that are not listed on an exchange or on Nasdaq.

Exchange, Nasdaq

OTCBB

See *OTC Bulletin Board Service*

Out-of-Pocket Loss

An Out-of-Pocket Loss is the actual loss that an investor or a trader has realized after selling a security they previously purchased, or closing out a short position.

Short, Realized Losses, Unrealized Losses

Out-of-the-Money

An option is Out-of-the-Money when the strike price is:

- Above the price of the underlying security for a call option
- Below the price of the underlying security for a put option

- When an option is Out-of-the Money, it does not have any intrinsic value, but can have a premium value.

Call Option, Intrinsic Value, Premium Value

Outplace

Firms frequently will attempt to Outplace people who are no longer needed in their organization. Outplacement often involves career counseling, assistance with resumes, interview practice and the identification of job opportunities. It does not guarantee a new job to the person being outplaced.

Downsize

Outsource

A firm is said to Outsource when it hires another firm to perform some function that was previously conducted internally.

Overbought

A stock is considered Overbought when investors or traders, through excessive buying, have driven the price of the stock to a market value above that which is widely believed to be its true value.

Oversold

Overdraft

An Overdraft occurs when an account holder attempts to withdraw more funds than the account actually has. This generally occurs by buying more securities than can be covered by the existing cash or margin, or by writing a check against an account that contains an insufficient amount of funds.

Overdraft Credit

A financial firm either has to cover an overdraft by issuing an Overdraft Credit, which is a formal loan, or by rejecting the trade or the check. The credit rules that are applied to this extension of credit are different for banks and brokers.

Loan, Margin

Override

An Override:

- As a noun, is added to a stated commission for a specific purpose
- As a verb, is entered into a system on top of another entry and which takes the place of the previous entry
- As a verb, is an action taken by someone with superior authority who changes a decision made by a subordinate

Oversold

A stock is considered Oversold when investors or traders, through excessive selling, have driven the price of the stock to a market value below that which is widely believed to be its true value.

Overbought

Over-the-Counter Firm

An Over-the-Counter Firm (OTC) is one that buys and sells securities in the Over-the-Counter market as opposed to on an exchange.

Over-the-Counter Market

Over-the-Counter Market

The Over-the-Counter Market (OTC) is a network of securities dealers who may or may not be members of a national exchange. OTC is primarily a dealers' market, is generally conducted using the Nasdaq system, (in the US) and by telephone, and trades unlisted securities.

OTC is the principal market for U.S. government bonds, municipals, and bank and insurance stocks.

Over-the-Counter Firm, Nasdaq

Overvalued

A stock is Overvalued when the current price is higher than its actual value or price/earnings ratio.

P&L Statement

See *Profit and Loss Statement*

P&S Department

See *Purchase and Sale Department*

PAC

See *Planned Amortization Class*

Pacific Clearing Corporation

The Pacific Clearing Corporation (PCC) is the clearing corporation of the Pacific Stock Exchange.

Pacific Stock Exchange

The Pacific Stock Exchange (PSE) is a stock exchange that operates in San Francisco and Los Angeles, and which lists primarily regional securities.

Paine Webber, Inc.

Paine Webber, Inc. is a US-based broker/dealer.

www.painewebber.com

Painting the Tape

Brokers Paint the Tape when they buy and sell among themselves to build up the volume of shares traded on a particular security to make it look interesting.

Panama Stock Exchange

The Panama Stock exchange is the primary stock exchange of Panama.

www.panamainfo.com/tables/stockex_stockex.html

Paper Profit

A Paper Profit is the unrealized profit that exists when a security or commodity can be sold for more than its cost basis.

Unrealized Profits

Par

See *Par Value*

Par Value

Par Value is different for various classes of securities:

- A bond is often said to be trading at Par Value when it trades for its face amount, which is typically $1,000.
- Par Value for common stock refers to an arbitrary dollar amount assigned to each share by the company's charter of incorporation. The par value has no significance to the market value of a stock unless it is used as a basis for some shareholders' rights.
- Par Value may also be defined as the amount to be received when a bond matures and is redeemed.
- Par Value is important for preferred stock and bonds since the preferred dividend and interest on the bond are often based on the Par Value that has been assigned to each issue.

Face Value

Parallel Processing

Parallel Processing is:

- A stream of input that has been broken down into separate independent streams that are acted upon individually
- A single task that has been broken into component parts with each of the parts being acted upon independently and then reassembled into a whole completed task

Parallel Testing

Parallel Testing is managed by the users and is usually the last test before a system goes live. If the new system is replacing an existing one, both systems are operated side by side for a pre-determined period of time to ensure that the output from both systems is the same, or that any differences are expected.

Testing, Systems Development Life Cycle

Pareto's Principle

Pareto's Principle, also known as the 80/20 rule, states that 80% of your problems usually come from 20% of your business activity, or that 80% of your profits come from 20% of your customers or products, etc.

Partial Redemption

A Partial Redemption occurs when an issuer redeems anything less than an entire issue of its securities.

Issue

Participant

A Participant is an entity that is an active member of a system such as a depository or clearing corporation.

Depository, Clearing Corporation

Participant Terminal System

The DTC offers a terminal-based product, called the Participant Terminal System (PTS), that provides direct terminal connectivity into the various DTC systems. DTC also provides computer to computer connectivity through two other methods, MDH and CCF.

Mainframe Dual Host, DTC

Participants Trust Company

The Participants Trust Company is the depository for GNMA securities. It has recently merged with the DTC.

GNMA, DTC

Participating Preferred Stock

Participating Preferred Stock grants to its holders the opportunity to "participate" in the growth of the company by receiving a dividend in addition to the amount normally authorized to be paid to preferred share holders. A company's Board of Directors must approve the additional payments made to participating preferred shareholders.

Preferred Stock

Participation Certificate

A Participation Certificate is a form of mortgage backed security which represents an interest in a group of mortgages purchased by a mortgage corporation. Participation Certificates trade similarly to GNMAs, but the market is much smaller.

Passed Dividend

A Passed Dividend occurs when a company's Board of Directors does not vote to pay a regularly anticipated dividend.

Dividend

Passive Management

Passive Management is an investment management style that is designed to match either an index or the general performance of the market.

Active Management

Pass-Through Asset Trust Security

Developed in 1996 by the Union Bank of Switzerland, the Pass-Through Asset Trust Security (PATS) bond was primarily sold to 144A investors as private placements and did not sell well in the open market since most investors did not want to have a trust in their portfolio.

144A, Private Placement

Pass-Through Security

A Pass-Through Security is a debt instrument backed by an interest in a pool of mortgages. The name comes from the fact that sponsoring organizations, such as the Government National Mortgage Association (GNMA), pass through the interest and principal that was collected from the mortgagors to the certificate holders on a monthly basis.

GNMA, Mortgagor

Password

A Password is a security code that permits individuals to access a system. A password is initially assigned by a securities administrator and must then be changed by the individual to ensure that only the individual knows the password.

Most firms have specific rules about how they issue passwords and how those passwords are used.

PATS

See *Pass-Through Asset Trust Security*

Paying Agent

A Paying Agent is an institution that, appointed by and acting on behalf of an issuer, makes a dividend, interest or principal payment to the holders of securities. Payment is made for bearer instruments and to holders of physical securities upon receipt of the bond's coupon. Payment for registered bonds/stocks is made to the holders listed on the issuer's record.

For securities that are held at the DTC, the payment is made to the DTC. The DTC then sends the appropriate amount to the banks and brokers, which then in turn credit the appropriate customers' accounts.

Bearer Instrument, Coupon, DTC, Physical Security

Payment

A Payment occurs when a monetary obligation has been made by the payor to the creditor, and both parties agree that the obligation has been satisfied.

Payment Date

The Payment Date is the date that a dividend will be paid to eligible shareholders. Eligibility is determined by the record date.

Record Date

PBGC

See *Pension Benefit Guarantee Corporation*

PC

The term PC can be used in two ways:

- See Participation Certificate
- See Personal Computer

PC Platform

PC Platform is the name of NSCC's data-entry and communications application that allows participants using a Personal Computer to directly access NSCC applications such as:

- CNS
- FITS
- Commission Billing
- ACATS
- Correspondent Clearing
- DCCage
- RECAPS
- Send transaction data and receive activity reports

NSCC, Personal Computer

Peak

A Peak is a temporary period of heightened activity. It could be an increase in transaction volume, an increase in errors, or high stock prices.

Valley

Pegging

See *Penalty Bid*

Penalty Bid

A Penalty Bid is an offer that has been made by the syndicate manager or underwriter to buy a security at a specific price during the distribution of a new issue. The bid stabilizes the price of the stock and makes the securities easier to distribute.

Penny Stock

A Penny Stock is a low-priced security, usually less than $1.00, that trades over-the-counter. These stocks are generally considered highly speculative.

Pension Benefit Guarantee Corporation

The Pension Benefit Guarantee Corporation (PBGC) is a regulated governmental agency, established by ERISA, that ensures payment of defined benefit plan benefits when qualified plans terminate without sufficient assets to pay their promised benefits. The PBGC is funded by premiums that are paid by the Qualified Plans.

ERISA, Qualified Plan

Pension Disbursing

Pension Disbursing is the department that is responsible for making payments to retirees who are beginning to receive regular benefit payments from a Pension Plan. This department keeps track of how much each person is due, as well as their current address, etc., and either sends a physical check or an ACH funds transfer each month.

ACH, Pension Plan

Pension Fund

See *Pension Plan*

Pension Plan

A Pension Plan is an employee retirement program that has been established in accordance with ERISA.

ERISA, Defined Benefit Program, Defined Contribution Program

Per Diem Interest

Per Diem Interest is interest that is calculated daily.

Performance Bond

A Performance Bond is a good faith deposit, or margin, that has been made to a regulated exchange to support an investor's obligations with futures and short options. The bond is monitored by the exchange, or its clearing house, and must be maintained at a certain percentage of the current market value of the investor's current positions. A performance bond can be made with cash, treasuries, a letter of credit, or some other high quality security.

Margin

Performance Measurement

Performance Measurement is the process that is associated with measuring an investment manager's total risk-adjusted performance.

Personal Computer

A Personal Computer is a device that typically sits on a desk and is dedicated to the use of one person. A Personal Computer generally has several components:

- A display terminal
- Operating Memory
- Operating System
- Data Storage
- Floppy Disk Drive (or other form of data input/extract device)

It may also have the following:

- Printer
- Modem
- Scanner
- Audio Card and speakers
- Fax Card

Personal Trust

A firm providing Personal Trust services generally offers the following Fiduciary and/or Agency Services:

- Safekeeping of property

- Processing of receipts and disbursements
- Accounting, record keeping, and asset management
- Fiduciary Services
- Estate Administration
- Personal Trust Administration
- Guardianships
- Agency Services
- Investment Advisory
- Custody Services

Philadelphia Depository

The Philadelphia Depository (Philadep) provided depository services to a small regional group of participants. It was merged into the DTC in 1997.

Philadelphia Stock Exchange

The Philadelphia Stock Exchange (PHLX) is an equities and options exchange in Philadelphia, Pennsylvania. The PSE is the Pacific Stock Exchange.

Philadep

See *Philadelphia Depository*

Physical Security

A Physical Security is one that is represented by a piece of paper that identifies the holder and the issuer. The industry is increasingly moving towards immobilizing and dematerializing securities.

Dematerialization, Immobilization

PIBOR

Pronounced Pie Bore

PIBOR is the abbreviation for the Paris Interbank Offered Rate, which is a rate established for overnight interest charged between financial institutions in Paris.

London Interbank Offered Rate

Pictet & Cie

Pronounced Pick tay and see

Pictet & Cie is a Swiss-based Private Bank.

www.pictet.com

Pink Sheet

A Pink Sheet, also called the Bulletin Board, is a daily quote list for over-the-counter stocks that are printed by the National Quotation Bureau. Quotes are collected from Market Makers.

Over-the-Counter Market

Pit

The Pit is a designated area of a commodity trading floor where a particular contract is traded.

PITI

PITI is an abbreviation for Principal, Interest, Taxes and Insurance, which are the components of a monthly mortgage payment.

Pixel

A Pixel is the smallest element that is used to construct a picture on a computer terminal. An individual pixel is a dot (or a very small square) on a terminal's screen that can be in various shades of gray or colors. The dots and their shading build a complete picture.

Pixels can be stored in a computer and recovered to re-form the original picture on paper or on a screen.

Screen

Plan

A Plan is:

- A logical list of tasks, milestones, resource assignments and dependencies that when performed, will attain a goal.
- A Pension Plan.

Goal, Task, Milestone, Project Plan, Pension Plan

Plan Sponsor

A Plan Sponsor is the firm that has established a Pension Plan and is responsible under ERISA for complying with the applicable regulations. The Plan Sponsor selects the investment manager and the custodian.

ERISA, Pension Plan

Planned Amortization Class

A Planned Amortization Class is a type of a collateralized mortgage obligation with somewhat certain prepayment characteristics.

Targeted Amortization Class, Derivative

Platform

A Platform is the hardware that is used to run a program or an application. A platform can be a PC, a minicomputer or a mainframe, and can be produced by different vendors.

PNC Bank Corporation

PNC Bank Corporation is a US-based bank.

www.pncbank.com

PO

See *Principal-Only Strip*

Point

A Point is:

- A price movement of one monetary unit. If an equity rises from 10 to 11, it has gone up one point. The monetary unit can be in any currency.
- An up-front fee that is paid by the borrower to the lender at the time that a loan is made. Each point equals one percent of the total loan amount.

Poison Pill

A Poison Pill is a tactic used by a firm to make the firm less desirable in a potential takeover. A poison pill gives the current shareholders the right to purchase additional shares at a reduced price if another firm acquires a pre-defined percentage of the firm's stock.

Policy

A Policy is established by a firm as a rule that sets a general direction, or which establishes actions that can not or should not be taken in certain circumstances. A policy differs from a procedure in that the policy sets the general guideline, while a procedure defines how something should be done.

Procedure

Pool Number

The Pool Number is the unique number that identifies the pools for mortgage backed securities such as GNMAs, FNMAs, etc. A pool is a group of asset backed securities (mortgages, for example) that are grouped together to distribute to investors the income and principal and income from the underlying loans.

Mortgage Backed Securities

Pooling

Mutual funds use Pooling to collect money from many individual investors in order to invest in an object oriented portfolio.

Mutual Fund

Population

Population is a statistics term that refers to all of the possible values in pool of data. A portion of a population is called a sample.

Sample

PORTAL

PORTAL is NASD's trading system for secondary market trading of 144A securities.

144A, NASD, Trading Systems

Portfolio

A Portfolio is a group of securities that are held in a single client's account, and can include various asset classes.

Portfolio Management System

A Portfolio Management System is one that has been designed to support the information needs of an investment manager's portfolio managers. These systems are basically record keeping systems that have the potential to support the portfolio manager's need to analyze the positions.

Portfolio Manager

A Portfolio Manager is an individual who is responsible for investing a pool of money for:

A Mutual Fund, in accordance with the fund's investment objectives

A High Net Worth Investor, in accordance with the investor's wishes. When investing for a HNWI, the Portfolio Manager is said to have discretion if they can make the investment decisions on their own authority.

A Pension Fund, in accordance with the Pension Fund's direction and objectives

High Net Worth Investors, Discretion, Pension Fund, Pooling

Portfolio Turnover

Portfolio Turnover is the ratio of buying and selling activity in a portfolio or account. The ratio is calculated with the net of the purchases and sales divided by the average balance.

Portfolio

POS

See *Principal-Only Securities*

Position Netting

Position Netting is a form of netting between trading partners that is not legally enforceable.

Trade Netting

Post Trade Processing

Post Trade Processing is a stage of the Trade Life Cycle.

Trade Life Cycle

Pounds

Pounds, previously called Pounds Sterling or Sterling, are the unit of currency in the United Kingdom.

Power of Attorney

A Power of Attorney is a legal document that authorizes one person to act on behalf of another.

A full Power of Attorney permits the person managing an account to deposit and withdraw securities and cash in addition to buying and selling securities.

A limited Power of Attorney permits the person managing the account to enter buy and sell orders but not move money out of the account.

PPI

Abbreviation for Producer Price Index

Prague Stock Exchange

The Prague Stock Exchange is the primary stock exchange of the Czech Republic.

Pre-Emptive Right

A Pre-Emptive Right specifies that the current owners of a stock must be given the opportunity to acquire additional shares in order to maintain their percentage of ownership if additional shares of the same class are issued. This right is normally specified in the corporation's charter.

Preference Stock

See *Preferred Stock*

Preferred Stock

Preferred Stock is a form of equity representing an ownership interest in the business, which has "preference" over common stock. The preferences include priority in the payment of dividends and/or the distribution of assets up to a certain fixed amount in the event of bankruptcy.

Preferred dividends are usually predetermined, and do not require approval from a company's Board of Directors The Board of Directors can, however, decide not to make or to delay a dividend payment for Preferred Stock.

Board of Directors, Common Stock

Preliminary Prospectus

See *Red Herring*

Pre-Matching Process

The Pre-Matching Process is a process of comparing trade or settlement information between counterparties before other matching or comparison procedures. The main difference between pre-matching and matching is that pre-matching tends to be informal and non-binding.

Matching

Premium

A Premium can be:

- The difference between the original offering price of a security and its price in the secondary market
- The amount a security sells for over its face value
- Any amount exceeding the face value that will not be repaid at maturity
- The opposite of a discount
- The amount in excess of the intrinsic value of an option
- The fee paid by a short seller to the lender of security that is sold short
- The amount at which a closed-end fund trades above its net asset value

Face Value, Secondary Market

Premium Price

Firms can charge a Premium Price when they offer a special level of service or a product that is in great demand.

Premium Value

See *Premium*

Prepaid and Deferred Assets

Prepaid and Deferred Assets include expenditures for future costs or expenses, such as insurance, interest or rent. These assets are amortized over a specific period of time.

Prepayment

Prepayment is the full or partial repayment of the principal on a loan before the contractual due date.

Prepayment Clause

A Prepayment Clause is an official statement in a contract or indenture permitting the borrower to pay all or part of the unpaid balance before it becomes due.

Prepayment Penalty

A Prepayment Penalty is a fee that is imposed upon the borrower when there is no prepayment clause that allows a debt to be repaid before it becomes contractually due.

Prepayment Clause

Prepayment Risk

Prepayment Risk is the risk that the mortgages behind a mortgage backed security will be prepaid during a period of declining rates.

Pre-Refunded Bond

A Pre-Refunded Bond is one that is secured by an escrow fund of US government bonds that is sufficient to pay off the entire issue at maturity. The rating of the refunded bond generally assumes the rating of the government securities that are placed in escrow.

Present Value

The Present Value of a future amount or a series of future amounts is their current value after adjusting each payment in the series for an assumed inflation or interest rate each year.

Pre-Syndicate Bid

A Pre-Syndicate Bid is a bid that was entered before the effective date of a secondary offering. This bid is made to stabilize the price during the primary distribution. This type of bid is permitted under SEC Rule 10b-7.

Secondary Offering

Pre-Trade

Pre-Trade functions occur before a trade is made and include:

- Obtaining Market Information
- Research
- Portfolio Management
- Analytics
- Modeling
- Risk Management

Preventive Controls

Preventive Controls, which are designed to prevent errors, fraud and mischief, include:

- Dual Control
- Dual Processing
- Batch-long Reconciliation
- Supervisory Review
- Passwords
- Check-Digits
- Automated Edits

Detective Controls, Compensating Controls

Previous Call

The Previous Call is the last date that a specific debt instrument was called.

Previous Day's Close

The Previous Day's Close is the last reported trade from the previous trading day.

Price

See *Market Price*

Price and Quotations Index

The Price and Quotations Index is a stock index derived from equities listed on the Bolsa Mexicana de Valores.

Price Index

The Price Index is a stock index derived from equities listed on the Societe de la Bourse de Luxembourg.

Price Limit

A Price Limit is the maximum price increase or decrease from the previous day's closing price that is permitted in one trading session for a security or a contract. Price limits are determined by the regulations of the exchange on which the security is traded.

Price Range

The Price Range for a security is defined by the highest price and the lowest price at which the security has traded during any specific period, such as a day, week, or year.

Price/Earnings Ratio

An equity's Price/Earnings Ratio (P/E) is its market price divided by its current or estimated future earnings per share. Price/Earnings Ratios are a method that is used to determine the value of a stock relative to other stocks.

Primary Distribution

See *Initial Public Offering*

Primary Market

The Primary Market is how firms bring their initial offers to the public. These offerings, called Initial Public Offerings (IPOs), are distributed to institutional and individual buyers through underwriters and participating brokers.

After an issue has been brought to the market in an IPO, all of the subsequent trading is conducted in the Secondary Market.

The Primary Market for a specific security is the primary exchange on which the security is listed.

Initial Public Offering, Secondary Market, Third Market, Fourth Market

Primary Research

When the research department of a firm engages in Primary Research, they spend a considerable amount of effort to understand in detail how the firm being studied works and its potential profitability. This includes:

- Examining financial information from the company
- Visiting the company
- Talking to customers and suppliers
- Attending company presentations
- Real-time information from the financial markets

Prime Rate

The Prime Rate is the interest rate extended by US commercial banks to their most credit-worthy and reliable corporate customers. Other interest rates are often pegged to the prime rate.

Principal

The term Principal can be used in several ways:

- A brokerage firm acts as a principal to the trade when they become responsible for the settlement of a customer's trade. Brokers like to function as a principal since they can then mark up a purchase price or mark down a sale price as they resell the security to their customer.
- Dealers, trading for their own account, act as a principal to the trade.
- The initial amount of money invested is the principal, excluding any earnings.
- The amount of debt, not counting interest, left unpaid on a loan is the principal.
- The face amount of a bond, payable at maturity

Dealer, Markdown, Markup

Principal Order

A Principal Order is an order by a broker/dealer that is buying or selling for its own account.

Principal Paydown

Principal Paydown occurs when a security has been constructed to return principal to the security holder through a series of periodic payments.

Asset Backed Security, Mortgage Backed Securities

Principal Payment Frequency

Principal Payment Frequency is the payment frequency of the principal balance on mortgage backed securities.

Mortgage Backed Securities

Principal Risk

Principal Risk is the risk that the buyer or seller of a security incurs when they deliver a security without simultaneous payment. Principal risk is minimized in settlement environments that use a Receive/Deliver vs. Payment process.

DVP, RVP

Principal Trades

See *Principal Order*

Principal Value

The Principal Value of a security is the amount that is inscribed on the face of a security, and which is used in the computation of regular interest payments.

Principal-Only Securities

Principal-Only (PO) Securities are usually mortgage backed securities that have payment streams derived solely from the principal portion of the underlying loans.

Principal-Only Strip

A Principal-Only (PO) Strip consists of the principal that has been separated from the interest of a mortgage backed security. A PO is traded separately from the Interest Only Security.

Strip, Interest Only Strip

Prior Period Adjustment

A Prior Period Adjustment is an accounting or operational entry that is made to correct an error in a previous accounting period.

Prior Preferred Stock

Prior Preferred Stock is a class of shares that have senior rights to dividends over other issues of preferred or common stock.

Common Stock, Preferred Stock

Private Bank

A Private Bank is a bank that is organized to provide services for high net worth investors, including:

- Traditional retail banking services
- Trust Accounts
- Securities purchases, sales and position maintenance
- Trading advice
- Discretionary Portfolio Management

High Net Worth Investors

Private Financing

See Private Placement

Private Label

Private Label processing is conducted by one bank for another bank. Banks selling this service provide back office services of cash management, trade processing, securities processing, etc., and produce statements and advices to the customers in the name of the bank that has bought the service. The buying bank's customers do not usually know that another bank is processing their transactions or maintaining their accounts.

Private Network

Firms create a Private Network by leasing lines from the major telecommunications companies and using their own hardware to connect.

Private Placement

A Private Placement involves the issuance of a security to a group of not more than 35 investors. The investors sign an Investment Letter, and rather than receive certificates indicating their purchase, are issued letter stock or letter bonds. Private Placements are usually associated with debt instruments.

SEC Rule 144A, Letter Stock

Private Sector Passthroughs

See *Pass-Through Security*

Procedure

A Procedure is established by a firm to specifically define how something should be done.

Policy

Process Improvement

A Process Improvement is any change to a firm's process that improves cost, quality, timeliness or the product/service itself.

Process Map

See *Flow Chart*

Process Mapping

See *Flow Chart*

Process Redesign

Process Redesign is the normal process that managers have used for years to identify incremental improvements to their areas of responsibility.

Reengineering, Business Redesign

Process Reengineering

See *Reengineering*

Processing Steps

The Processing Steps are the individual actions that are taken in order to complete a process.

Processor

A Processor is:

- A person performing a task

Central Processing Unit

PROCTOR

See *Professional Certification Testing Organization*

Professional Certification Testing Organization

The Professional Certification Testing Organization (PROCTOR) is the NASD's process to test, administer appointments, and authorize grades for the licenses granted by the NASD. There is a network of PROCTOR test delivery centers throughout the US.

Profit and Loss Statement

The Profit and Loss Statement describes a firm's current revenues and expenses, and in conjunction with the Balance Sheet, presents a firm's financial condition.

Balance Sheet

Profit Dynamics

Profit Dynamics describe the interplay of revenue and expense in a given business, and explains how a business actually makes a profit. The profit dynamics for different segments of the securities business vary considerably.

Different segments can make money through spreads, fees, commissions, markups, etc.

Spread, Commission, Markup

Profit Sharing Plan

A Profit Sharing Plan is a form of defined contribution retirement plan. The employer can make a contribution to the plan when the company's profits are sufficient to do so. Contributions to a profit sharing plan are made at the firm's discretion, and can range from nothing to an allowable maximum.

Defined Contribution Program

Profit Taking

Profit Taking occurs when the holder of a security that has appreciated since its purchase actually sells it. Profit Taking transfers an unrealized gain into a realized gain.

Program

The term Program can be used in two ways:

- A Program is a group of lines of code that is designed to perform a specific task. A group of programs working together is an application.
- A Program is a series of related events that is intended to achieve a specific goal and to maintain that goal over a period of time. A Program has a start date, but usually does not have a designated end date.

Project

Program Trading

Program Trading includes a range of different computer-based portfolio trading strategies that involve the purchase or sale of 15 or more stocks with a total market value of $1,000,000 or more. Some examples of program trading include:

- Index arbitrage, or the purchase or sale of a basket of stocks along with the sale or purchase of a derivative product
- Liquidation of stock positions
- Portfolio management, including portfolio realignment and portfolio liquidations

Project

A Project is a series of related events that are intended to achieve a specific goal in a specific period of time. A Project has a start date and an end date.

Program

Project Plan

A Project Plan is the list of activities that must be performed in order to accomplish a project's objectives. Project Plans can take many forms, although almost all of them contain at least:

- Tasks
- People responsible for the completion of the tasks
- Due dates for the tasks
- Dependencies of the task with other tasks

Project Risk

There are eight possible outcomes of any project, and only one of them is good. All of the others are categories of risk that can result from a project.

Project is late and/or over budget

- Cancelled during development
- Goes live, but blows up
- Goes live and is a success

- Goes live but is cancelled before reaching its payback
- Project is on time and within budget
- Cancelled during development
- Goes live, but blows up
- Goes live and is a success
- Goes live but is cancelled before reaching its payback

Prompt

The term Prompt can be used in two ways:

In a text-based program, a Prompt is the word or symbol that is used to tell the user that they must enter input.

In Windows, a Prompt is the flashing icon that identifies where the cursor is at any point in time.

Icon, Cursor

Prompt Delivery

See *Prompt Receipt*

Prompt Receipt

Prompt Receipt occurs when the securities involved in a trade are delivered by the selling party at or before the settlement date.

Proof

A Proof is a formal accounting reconcilement that can be conducted daily, weekly, monthly, etc. A proof is generally one sub-set of a firm's general ledger and is typically related to some specific operational activity.

General Ledger

Proprietary Systems

A Proprietary System is a computer application that is written by a firm for its own use.

Open Systems, Application

Proration

Proration is the process used by an issuer if more shares are surrendered than the issuer wants to obtain in a tender offer. The Proration is a percentage that is applied to all of the securities that are offered, and the balance is returned to the customer.

Tender Offer

Prospectus

A Prospectus is a legal document that explains the history, business plan, current status and terms of a security issue, or a mutual fund. A prospectus must be made available to all interested purchasers in advance of a public offering for securities that are covered by the Securities Act of 1933.

Initial Public Offering, Mutual Fund

Protect Period

The Protect Period is the time that is available after a tender offer expires to allow for the late delivery of certificates. On the New York Stock Exchange, the protect period is usually three to five business days.

Tender Offer

Protocol

A Protocol is a standard set of instructions to facilitate telecommunications. Some typical instructions in a protocol are:

- Baud Rate
- Parity
- Number of data bits
- Stop bit
- Duplex type

Prototype

A Prototype is an early version of a product or an application which gives some of the look and feel of the finished product. A prototype is usually developed in a short period of time and for a fraction of the cost of the final product, but does not have the complete functionality of the finished product.

Provisional Transfer

A Provisional Transfer is a transfer that is conditional in that one or both parties to the transfer have the right to rescind it.

Proxy

A Proxy is a written form that is given by a shareholder to record their vote or to authorize someone else to vote in their place at a stockholder's meeting.

Proxy Statement

Proxy Fight

A Proxy fight can occur when a group of stockholders attempt to collect the proxies (votes) of other shareholders to force the management of a firm to take a specific action.

Proxy

Proxy Statement

The Securities Exchange Commission requires that a security's issuer provide a Proxy Statement to their stockholders before a vote is solicited.

Proxy

Prudent Investor Rule

The Prudent Investor Rule requires people who makes investment decisions on behalf of others to exercise the same care that any professional investor would take, but to not miss opportunities by only investing in totally safe securities.

Prudent Man Rule

The Prudent Man Rule was a federal and state regulation that required trustees and portfolio managers to make financial decisions in the manner of a prudent man, e.g., with intelligence and discretion. This typically led to extremely safe investments that failed to match the average returns in the industry.

This has been placed by the concept of a prudent investor.

Prudent Investor Rule

Prudential Securities

Prudential Securities is a US-based broker/dealer.

www.prusec.com

PSA

See *Bond Market Association*

PSE

See *Pacific Stock Exchange*

PT Kliring Deposit Efek Indonesia

PT Kliring Deposit Efek Indonesia (KDEI) is the clearing organization of Indonesia.

PTC

See *Participants Trust Company*

PTC Contra ID

The PTC Contra ID is the code that is used to identify the trading counterparty at the Participants Trust Company.

Participants Trust Company

PTS

See *Participant Terminal System*

Public Float

Public Float is the total of a company's shares that are owned by public investors. This does not include shares held by company officers, directors, or any investors who hold a controlling interest in the company.

Public Network

A Public Network is a telecommunication network that is directly accessed by the public. Public networks may also sell line access to a firm that will create its own private network.

Private Network

Public Offering Date

The Public Offering Date is the first day a new issue is offered to the public.

Public Securities Administration

See *Bond Market Association*

Purchase and Sale Department

The Purchase and Sale Department is the back office area of a brokerage firm that is responsible for figuration, trade comparison, and issuing confirmations.

DK, Figuration

Put

A Put is an option that gives the owner the right to sell a specific amount of the option's underlying security at a specific price up to a specific point in the future.

Underlying Security

Put Bond

A Put Bond is a bond that is sold with an attached put that cannot be traded separately from the bond.

Reset Put Security

Put Frequency

The Put Frequency defines how often a given put bond with a put provision may be presented to the issuer for payment under the provision.

Put Bond

Put Option

A Put Option can be either:

- A portion of a contract that gives the owner the right to sell a fixed number of shares or bonds at a fixed price within a stated time period.
- An option that provides the right but not the obligation to sell the underlying security at a specific price up to a specific point in time.

QDS

See *Quote Dissemination System*

QT

See *Questionable Trade*

Qualified Institutional Investor

A Qualified Institutional Investor is an institutional investor that is permitted by SEC rules to trade privately-placed without registering the securities with the SEC.

One SEC requirement for a qualified institutional investor is that they must have at least $100 million in assets under management.

Qualified Plan

A Qualified Plan is a retirement plan that meets certain IRS guidelines, and which receives special tax treatment under Section 401 of the Internal Revenue Code.

Companies may deduct their contributions to the plan, and employees do not pay taxes on their contributions or on the fund's earnings until they take money out of the fund.

Non Qualified Plan

Quality

Quality is defined as adhering to predefined standards. Any product or service meets its quality objectives if it adheres to its own standards. Quality is not the same as value.

Quality Indicator

A Quality Indicator is a measurable activity that is covered by a quality standard.

Quantitative Analysis

Quantitative Analysis is the technique that analyzes a security or corporation based on measurable (quantifiable) factors rather than on subjective factors.

Quarter

A Quarter can be:

- A period of three calendar months
- One-fourth of a point

Questionable Trade

A Questionable Trade is one that cannot be compared by the morning of trade date plus one.

Queue

A Queue is a line of things (people, documents, files, etc.) waiting their turn for processing.

Quotation

See *Quote*

Quotation Size

Quotation Size is the maximum number of shares that a market maker covers in their bid and asked price.

Asked, Bid, Market Maker

Quote

A complete Quote includes the highest bid and the lowest offer for a specific security at a specific time.

Bid, Offering Price

Quote Dissemination System

The QDS system electronically provides quotations that are made by a Nasdaq market maker to outside services and vendors.

Market Maker

Quote Vendors

Quote Vendors are firms that electronically provide real-time prices from recognized exchanges, for a fee.

Market Data Vendors

Quoted Price

The Quoted Price is the price at which the last trade of particular security or commodity took place.

QWERTY

Pronounced Quert ee

QWERTY describes the typical keyboard that has the letters, Q W E R T Y in sequence in the upper left hand corner.

RAID

See *Redundant Array of Inexpensive Disks*

Raider

A Raider is a person or a firm that tries to acquire another firm against that firm's will.

Railroad Bonds

Railroad Bonds are industrial bonds, or equipment trust bonds that have been issued by a railroad.

Equipment Trust Bond

Rally

The term Rally can be used in two ways:

- A Rally in the stock market occurs when active buyers drive the general price of shares upward.
- A Rally in the bond market occurs when interest rates drop and the price of bonds moves upward.

RAM

Random Access Memory is the fastest method that is used to store and access information in a computer. It is only temporary storage, and is usually lost when the computer is turned off.

Memory

RAN

See *Revenue Anticipation Note*

Range

A Range is the difference between the highest and lowest number in a related series of numbers over a defined period of time. A range could identify:

- Price movements during a trading session
- Interest rates over a period of time
- Volume of transactions processed in a specific period of time, etc.

Range Forwards

See *Collar*

Rate

The term Rate is usually used to identify the ratio of interest earned divided by the principal during a specific period of time. Rates are usually presented as a percentage.

Rate could also be used to identify error rates (number of errors divided by the total of errors), attendance rates, or any relationship of similar data.

Interest Rate

Rate Change Frequency

The Rate Change Frequency is the frequency with which an issuer can change the rate on a variable or floating rate debt instrument.

Variable Rate, Floating Rate Instruments

Rate of Interest

See *Interest Rate*

Rate of Return

See Return on Investment

Ratio

A Ratio is the mathematical comparison of two values.

RCMM

See *Registered Competitive Market Maker*

Read Only Memory

Read Only Memory is a type of computer or electronic memory that can only be written on once, and then is available to be read many times.

CD ROM

Real Estate Investment Trust

A Real Estate Investment Trust (REIT) is a firm that invests almost exclusively in real estate. A REIT must pay out 90% of its income to shareholders if it wants to retain its tax exemption.

Real Estate Mortgage Investment Conduit

A Real Estate Mortgage Investment Conduit (REMIC) is a form of Collateralized Mortgage Obligation that provides tax advantages for the issuer.

The terms REMIC and CMO are now used interchangeably.

Collateralized Mortgage Obligation

Real Return

The Real Return on an asset is the rate of return adjusted for changes in price levels and inflation.

Nominal Return

Realized Losses

Realized Losses occur when a security is sold at a price below its cost basis. Until the security is sold, the loss is considered unrealized.

Cost Basis, Unrealized Losses

Realized Profits

Realized Profits occur when a security is sold at a price above its cost basis. Until the security is sold, the gain is considered unrealized.

Cost Basis, Unrealized Profits

Real-time Price

The Real-time Price is the up-to-the-minute price of trades being conducted throughout the day.

Real-time Processing

Real-time processing is:

- The processing of instructions on an individual basis at the time they are received rather than at some later time
- The individual processing of transactions by a computer as they are input

Batch

Real-time Trade Reporting

Real-time Trade Reporting is a NASD requirement that market makers report each trade to Nasdaq no later than 90 seconds after the trade was executed.

Market Maker, NASD

Receive Free

A Receive Free occurs when a trade is settled in which securities are delivered from the opposing settlement party without payment.

Receive vs. Payment, RVP

Receive vs. Payment

Receive vs. Payment (RVP) is a trade settlement in which securities and cash move simultaneously and in opposite directions between the settlement parties. With RVP, a custodian is instructed to receive securities and pay the settlement amount.

RVP, DVP, Deliver versus Payment

Receiver of Securities

The Receiver of Securities is the institution to whom a custodian or agent will deliver securities. The Receiver of Securities is usually the executing broker's clearing agent and is named in the delivery instructions.

Delivery Instructions

Recission

A right of Recission exists in the following circumstances:

- Individuals may use the Automated Clearing House's direct debit program to pay recurring charges such as mortgages, lease payments, etc. The right of Rescission allows consumers to reject an ACH debit to their account for up to sixty days from the date of the transaction if they do not recognize the charge or believe that it is incorrect.
- With certain kinds of commercial loans, under the provisions of the Truth-in-Lending Act, the borrower has the right to cancel the loan within three business days of signing for the loan.

Reconcilement

Reconcilement occurs when a clerk or a system compares two different groups of information (e.g., outgoing orders vs. incoming confirmations, positions on internal books vs. positions with a custodian, etc.). Reconcilement can cover the following areas:

- Daily, weekly, monthly, etc.
- Balances or Transactions
- Positions or Accounting

Reconfirmation and Repricing Service

Reconfirmation and Repricing Service (RECAPS) is an NSCC process that reconfirms and reprices participants' aged equity, municipal bond and zero coupon security transactions that have failed to settle. The service nets any open fails and assigns new settlement dates.

Record

A Record is a collection of related data elements in a file.

Record Date

The Record Date is the day that an investor must be registered as the owner of record in order to be entitled to an announced dividend, liquidation distribution, reverse split, capital gains, etc.

Payment Date

Record Status

Record Status is a record's level of completion.

Record

Recording

Recording is the act of entering data into a file, either manually or through an automated process.

Recordkeeper

The term Recordkeeper can be used in several ways:

- A custodian acts as a Recordkeeper by maintaining the records of their customers' buys and sells, income, corporate actions, etc.
- A firm that maintains 401(k) date for its clients also acts as a Recordkeeper.

- A firm that keeps records of investors' subscriptions and redemptions in a Mutual Fund also acts as a Recordkeeper.

Red Herring

A Red Herring is a preliminary prospectus for an initial public offering.

Initial Public Offering

Redemption

A Redemption is the payment that is made by the issuer on the designated maturity date of a debt instrument. Redemption includes the principal amount plus any accrued interest on the debt security.

Redemption Agent

A Redemption Agent is an institution authorized to redeem preferred stock.

Redundancy

See *Redundant*

Redundant

A position or a person may become Redundant when their services are no longer required by the firm that has employed them.

Downsize

Redundant Array of Inexpensive Disks

A Redundant Array of Inexpensive Disks (RAID) is a device that includes multiple inexpensive hard disks or CDs and the software that is necessary to manage them.

Rather than use a single large expensive hard drive, a user may elect to use a RAID solution.

Reengineer

When firms Reengineer their processes, they are looking to make a radical change in how they operate. The new process may involve significant automation, or a process flow that has several fewer steps than what was previously required.

Process Redesign

Reengineering

See *Reengineer*

Refinancing

Refinancing is the process of paying off one loan with the proceeds from a new loan. Refinancing is normally done during a period of low interest rates when the debt being refinanced is at a higher interest rate.

Refunding

Refunding occurs when an issuer replaces an existing debt instrument with a new debt instrument. An issuer will normally do this when the current interest rate is lower than the interest rate on the existing issue.

Interest Rate

Refunding Bond

A Refunding Bond is a bond that has been issued for the express purpose of retiring an outstanding bond.

Region

A Region can be:

- A geographical portion of the world or a country
- A segmented portion of a computer that can be allocated for a specific application or applications

Registered Bond

A Registered Bond is one that is registered in the name of the bondholder, or the bondholder's nominee, such as a bank or a broker, or the DTC.

These bonds must be endorsed by the registered owner in order for ownership to be transferred.

Bond, Bearer Bond

Registered Competitive Market Maker

A Registered Competitive Market Maker (RCMM) is a member of the New York Stock Exchange who has a specific obligation to enhance the quality of the NYSE market by using their own or their firm's capital during difficult market-making situations.

If requested by the exchange, an RCMM must make a bid or offer that narrows an existing quote spread or improves its depth. An RCMM may also be asked by the exchange to assist a commission broker or floor broker in executing a customer's otherwise unexecutable order.

Registered Form

A security is in Registered Form when ownership is recorded on the issuer's central securities ledger.

Registered Market Maker

See *Market Maker*

Registered Representative

A Registered Representative is a person who has met the requirements of an exchange and who has passed a Series 7 test.

Series 7, Account Executive

Registered Trader

See *Competitive Trader*

Registrar

A Registrar is a trust company or bank that records the issuance of the securities that are authorized by an issuer. The registrar works closely with the transfer agent to maintain the record of the owners of a company's bonds and stocks. The registrar must ensure that only the authorized amount of stock is in circulation.

If the registrar and transfer agent are the same firm, a 'Chinese Wall' must be established to separate the two functions.

Registration, Transfer Agent, Chinese Wall

Registration

There are two types of registration. One for new securities and one for the owners of securities.

Before an initial public offering, a security must be registered under the Securities Act of 1933, which records the recording of ownership of securities in the issuer's official register or in a central securities depository. This task is often performed by an official registrar or transfer agent. Actual registration may be made by stamping the name of the customer's account at a central depository on the certificates.

Central Securities Depository, Registrar, Registration Statement, Transfer Agent

Registration Statement

The Registration Statement is a document that must be filed with the Securities and Exchange Commission to explain the details about a pending issue as well as identify the issuer. The SEC uses this statement to either approve or decline the issue.

Regular Dividend

A Regular Dividend is a dividend that has been fixed by a corporation and is usually paid quarterly or semiannually.

Dividend

Regular Way

See *Regular Way Contract*

Regular Way Contract

The Regular Way Contract is the NSCC contract sheet that lists compared, uncompared, and advisory data about trades.

Uniform Practice Code

Regular Way Delivery

The normal method of trading and settling is called Regular Way Delivery. It varies by instrument type. For example, DTC eligible equities and bonds settle on the third business day after the trade; government bonds and options settle on T+1; mortgage backed securities settle once a month, etc.

Regulation

A Regulation is a rule that has been made by the government or a government agency and which, if violated, can result in a fine or imprisonment.

Rules

Regulation 9

See *OCC Regulation 9*

Regulation G

See *Fed Regulation G*

Regulation T

See *Fed Regulation T*

Regulation T Excess

Regulation T Excess is the amount of a margin loan value that is greater than the debit balance in a margin account.

Regulation T

Regulation U

See *Fed Regulation U*

Regulation X

See *Fed Regulation X*

Reinvestment Privilege

A Reinvestment Privilege allows investors to automatically reinvest dividends and capital gains without being charged a commission.

DRIP, IRIP

Reinvestment Risk

Reinvestment Risk is the risk that interest income or principal repayments will have to be reinvested at lower rates in a declining rate environment.

REIT

See *Real Estate Investment Trust*

Rejected Option Trade Notice

A Rejected Option Trade Notice (ROTN) is the form and process that is used to return a listed option trade that can not be compared to the broker who executed the trade so that the discrepancy can be resolved.

Relationship

Any two entities that are associated in any way could have a Relationship. In financial services, a firm wants to develop a relationship in order to turn a customer into a client.

Customer, Client

Relationship Manager

A Relationship Manager is an employee of a firm who is responsible for a relationship with a specific client, or clients.

Remainderman

A Remainderman is the designated beneficiary of a trust fund who receives any proceeds that cannot be distributed to the main beneficiaries of the fund when the Trust is closed.

Trust

REMIC

See Real Estate Mortgage Investment Conduit

Removable Disk

A Removable Disk is any form of computer memory that can be removed from one machine and transported to another. Removable Disks include:

- Floppy disks
- High capacity disks
- Removable hard drives

Removable Media

See *Removable Disk*

Render

When a firm Renders something, they are producing it for delivery to another entity, such as a customer.

Reorg

See *Corporate Reorganization*

Reorganization

See *Corporate Reorganization*

Repair

A message or a transaction may need to be Repaired if there are errors in content or format. The repair function is usually manual.

Replacement Cost Risk

Replacement Cost Risk is the risk that a firm's counterparty will fail to deliver or pay on the settlement date. If the buyer has to perform for the delinquent counterparty, the risk is that the cost of the undelivered security will rise or that exchange rate will change in the meantime.

Repo

See *Repurchase Agreement*

Report

A Report is any form of organized information, either from an office or a department.

REPS

See *Reset Put Security*

Repurchase Agreement

A Repurchase Agreement (Repo) is a short term contract, frequently overnight, that is used to finance government and money market inventory positions by agreeing to sell and subsequently repurchase securities at a specified date and price.

Research

Research is the process of gathering information regarding a particular security or firm.

Primary Research, Secondary Research

Research Department Rating

The Research Department Rating is the rating given by an internal research department to a specific issue.

Reset Put Security

A Reset Put Security is an instrument composed of a bond and an associated put which can be separated and traded independently. Typically, with this instrument, the investment bank keeps the put and uses it in its own derivatives unit and discounts the bond for the price that the put would have received on the open market.

Since not every bond buyer can use the put to its full advantage, the full value of the put is not always realized until it is separated from the bond.

Resident Alien

A Resident Alien is a person who is not a US citizen and who resides in the US.

Non Resident Alien

Resistance Level

The Resistance Level is the theoretical point at which sellers start to outnumber buyers and the market peaks.

Support Level

Response Time

The Response Time of a system consists of three elements:

- The time it takes a program to access and retrieve data
- The time it takes the program to process the data
- The time it takes to display the data

Response time is affected by the access time of the hard drive, the processing speed of the CPU and the interaction the program has with other programs or users who are simultaneously using the computer resource.

CPU, Hard Drive

Restricted Account

A customer's margin account is classified as a Restricted Account under Regulation T when the debit balance exceeds the loan value of the securities in the account.

Retail Bank

A Retail Bank is a bank that concentrates on selling services to retail customers. These services typically include:

- Checking

- Savings
- Unsecured Lending
- Secured Lending
- Certificates of Deposit

Retail Investor

See *Individual Investor*

Retail Shareholder

See *Individual Investor*

Retirement

Retirement can relate to an individual or to a bond:

- A person retires when they formally stop working as a result of length of service, age, or disability. This can initiate a series of regular retirement benefit payments.
- A Bond is retired when it matures or is called by the issuer.

Maturity, Call, Pension Disbursing

Return on Investment

An investor's Rate of Return is the ratio of their profit to their initial investment. This is usually expressed in annual terms.

Revenue

Revenue is the income that is earned by a firm.

Revenue Anticipation Note

A Revenue Anticipation Note (RAN) is a form of short term debt issued by a municipality, that is designated to be redeemed with some anticipated revenue.

Revenue Bonds

Revenue Bonds are issued to finance a specific revenue producing project such as toll roads, bridges, power plants, etc. The interest and redemption of these bonds is intended to be paid with the revenue from these projects.

Municipal Bond

Reverse Split

A Reverse Split occurs when a firm issues new shares at a higher cost to replace the older ones. Holders of the older shares receive a smaller number of new shares.

For example, if a stockholder has 100 shares of a stock with a market price of $2.00, and the issuing company announces a one-for-two reverse split, the stockholder will now own 50 shares that are valued by the market at $4.00. Reverse Splits are done by firms that wish to make their stock price seem more substantial.

Right

While a Right can be any form of benefit granted by a company to its stockholders, it generally refers to an opportunity to buy additional shares. Current shareholders can be given the opportunity to purchase additional equity in advance of the issue of additional shares. When this occurs, the evidence of this privilege is a document called a right.

Rights are generally offered at a price below the current market price. As a result, the rights have a short term intrinsic value and can be traded in the open market. If a right has not been exercised prior to its expiration date, it becomes worthless.

Pre-Emptive Right

Rights Offering

See *Right*

Rio de Janeiro Stock Exchange Index

The Rio de Janeiro Stock Exchange Index (IBV) is a stock index derived from equities listed on the Bolsa de Valores de Rio De Janiero.

Risk Arbitrage

See *Arbitrage*

Risk Management

Risk Management is a function concerned with minimizing a firm's exposure to several categories of risk, including:

- Market
- Interest Rate
- Price
- Currency
- Settlement
- Credit
- Lending
- Counterparty
- Default
- Issuer
- Performance
- Country/Sovereign
- Fiduciary
- Legal, regulatory and compliance
- Event
- Call
- Liquidity

Market Risk, Event Risk, Call Risk, Liquidity Risk, Credit Risk, Default Risk

Risk Tolerance

Risk Tolerance is an investor's propensity to accept risk. An investor's philosophy can be Aggressive, Moderate or Conservative.

Aggressive, Moderate Investor, Conservative Investor

Road Show

A Road Show is a series of presentations by a firm and their investment banker that is given to potential investors prior to an initial public offering.

Investment Banker, IPO

Roadkill

Roadkill is a term recently used to describe people who are avoiding the internet or who do not accept its future potential. It is usually used by journalists in the context: "Roadkill on the Information Superhighway."

Information Superhighway

Robertson Stephens

Robertson Stephens is a US-based broker/dealer.

www.rsco.com

ROI

See Return on Investment

Rolling Option

A Rolling Option is a process whereby one option position is closed and a new option position is opened with different terms but which is based on the same underlying security. The terms that change can be the strike price and the expiration date.

Option

Rolling Settlement

Rolling Settlement is a daily settlement process that occurs a specific number of days after a trade. Rolling Settlement differs from a settlement process that occurs once a week, fortnightly or monthly.

Rollover

The term Rollover is used in two ways:

- An investor may Rollover their investment as it becomes mature by automatically reinvesting the proceeds in another, similar investment.
- The transfer of a futures or options position from one delivery month to a later month is also called a Rollover.

ROR

See Rate of Return

Roth IRA

Created as part of the Taxpayer Relief Act of 1997, the Roth IRA is an individual retirement account that allows its holders to make post-tax contributions while receiving tax-free distributions. The Roth IRA has no minimum distribution requirements and does not impact the holder's adjusted gross income during the term of distribution.

Round Lot

A Round Lot is the usual unit for trading equities and bonds. Round Lots consist of groups of 100 shares for equities, although inactive securities often trade in round lots of 10 shares.

A round lot of bonds in the over-the-counter market consists of 5 bonds.

Odd Lot

Route

An individual or an application will Route, or direct, a transaction to the next step in the process. This term is used in workflow analysis and messaging.

Royal Bank of Canada

The Royal Bank of Canada is a Canadian-based bank.

www.royalbank.com

Royal Bank of Scotland

The Royal Bank of Scotland is a UK-based Universal bank.

www.rbs.co.uk

Rule 10b-21

See *SEC Rule 10b-21*

Rule 10b-4

See *SEC Rule 10b-4*

Rule 10b-6

See *SEC Rule 10b-6*

Rule 10b-6A

See *SEC Rule 10b-6A*

Rule 12b-1

See *SEC Rule 12b-1*

Rule 13d

See *SEC Rule 13d*

Rule 144A

See *SEC Rule 144A*

Rule 15c3-1

See *SEC Rule 15c3-1*

Rule 15c3-3

See *SEC Rule 15c3-3*

Rule 15c6-1

See *SEC Rule15c6-1*

Rule 17a-3

See *SEC Rule 17a-3*

Rule 17a-4

See *SEC Rule 17a-4*

Rule 19b-4

See *SEC Rule 19b-4*

Rule l0b-13

See *SEC Rule l0b-13*

Rule l0b-2

See *SEC Rule l0b-2*

Rule-based

A Rule-based system is one that uses a table of rules, such as accounting, tax, settlement instructions, etc., and which is accessed by a program when the data is needed. The table is usually maintained by the system's users.

Rules

Rules are established by non-governmental entities to inform persons or firms bound by the rules of what they can and can not do. Violation of these rules may involve a sanction or a fine, but do not involve prison time.

Regulation

Rules of Fair Practice

The Rules of Fair Practice are NASD's rules that define how members should deal with their customers.

Uniform Practice Code, NASD By-Laws

RVP

See *Receive vs. Payment*

S&L

See *Savings and Loan Association*

S&P

See *Standard & Poor's Corporation*

S&P 425 Index

See *Standard & Poor's 425 Index*

S&P 500 Index

See *Standard & Poor's 500 Stock Price Index*

S&P CNX Nifty

The S&P CNX Nifty is a stock index derived from equities listed on the National Stock Exchange of India.

S.W.I.F.T.

Pronounced Swift

See *Society for Worldwide Interbank Financial Telecommunication*

S.W.I.F.T. Gateway

The S.W.I.F.T. Gateway is a device or system that actually interfaces to the S.W.I.F.T. network.

S.W.I.F.T. Interface Device

S.W.I.F.T. Interface Device

In order for a firm to connect to the S.W.I.F.T. network, they must use a S.W.I.F.T. Interface Device that is sold by S.W.I.F.T. and by other vendors. The device manages the protocols needed to connect to the network.

S.W.I.F.T.

Safe Harbor

The Private Securities Litigation Reform Act of 1995 provided the "Safe Harbor for Forward-Looking Information." The rule allows a company's managers to discuss their company's prospects and financial projections with analysts and investors without the risk of being sued.

Safekeeping

Safekeeping is the generic service that is provided by banks for a fee whereby securities and valuables are stored in the bank's vaults. When securities are held in safekeeping, the process is generally referred to as custody.

Custody

Safekeeping Account

A Safekeeping Account is the account at a custodian or sub-custodian where a client's assets are held. A client may have separate cash and securities safekeeping accounts.

Custodian, Sub-Custodian, Cash Account, Securities Account

Sales Function

A firm's Sales Function is used to distribute the firm's inventory in either the primary market or the secondary market. A sales person works closely with the firm's traders to sell securities in the firm's inventory to customers.

Sallie Mae

See *Student Loan Mortgage Association*

Salomon Smith Barney

Salomon Smith Barney is the broker/dealer subsidiary of Travelers Insurance.

www.salomonsmithbarney.com

Same Day Funds

Same Day Funds is the process that is used throughout the world for payment transfers. The money is transferred today and is immediately available for use.

Next Day Funds

Sample

In statistics, a Sample is a small segment of a population that can be measured.

Population

Sao Paulo Bovespa Index

The Sao Paulo Bovespa Index is a stock index derived from equities listed on the Bolsa de Valores de Sao Paulo.

Savings Account

A Savings Account is an account opened by an individual in a commercial bank, a savings and loan association, or a savings bank. Typically, funds in these accounts may be increased or withdrawn in any amount. While the funds can usually be withdrawn without notice, a bank may require advance notice for large withdrawals.

Interest on a savings account is calculated from the deposit date to the withdrawal date and is credited to the account either quarterly or semiannually.

Savings and Loan Association

Savings and Loan Association

A Savings and Loan Association (S&L) is a financial institution that is chartered by the state or federal government and owned by depositors and/or stockholders. S&L's were created to provide mortgage loans and to provide government-insured, interest bearing savings accounts to individuals.

S&L's generally collect deposits from a local community and then recycle the funds by making local mortgage loans. The business of S&L's changed significantly in the 1980's after a large number were forced to close due to bankruptcy and mismanagement.

Bank

SAX Index

The SAX Index is a stock index derived from equities listed on the Bratislava Stock Exchange.

SBF Paris Bourse

The SBF Paris Bourse is the primary stock exchange of France.

www.bourse-de-paris.fr

SBI Share Index

The SBI Share Index is a stock index derived from equities listed on the Ljubljanska Stock Exchange.

SBIC

See *Small Business Investment Companies*

Scanner

A Scanner is a device that converts a photograph or document into pixels so that it can be electronically transported and stored by a computer, and then recovered in a way that reconstructs the image on a screen or on paper.

Used in conjunction with OCR, scanning is being increasingly used for securities processing.

Pixel, OCR

Scanning

See *Scanner*

SCCP

See *Stock Clearing Corporation of Philadelphia*

Screen

A Screen can be:

- An abbreviation for Terminal Screen
- A piece of material onto which an image can be projected by an overhead projector or other device

Scrip

Scrip is a temporary certificate, representing fractional shares, that is issued to stockholders. Before the expiration date of the scrip, stockholders must decide to round to full shares by either buying an additional fraction or selling their fraction.

Scrip Agent

A Scrip Agent is required for the issuance of scrip for fractional shares. This role will normally be performed by the Corporate Trust department of a bank.

Scrip, Corporate Trust

SCSI

SCSI, pronounced scuz-ee, is the common term used for the small computer system interface. This interface standard is used by computers when they work with attached hard drives, scanners, etc.

SD

See *Settlement Date*

SD INDEVAL, SA de CV

SD INDEVAL, SA de CV, is the central securities depository of Mexico and also acts as the institution responsible for clearing trades between domestic parties.

SDLC

See *Systems Development Life Cycle*

Sealed Bid

A Sealed Bid is a confidential offer that is made to purchase securities.

SEAQ

SEAQ is the automated trading system that is used by the London Stock Exchange.

London Stock Exchange

Seasoned Mortgage

A Seasoned Mortgage is a mortgage in which the required payments have been made as scheduled over a long period of time.

Seat

A Seat is a generic term that indicates membership on a national exchange. A membership on the New York Stock Exchange is traditionally referred to as a "seat" because in the early years of its existence members sat in assigned chairs during the roll call of stocks. The term lost its literal meaning when continuous trading began in 1871.

Seats may be sold or leased by their owner, although buying a seat does not guarantee membership. Candidates for a seat must meet high standards of personal and financial integrity and demonstrate their knowledge of the securities business. Once admitted, members' activities are subject to continuous oversight by the exchange and government regulators to assure compliance with securities regulations.

SEC

See *Securities and Exchange Commission*

SEC Form 10 K

See *Annual Report*

SEC Form 10 Q

The Form 10Q is a quarterly report that provides unaudited financial information about a firm as well as other selected material for the SEC and investors.

SEC Form 20-F

SEC Form 20-F is a registration statement and annual report form that is typically used by foreign issuers.

SEC Form 6-K

SEC Form 6-K is used by non-US issuers to make periodic reports.

SEC Form F-1

Form F-1 registers the securities of a non-US company to be issued in a public offering.

SEC Rule 10b-21

SEC Rule 10b-21 prohibits a firm from covering a short position in a security with stock purchased from a new offering of the security.

SEC Rule 10b-4

SEC Rule 10b-4 prohibits the tendering of stock through a short sale.

SEC Rule 10b-6

SEC Rule 10b-6 prohibits persons engaged in a distribution of securities from bidding for or purchasing those or similar securities until the distribution is completed.

SEC Rule 10b-6A

SEC Rule 10b-6A permits broker/dealers engaged in the distribution of a security to make certain types of transactions in the security being distributed without violating Rule 10b-6.

SEC Rule 12b-1

SEC Rule 12b-1 was established in 1980 to define the charges that mutual funds can levy on the fund's assets. Acceptable charges include:

- Distribution Costs
- Marketing Expenses
- Commissions to Salespeople

12b-1 Fees are defined by the SEC as those paid by a fund for distribution costs, such as advertising and commissions paid to dealers. These costs must be defined in the fund's prospectus if they are charged.

NASD rules define two maximums for 12b-1 fees.

- An annual distribution cost limit of 0.75 % of a fund's assets. This includes a 0.25 % service fee which may be "paid to brokers or other sales professionals in return for providing ongoing information and assistance to investors."
- A rolling cap on total sales charges, that is 6.25 % of new sales plus interest for funds that pay the service fee, and 7.25 % plus interest for funds that do not pay a service fee.

Mutual Fund

SEC Rule 13d

SEC Rule 13d requires that anyone who acquires a beneficial ownership of 5% or more in any equity security that is registered with the SEC, disclose this ownership to the SEC.

SEC Rule 144

SEC Rule 144 stipulates that a person who owns a large amount of their firm's stock which has not been bought in the open market, is permitted to sell a portion of the stock every six months following a holding period of two years without filing a formal registration statement with the SEC.

SEC Rule 144A

Certain unregistered securities that are defined by the Securities Act of 1933 are exempt from registration, and the prospectus delivery requirement are defined in SEC Rule 144A.

SEC Rule 15c3-1

SEC Rule 15c3-1, the Net Capital Rule, requires broker/dealers to maintain no more than a 15 to 1 ratio of indebtedness to liquid assets.

Categories of indebtedness include:

- Money owed to the firm
- Margin loans
- Commitments to purchase securities
- Liquid assets include:
- Cash
- Other assets that are easily convertible to cash

Securities Operations Forum (www.soforum.com) offers classes to help brokers understand this rule.

SEC Rule 15c3-3

SEC Rule 15c3-3, the Customer Protection rule, requires that the broker/dealer:

- Has possession or control of customers' securities, and properly segregates these securities from the securities the firm owns
- Deposits customers' funds in a special reserve bank account
- Cannot use customer balances to finance their own trading

Securities Operations Forum (www.soforum.com) offers classes to help brokers understand this rule.

SEC Rule 17a-3

SEC Rule 17a-3 specifies the books and records that brokers/dealers must keep current.

SEC Rule 17a-4

SEC Rule 17a-4 specifies the time period that broker/dealers must preserve SEC Rule 17a-3 records and other documents pertaining to their business.

SEC Rule 17a-3

SEC Rule 19b-4

SEC Rule 19b-4 provides the procedures that self regulatory organizations must use to propose rule changes to the SEC.

SEC Rule l0b-13

SEC Rule l0b-13 prohibits a firm making a tender offer or an exchange offer from acquiring the security from any other source until after the offer has expired.

SEC Rule l0b-2

SEC Rule l0b-2 prohibits firms engaged in a primary or secondary distribution from soliciting any orders for the issue by any means other than through a prospectus.

SEC Rule15c6-1

SEC rule 15c6-1 requires a standard three day settlement period in the US.

Second Mortgage

A Second Mortgage is an additional mortgage placed on a property. A second mortgage has rights that are subordinate to the first mortgage.

Second Put Date

The Second Put Date is the second date on which a Put can be used on an option.

Put

Second Put Value

The Second Put Value is the price of an option's second put.

Put

Secondary Market

The Secondary Market includes the exchanges and over-the-counter markets where securities are bought and sold after they are brought to market through an original issuance in the primary market.

Nasdaq, Exchange, Primary Market

Secondary Offering

A Secondary Offering is an officially registered offer of a large block of an existing issue that is being made by large investors or institutions. Since these shares are already owned by a firm other than the original issuer, the selling firm gets all income from the sale.

Secondary Research

When the research department of a firm engages in Secondary Research, they use existing published sources of information to understand how the firm being investigated works and its potential profitability. Secondary Research includes:

- Analyst opinions and research reports
- News reports
- Company press releases
- Newsletters
- Primary Research

Section 112

See *Federal Deposit Insurance Corporation Improvement Act*

Section 401 (h)

See *IRS Section 401(h)*

Section 401 (k) Plan

See *IRS Section 401(k) Plan*

Section 403 (b) Plan

See *IRS Section 403(b) Plan*

Section 501 (c) (9)

See *IRS Section 501(c)(9)*

Sector

A Sector is a group of companies that are engaged in a similar industry.

SECTOR

See *Securities Telecommunications Organization*

Sector Fund

A Sector Fund is a mutual fund that concentrates its investments among securities or other assets sharing a common interest.

Securities Account

A Securities Account, also known as a safekeeping account, is the account name and number at the custodian or sub-custodian where a client's securities are held. A client may have separate cash and securities accounts.

Cash Account, Safekeeping Account

Securities Act of 1933

The Securities Act of 1933 is an Act of Congress that was created to provide full and fair disclosure concerning the characteristics of all securities sold to the public, and to prevent fraud.

Securities Acts, SEC

Securities Acts

The Securities Acts are the Federal laws that are enforced by the Securities and Exchange Commission to protect investors. They include:

- Investment Advisors Act
- Investment Company Act
- Securities Act of 1933
- Securities Exchange Act of 1934
- Trust Indenture Act
- Public Utilities Holding Company Act

SEC, Investment Advisors Act of 1940, Investment Company Act of 1940, Securities Act of 1933, Securities and Exchange Act of 1934, Trust Indenture Act

Securities Acts Amendments of 1975

The Securities Acts Amendments of 1975 significantly extended the Securities and Exchange Act of 1934. These amendments ended fixed commission rates, started the development of a national market system, and granted the SEC approval authority over adoption of rules by any self regulating organization.

Self Regulating Organization

Securities Analyst

A Securities Analyst is an individual who researches investment alternatives and recommends that investors buy, sell, or hold selected securities. Analysts usually specialize in a few specific companies, a single industry or a business sector.

Sector

Securities and Exchange Act of 1934

The Securities and Exchange Act of 1934 regulates securities exchanges and over-the-counter markets that operate interstate. The regulations are designed to prevent inequitable and unfair practices within these exchanges and markets.

The Securities and Exchange Act of 1934 created the SEC, and granted more authority to the Federal Reserve's Board of Governors who are now responsible for establishing and monitoring margin requirements. The 1934 Act governs key factors, such as:

- The lending of money by brokerage firms (Regulation T)
- Short-sale (up tick) rule
- Requirements regarding insiders or controlled persons

An amendment to the 1934 Act, the Maloney Act of 1938, established self regulating organizations.

The Securities and Exchange Act of 1934 was passed one year after the primary act that regulated the securities industry, Securities Act of 1933.

Maloney Act of 1938, Regulation T, Securities Act of 1933, Self Regulating Organization

Securities and Exchange Commission

The Securities and Exchange Commission (SEC) is the primary regulatory body that governs the securities industry. Created by Congress with the Securities Exchange Act of 1934, the SEC is an independent, bipartisan, quasi-judicial agency of the United States Government. The SEC is managed by a five person Board of Governors which is led by a chairman.

The laws administered by the SEC deal with securities and finance and seek to provide protection for investors in their securities transactions. Criminal violations are prosecuted by the U.S. Department of Justice.

Securities and Exchange Act of 1934

Securities and Futures Association

The Securities and Futures Association (SFA) reports to the SIB and has the responsibility to authorize firms to carry out agreed investment business in the UK, to register all investment staff and ensure their fitness for the industry, to monitor firms compliance with all SFA rules, and to investigate and discipline firms who breach these rules.

Securities and Investments Board

Securities and Investments Board

The Securities and Investments Board (SIB) is the regulatory authority responsible to the UK Treasury as a result of the UK's Financial Services Act 1986.

Securities Borrowing

See *Securities Lending*

Securities Clearing and Computer Services Ltd.

Securities Clearing and Computer Services Ltd. (SCCS) is an auxiliary company of the Stock Exchange of Singapore that provides clearing facilities and computer services between the Exchange and its member companies.

Securities Clearing Automated Network Services

Securities Clearing Automated Network Services (SCANS) is a subsidiary of the Kuala Lumpur Stock Exchange that provides clearing services for the members of the Exchange.

Securities Clearing Corporation of Philadelphia

The Securities Clearing Corporation of Philadelphia (SCCP) was a clearing corporation that supported a small, regional participant base. In 1997 it was merged into the NSCC.

NSCC

Securities Depository

See *Central Securities Depository*

Securities Exchange

See *Exchange*

Securities Industry Association

The Securities Industry Association (SIA) is the primary industry association for participants in the securities industry, representing more than 500 brokerage and investment banking firms. It supports its participants, provides education, and represents the industry to the SEC and other regulatory agencies.

The SIA has several divisions that focus on specific areas of business, including:

- Dividend Division
- Reorganization Division
- Data Management Division

www.sia.com

Securities Industry Automation Corporation

Securities Industry Automated Corporation SIAC) manages the data centers and applications that are used by New York Stock Exchange, American Stock Exchange, NSCC, and PCC.

NYSE, AMEX, NSCC, Pacific Clearing Corporation

Securities Investor Protection Corporation

SIPC is a non-profit corporation established by Congress in 1970 through the Securities Investor Protection Act. SIPC's mission is to protect customers' securities and cash held by broker/dealers in the event a broker/dealer defaults and is liquidated.

The fund, which is maintained by annual assessments of US broker/dealers, guarantees the replacement of securities held in the account up to $500,000, and cash up to $100,000.

FDIC, Securities Investors Protection Act of 1970

Securities Investors Protection Act of 1970

The Securities Investors Protection Act of 1970 created the Securities Investors Protection Corporation, which resembles the FDIC in that it insures investors who are customers of a brokerage firm against the liquidation of that firm.

Securities Investor Protection Corporation

Securities Lending

Securities Lending is the process that firms use to loan securities to each other. Firms that borrow securities, usually do so to cover obligations resulting from, or to take advantage of opportunities presented by:

- Fails and short sales
- Arbitrage
- Index and options arbitrage
- Dividend Reinvestment Plans (DRIP)

Lenders are willing to lend their securities in order to increase their return.

Securities Lending is subject to specific industry rules, such as:

- Loan can be terminated by the lender at any time
- Recalls generally within three days
- Cash collateral posted by the borrower
- Lender receives dividends and other distributions
- Securities must be recalled in order to be voted

Dividend Reinvestment Program, Short Sale

Securities Market Automated Regulated Trading Architecture

The Securities Market Automated Regulated Trading Architecture (SMART) is an architecture that defines how NASD's technology base should be restructured using modular applications, an enterprise-wide database structure, an organization-wide application topology, and an open systems environment.

Open Systems, Application Topology

Securities Operations Forum

Securities Operations Forum, a subsidiary of The Summit Group which publishes this glossary, is a privately owned organization that provides operationally-oriented publications, training and conferences to the securities industry.

www.soforum.com

The Summit Group

Securities Settlement System

A Securities Settlement System is a system in which the settlement of securities takes place. Often the SSS is a Central Securities Depository.

Central Securities Depository

Securities Telecommunications Organization

The Securities Telecommunications Organization (SECTOR) is a division of SIAC that provides the financial industry with communications lines.

SIAC

Securitization

Securitization is the process of converting some form of debt or receivable into a security.

Security

A Security is an investment contract that exchanges certain rights for money. A security signifies ownership, a creditor relationship or identifies other financial obligations.

Equity, Bond

Security Group

A Security Group is the sector to which an issue is assigned.

Sector

Security Instructions

Security Instructions are the detailed delivery instructions for a securities account. Security Instructions include an account name, account number and an agent name and number.

Delivery Instructions, Securities Account

Security Stock Split

See *Split*

Security Valuation Model

A Security Valuation Model is usually based on the concept that the current value of a share of common stock can be calculated as the sum of the discounted present value of the estimated future stream of dividends.

Present Value

SEDOL

Pronounced Say Doll

SEDOL is a securities numbering method primarily used by the London Stock Exchange (International Stock Exchange) in the UK. Many globally traded securities have SEDOL numbers.

SEGA

Pronounced Say Ga

SEGA is the Swiss Central Securities Depository.

Segregation

Segregation is the process of separating different categories of securities in an account. A securities firm has two categories of securities in its records:

- Securities that can be loaned or hypothecated
- Securities that are fully paid and which belong to their customers (or that portion of a margin account in excess of loanable securities)
- The shares that belong fully to the customers must be segregated from the other securities in order to ensure that they are not accidentally loaned or sold.

SelectNet

SelectNet is an automated Nasdaq market service that electronically connects trading desks at Nasdaq firms. SelectNet supports order routing, negotiation of terms, and trade execution.

Self Audit

A Self Audit is a formal process conducted by managers to ensure their:

- Readiness for an audit by internal auditors
- Readiness for an audit by external auditors
- Compliance with FDICIA

Internal Audit, External Audit

Self Regulating Organization

The Securities and Exchange Act of 1934 establishes the right for participants in the securities industry to establish their own rule making organizations, called Self Regulating Organizations. A Self Regulating Organization is one that has been established by the Maloney Act of 1938, and which is supervised by the SEC. SROs present their rules to the SEC for final approval.

An SRO can be an exchange, a clearing agency or a depository and have the following functions:

- Defines rules, qualifications, record keeping, etc.
- Compliance monitoring
- Industry representation

NASD is the only over-the-counter entity that is an SRO.

SEC, Maloney Act of 1938, Nasdaq, Exchange, Clearing Agencies, Depository

Self-Collateralized

Self-Collateralized refers to securities that can be used as their own collateral when they are being transferred. Self-collateralized securities are used to limit the risks involved in the transfer process.

Transfer

Sell Short

See Short Sale

Sell Side

The Sell Side consists of brokers who sell their services to the Buy Side.

Buy Side

Sell Side Trader

A Sell Side Trader is a brokerage employee who buys and sells securities in the institutional market.

Buy Side Trader

Sell Stop

A Sell Stop order is entered below the current market price to limit losses or protect a profit. It is a memorandum order that becomes a sell order when the set price is reached.

Buy Stop

Seller's Option

A Buyers Option gives the buyer the right to set the settlement date, using one of the available forms:

- Regular Way
- Cash Settlement
- Next Day Settlement
- Future Settlement

Buyer's Option

Seller's Option

A Seller's Option gives the seller the right to deliver a specific stock or bond at any time within a specified period from two business days to 60 business days.

Uniform Practice Code

Selling Against the Box

See *Against the Box*

Sensitivity

The Sensitivity of a portfolio is the measurement of a portfolio's volatility compared against the overall market.

Volatility

Separate Purchase of Registered Security and Principal

See *Strip*

Sequential Effort Priority

Sequential Effort Priority is the process of organizing tasks based on their importance with regard to the allocation of resources.

In the case of a Sequential Effort Priority, a project manager can decide that they will either first work on the tasks that require the least effort, or on the tasks that require the most effort.

Sequential Finish Priority

Sequential Finish Priority

Sequential Finish Priority is the process of organizing tasks based on their importance with regard to sequence of completion.

In the case of Sequential Finish Priority, a project manager can decide that they will either work on the tasks that can be completed first and then on the tasks that cannot be finished until later, or they will work on the long lead-time items first.

Lead Time, Sequential Effort Priority

Serial Bond

A Serial Bond is a bond issue that matures in specific steps over several years at stated intervals.

Serial Options

Serial Options are options which are traded in specified months other than the existing four principal quarterly delivery months, which are March, June, September, and December.

Series

A Series can be:

- Option contracts that have the same underlying security, unit of trade, expiration date, and strike price
- A group of mortgages that are contained in a tranche

Series 7

Series 7 is the nation-wide test that must be passed to become licensed as a Registered Representative.

Registered Representative

Series Funds

Series Funds are those mutual funds that are established with separate portfolios of securities, each of which has a separate investment objective.

Server

A Server is an independent personal computer or workstation on a LAN that performs a specific function. Some of the functions that can be performed by a server are:

- File Server
- Communications Server
- Fax Server

Client, Client/Server

Service Level Agreement

A Service Level Agreement is generally established between two firms (or two departments) to define each department's responsibilities, and to define the required level of timeliness and quality.

Servicio de Compensación y Liquidación de Valores

Servicio de Compensación y Liquidación de Valores (SCLV) is the central securities depository of Spain.

SES All Singapore Index

The SES All Singapore Index is a stock index derived from equities listed on the Stock Exchange of Singapore.

New Straits Times Industrial Index

SET Index

The SET Index is a stock index derived from equities listed on the Stock Exchange of Thailand.

Settlement

Settlement is:

- The final process of exchanging money and securities between the counterparties to a transaction. Settlement usually takes place between agents for the counterparties.
- The conclusion of a real estate transaction that includes the delivery of a deed security instrument, signing of legal documents and the disbursement of the funds necessary to finalize the sale of a property.

Clearance, Agent, Settlement Agent,

Settlement Agent

A Settlement Agent is an intermediary, usually a bank, that acts with a buyer and seller to settle transactions. A settlement agent is also known as a clearing agent, sub-agent, sub-custodian, or clearing broker.

Sub-Agent, Sub-Custodian, Clearing Agent

Settlement Amount

The Settlement Amount is the trade amount (trade price multiplied by quantity) minus the total of commissions, fees and taxes. Settlement amount is also known as the net amount.

Settlement Balance Order

The Settlement Balance Order is a settlement system provided to its participants by the Mortgage Backed Securities Clearing Corporation. Settlement Balance is an extension of the MBSCC's Trade-for-Trade settlement system.

MBSCC, Trade-for-Trade

Settlement Cycle

The Settlement Cycle is the sequence of events that occurs after a trade, and which leads to the exchange of securities and payments. The normal settlement cycle varies country by country and for different categories of instruments. In the US, listed equities and corporate bonds settle on Trade Date plus three days (T+3).

Trade Date

Settlement Date

The Settlement Date is the contractual date on which the final consummation of a securities transaction takes place and payment is made in exchange for delivery of the security. In the US, settlement day for listed equities and corporate bonds is usually three business days following the trade date.

The settlement date for a trade varies by instrument, and can be any date upon which both the buyer and seller agree.

Regular Way, Trade Date

Settlement Date Inventory

Settlement Date Inventory is the total of a firm's position in a specific security held on settlement date. This includes all of the securities that are held in the firm's depository accounts, vault, out to transfer, etc.

Stock Record

Settlement Guarantee Fund

The Settlement Guarantee Fund has been established by the NSCC, with funds provided by its members, to cover trade errors and defaults.

Settlement Interval

Settlement Interval is the amount of time that exists between trade date and settlement date.

Settlement Location

The Settlement Location is also known as the clearing method. Settlement Location indicates the actual place of settlement, which can be either a central securities depository or the country where the trade will settle.

Central Securities Depository

Settlement Price

The Settlement Price is a closing price (or for commodities it is a range of closing prices) that is used to:

- Determine the next day's price limits
- Invoice for commodity deliveries when a notice of intention to deliver is scheduled for that day

Settlement Risk

Settlement Risk is the risk that settlement in a transfer system will not take place as expected. This risk may include credit and liquidity risk.

SFA

See Securities and Futures Association

SFE

See Sydney Futures Exchange

Shanghai Index of A Shares

The Shanghai Index of A shares is a stock index derived from class A equities listed on the Shanghai Securities Exchange.

Shanghai Index of B Shares

The Shanghai Index of B shares is a stock index derived from class B equities listed on the Shanghai Securities Exchange.

Shanghai Securities Exchange

The Shanghai Stock Exchange is a primary stock exchange of China.

Share

A Share is the smallest whole unit of equity that represents the owner's interest in a corporation.

Equity

Share Classes

See *Classes of Shares*

Shareholder of Record

The Shareholder of Record is the individual or entity registered by an issuer listed as the owner of its securities.

Beneficial Owner

Shares Outstanding

Shares Outstanding include all of the company's shares that are held by investors. Shares outstanding do not include Treasury shares. Authorized but unissued stock is not considered to be outstanding.

Treasury Stock

Shelf Registration

A Shelf Registration is an IPO issued under SEC Rule 415. Shelf Registrations are single registrations that have been created by issuers, and which have been established to cover longer term needs. All of the securities issued under a shelf registration must be issued within two years.

IPO

Shell

A Shell is a special envelope that has been designed to hold bearer bonds or bearer coupons when they are being redeemed.

Bearer Bond, Coupon

Shenzhen A Share Index

Shenzhen A Share Index is an index derived from class A shares listed on Shenzhen Stock Exchange.

Shenzhen Stock Exchange

The Shenzhen Stock Exchange is a primary stock exchange of China.

Short

See *Short Sale*

Short Covering

Short Covering is the process of purchasing a security in order to return the security that was previously borrowed to make delivery on a short sale.

Short Exempt

Short Exempt refers to short sales that are exempt from the normal rules covering the procedure. Exempted short sales include:

- Buying a convertible preferred equity
- Submitting conversion instructions
- Selling common stock before the stock is actually received

Short Sale Rules

Short Interest

A firm's Short Interest is the net position of a security that has been sold short by customers and which has not been repurchased to settle the short positions.

Short Option Position

An option writer has a Short Option Position when they have written more options for a specific underlying security than they have bought.

Short Position

A Short Position can be when either:

- A customer's account does not have securities that they sold, and has borrowed them from the broker in order to settle
- A security position on a broker's records that has a credit balance

Long Position, Short Sale

Short Sale

A Short Sale is the sale of a security that the seller does not own.

Short sales are conducted in anticipation of a decline in the price of a security. Because the seller cannot actually sell what he does not own, he must borrow the security in order to make the delivery to the buyer. As a result, the short seller must pay interest on the loan of the securities.

If the price of the security does go down, the short seller makes a profit when he buys the security back at the lower price. If the price of the security rises, the short seller will incur a loss.

Securities Lending, Short Position

Short Sale Rules

There are two different Short Sale Rules:

- SEC regulations allow investors to sell short only when a stock price is moving upward. This regulation is designed to prevent a broker from driving down the price of a specific stock by short-selling and then buying the shares at the lower price for a profit.
- Nasdaq has a short sale rule that prohibits NASD members from selling a stock at or below the inside best bid when that price is lower than the previous inside best bid in that stock.

Best Bid

Short Tender

A Short Tender, which is prohibited by SEC Rule 10b-4, occurs when a firm or individual who has borrowed shares to cover a short position, presents the borrowed shares during a tender offer.

SEC, Rule 10b-4, Tender Offer

Short Term Bond

A Short Term Bond is a debt security with a holding period less than 5 years to maturity.

Short Term Investment Fund

A Short Term Investment Fund is an overnight cash investment vehicle for institutional accounts.

SIAC

Pronounced Sy Ack

See *Securities Industry Automation Corporation*

SIB

See Securities and Investments Board

SIC

Pronounced Sick

SIC is an abbreviation for the Securities Industry Classification.

Standard Industrial Classification

SICOVAM

SICOVAM is the central depository for the SBF-Bourse de Paris.

SID

See *Standing Instruction Database*

SIMEX

See Singapore International Monetary Exchange

Singapore International Monetary Exchange

The Singapore International Monetary Exchange (SIMEX) is the physical exchange using open outcry and automated trading of financial and energy futures and options contracts in Singapore.

Sinker

See *Sinking Fund*

Sinking Fund

A Sinking Fund is a trust established by the issuer of a bond with the purpose of accumulating capital for the annual future repayment of principal. Sinking funds obligate the issuer to make periodic contributions to the trust, and are usually established when the credit worthiness of the issuer is in doubt.

SIPC

See *Securities Investor Protection Corporation*

Size

When a market maker makes a complete quote with a bid and an offer price, they must also identify the Size of the order that is acceptable at the quoted prices. For example, when a market maker quotes "XYZ at 15 1/2 to 5/8 100 by 500," they have defined the bid and offer price as well as the minimum and maximum acceptable size of the bid and offer.

Bid, Market Maker, Offering Price

SLA

See *Service Level Agreement*

SLMA

See *Student Loan Mortgage Association*

Small Business Administration

The Small Business Administration was created as a governmental agency in 1953 to provide "financial, procurement, and management assistance to small business concerns and also to assist victims of natural and other disasters."

Small Business Investment Companies

Banks can form Small Business Investment Companies as a way to finance small businesses, using government-secured loans. By forming a SBIC, banks can loan up to 50% of the pre-investment capital needed by new firms.

Small Cap Stocks

Small Cap Stocks are the equities issued by a relatively small firm with little equity and few shares of common stock outstanding. The prices of Small capitalization stocks tend to fluctuate widely and have the opportunity for significant gains or losses

Small Order Execution System

Small Order Execution System is the automated execution system that is used by Nasdaq to process trades of up to 1,000 shares.

SMART

See *Securities Market Automated Regulated Trading Architecture*

Smart Terminal

See *Terminal*

Socially Responsible Fund

A Socially Responsible Fund is a mutual fund that limits the portfolio manager to invest in the securities of firms that meet pre-defined social standards. These mutual funds most often avoid purchasing stocks in cigarette manufacturers, alcohol manufacturers, etc.

Societe de la Bourse de Luxembourg

The Societe de la Bourse de Luxembourg is the primary stock exchange of Luxembourg.

Society for Worldwide Interbank Financial Telecommunication

S.W.I.F.T., which was established in 1977, is an international cooperative organization that is owned by over 2,000 member banks around the world. It provides message standards and a message transfer platform that connects nearly 6,000 institutions worldwide with over 600 million messages annually.

S.W.I.F.T. has a dedicated telecommunications network, and it guarantees the rapid, cost-effective, secure and reliable transmission of financial data.

S.W.I.F.T. provides:

- Standards
- Modern telecommunications network
- Network compatible terminals, interfaces and value-added products

The S.W.I.F.T. message types are in several categories:

- Payments
- Forex
- Money markets
- Securities
- Trade finance

ISO, ISO 7775

SOES

See *Small Order Execution System*

SOES Bandit

A SOES Bandit is a trader that seeks to use the SOES system to find arbitrage opportunities.

Small Business Order System

SOF

See *Securities Operations Forum*

Soft Dollars

The term Soft Dollars is used to identify that portion of a commission that is available to be used to purchase other services. When an institutional investor pays a full commission, one part of the commission is taken by the broker for a transaction fee, and the remainder is "saved" in a special account that can be used to buy other services that are offered by the broker, such as research.

Soft dollars were created when commissions were deregulated, as a way for brokers to continue to maintain a higher brokerage fee.

Software

Software is any type of computer program, including:

- Operating Systems
- Applications
- Utilities

Vaporware, Hardware, Operating System, Utility

Solicitation Fee

A Solicitation Fee is a commission that is paid to a broker/dealer for soliciting a tender offer from their clients.

Tender Offer

SOP

See *Standard Operating Procedure*

Sort Routine

A Sort Routine is a computer utility or program that is used to sort columnar data into some ascending or descending order, by using the data in one of the columns as the base for the sort.

Sound Card

A Sound Card is a board that can be added to a personal computer which converts data into sound that can then be output to a speaker.

Source Code

A system's Source Code is a list of separate instructions that tell a computer how to execute a task. While people can read source code, computers must convert it into machine readable language in order to operate.

Object Code, Compile

SPAN

See Standard Portfolio Analysis of Risk

SPDRs

Pronounced Spiders

See *Standard & Poor's Depositary Receipts*

Special Assessment Bonds

Special Assessment Bonds are often used to finance sewers and water improvement, and are repayable from any special tax assessments that are made for these purposes.

Municipal Bond

Special Situation

A Special Situation is a term that is often used to describe an investment opportunity that arises because of some unique circumstances such as a merger, oil discovery, new product development, etc.

Special Tax Bonds

Special Tax Bonds are instruments whereby all interest and principal payments are only authorized to come from the proceeds of a particular tax or some other specific source of funds.

Specialist

A Specialist is a member of an exchange who is required to make a market in the securities assigned to him and who has the following functions:

- Maintain an orderly market
- Act as a broker's broker

To perform its role properly, the specialist will do the following:

- Maintain current bid and asked prices for their assigned stocks which are electronically published
- Act as an agent for a floor broker and execute trades such as limit orders for them
- Buy or sell for their own accounts when there is a temporary shortage of either buyers or sellers
- Bring buyers and sellers together

Specialists are required to place and execute public investor orders ahead of their own, and if there are not enough buyers or sellers the specialist must make the market as liquid as possible by using their own capital or inventory to complete a transaction.

Two-Dollar Broker

Specialist Manager

A Specialist Manager is an investment manager who researches a single class of investments or concentrates on a more defined strategy than does a balanced manager.

Specialized Fund

A Specialized Fund is a mutual fund that concentrates on one particular country, region or sector.

Specific Risk

Specific Risk is the risk that is unique for a specific investment or security.

Systemic Risk

Speculation

See *Speculator*

Speculation Objectives

An investor has a Speculation Objective when they have a strategy that assumes a higher than normal market risk with the anticipation of a commensurate higher return.

Speculator

Speculator

A Speculator is an individual or a firm that is willing to exchange higher risk for a potentially higher profit.

Spin Off

A Spin Off occurs when a portion of a company is removed from its parent and established as a separate legal entity. The new firm, if established as a corporation, has its own capital structure.

Split

See *Stock Split*

Split-up

See *Stock Split*

Spot

Spot trades of currency are conducted between two parties using the current foreign exchange rate, and typically settle in one or two days.

Spot Market

The Spot Market, also called the cash market, is where trades are settled the same day they are traded.

Spread

The Bid and Asked Spread is:

- The difference between what the underwriter pays to the issuer and the price at which the underwriter sells the security to the public.
- The difference between a market maker's bid and asked price. The spread, which narrows or widens due to supply and demand, is the market maker's profit margin in an efficient market.
- A simultaneous long and short option using either puts or calls on the same underlying security but with a different strike price or different expiration dates. There are a variety of combinations or spreads and strategies for trading options.

Asked, Bid, Market Maker, Straddle

SRO

See *Self Regulating Organization*

SSAN

Abbreviation for Social Security Number, the US tax identification number for individuals.

SSN

Abbreviation for Social Security Number, the US tax identification number for individuals

SSS

See *Securities Settlement System*

Staffing for Peaks

A manager may decide to use the strategy of Staffing for Peaks by having enough people working at all times to ensure that peak volumes can be handled. Managers usually prefer to staff to average volumes and then supplement their work force with temporary help if necessary.

Peak

Stamp Duty

A Stamp Duty is a tax that is payable to the local government for securities transactions. This originally referred to the fee that was charged for stamping the securities certificates during the physical Registration process.

Stamp Duty is still collected in many countries with dematerialized securities.

Registration, Dematerialized Security

Standard

A Standard is a prescribed way of presenting information or performing a task. There are a variety of standards used in the securities industry, such as pricing, messaging and numbering standards.

International Standards Organization

Standard & Poor's 425 Index

The Standard & Poor's 425 Index is an index of the 425 industrial stocks based upon the S&P 500 and calculated by Standard & Poor's Corporation.

Standard & Poor's Corporation

Standard & Poor's 500 Stock Price Index

The Standard & Poor's 500 Stock Price Index is a value weighted index of stock prices that is calculated by the Standard & Poor's Corporation and consists of a list of 400 industrial stocks, 40 utilities, 20 transportation and 40 financial stocks.

Standard & Poor's Corporation

Standard & Poor's Corporation

The Standard & Poor's Corporation is a for-profit business that provides information for firms in the financial services industry.

Standard & Poor's Depositary Receipts

Pronounced Spiders SPDRs represent an ownership position in the SPDR Trust, which is a long term unit investment trust that holds a portfolio of common stocks that are intended to track the price performance and dividend yield of the Standard & Poor's 500 Stock Price Index.

SPDRs were first traded on the American Stock Exchange on January 29, 1993.

Standard & Poor's 500 Stock Price Index

Standard Deviation

The Standard Deviation is a statistical measure of the variability of securities returns when compared to the mean. The higher the standard deviation, the riskier the security.

Mean

Standard Industrial Classification

The Standard Industrial Classification (SIC) is a numbering system that has been established by the US Office of Management and Budget to identify a company's industry.

Standard Operating Procedure

A Standard Operating Procedure is a predefined set of actions that are always to be taken in certain pre-defined circumstances.

Standard Portfolio Analysis of Risk

The Standard Portfolio Analysis of Risk (SPAN) is a method of calculating the initial margin required for futures and options by evaluating portfolio risk under a number of scenarios. Originally developed by the Chicago Mercantile Exchange, SPAN is also used by LIFFE to calculate the initial margin for all contracts.

Stand-By Underwriting

Stand-By Underwriting occurs when a new issue is offered to the public for up to 20 days before the underwriter is committed to purchase the remaining shares.

Standing Instruction Database

The DTC has established their Standing Instruction Database (SID) as a central repository of settlement instructions that can be accessed and used by banks, brokers and investment advisors to reduce the potential for errors during the settlement process.

DTC, ID, IID

Standing Instruction Databases

Standing Instruction Databases are electronic databases that contain all of the delivery instruction data required to effect an automated settlement. A major gap in the industry's drive for straight through processing has been in the area of delivery instructions.

Today, four factors are important for the successful introduction of an automated solution for delivery instructions:

- Collecting and maintaining the data from all affected firms
- Reliable connectivity
- Multiple, easy ways to access the data
- Critical mass

Delivery Instructions, Straight Through Processing

State Street Bank and Trust

State Street Bank and Trust is a US-based bank and Global Custodian.

www.statestreet.com

Step-Up Privilege

When an investor has a fractional share of a security as a result of a rights offering, they can use a Step-Up Privilege to obtain an additional fractional share in order to round up to a whole number.

STIF

Pronounced Stiff

See Short Term Investment Fund

Stock

See *Equity*

Stock Borrow Program

The NSCC's Stock Borrow Program allows participant firms to lend stocks and corporate bonds from their DTC account to cover temporary shortages in NSCC's CNS System.

Participants can earn interest on the current market value on any of their DTC positions that are borrowed by NSCC.

Securities Lending

Stock Certificate

See *Certificate*

Stock Clearing Corporation of Philadelphia

The Stock Clearing Corporation of Philadelphia (SCPP) was the clearing corporation of the Philadelphia Stock Exchange. In 1997, it was merged into the NSCC.

Stock Dividend

A Stock Dividend occurs when a dividend is paid in shares of stock instead of cash. The amount of the dividend is granted as a percentage of the outstanding shares, and every shareholder gets a pro rata share of the dividend.

Stock dividends are usually paid by corporations that wish to conserve capital for expansion or other purposes.

Stock Exchange

See *Exchange*

Stock Exchange Clearing House

The Stock Exchange Clearing House provides automated trading and clearing for securities in Israel.

Stock Exchange of Hong Kong

The Stock Exchange of Hong Kong, LTD is the primary stock exchange of Hong Kong.

Stock Exchange of Singapore

The Stock Exchange of Singapore is the primary stock exchange of Singapore.

www.ses.com.sg

Stock Exchange of Thailand

The Stock Exchange of Thailand is the primary stock exchange of Thailand.

www.set.or.th

Stock Loan and Borrow

A firm's Stock Loan and Borrow unit is responsible for lending excess segregated stock and for obtaining stock when it is needed by the firm. This function is typically a part of the cashiering department.

Segregation

Stock Power

A Stock Power is the official form that is used instead of a formal endorsement on the back of a security's certificate. The security can be delivered or transferred after the Stock Power is properly completed and attached to the certificate.

Stock Price

See *Market Price*

Stock Record

A Stock Record is a detailed ledger that is used by brokers to record all of their movements for a specific security. A stock record has two formats:

- Previous day movements
- Current security positions

Stock Split

A Stock Split occurs when a corporation with board approval decides that it wishes to reduce the price of its current shares by issuing more shares. Stock splits generally are on a two-for-one, or three-for-one basis, where the original holder is issued two or three times as many shares, with each share worth one-half or one-third, respectively, of its previous price.

For example, if a stockholder has 100 shares of a stock with a market price of $50, and the issuing company announces a two-for-one split, the stockholder will now own 200 shares that are valued by the market at $25.

Stock splits do not increase or decrease the total capitalization of the company.

Reverse Split

Stock Symbol

A Stock Symbol is a unique three, four or five letter symbol that is used to identify a specific security.

Stock Transfer

Stock Transfer is the registration process that identifies the ownership of a security.

Float, Registration

Stockholder

A Stockholder is the person or entity owning one or more shares of corporate equity. Stockholders are generally entitled to:

- A proportionate share of the company's assets
- Dividends when declared by the Board of Directors
- The right of proportionate voting power
- Possible opportunities to subscribe to additional stock before public offerings are made

Pre-Emptive Right

Stockholder of Record

See *Shareholder of Record*

Stockholm Stock Exchange

The Stockholm Stock Exchange is the primary stock exchange of Sweden.

www.public.se/finans/stock.english

Stockholm Stock Exchange Index

Stockholm Stock Exchange Index is a stock index derived from securities listed on the Stockholm Stock Exchange

Stop Limit Order

See *Stop Order*

Stop Loss Order

See *Stop Order*

Stop Order

A Stop Order is an order to buy or sell on an exchange that becomes effective as soon as a security reaches a certain price.

Buy Stop, Sell Stop

Storage

Storage of data in electronic form can occur on several different types of media, including:

- Microfiche
- Tape
- Floppy Disk
- Hard Drive
- CD ROM

Each type of storage has a different cost per unit and a different retrieval time.

Generally the faster the information must be retrieved, the more the storage media will cost.

STP

See *Straight Through Processing*

Straddle

A Straddle is the simultaneous purchase or sale of the same underlying security, based upon any one of the following:

- Long or short positions of puts and calls
- Strike price differences
- Differences in expiration dates

Spread, Series

Straight Through Processing

Straight Through Processing (STP) is the process of automating the entire flow of securities processing information from orders through to settlement and reconciliation.

STP has been defined as:

- Processing without human intervention
- End-to-end computing
- Paper-less processing
- Exception-only processing

Strangle

A Strangle is an option strategy that uses one call and one put with different strike prices but with the same expiration date.

STRAP

A STRAP is an option strategy where the investor buys two calls and one put on the same security.

STRIP

Street

Originally referring to Wall Street and the New York financial district, the term "Street" is now a general reference encompassing all activity throughout the securities industry.

Street Name

When securities are registered on behalf of a client in the name of a broker, bank or depository, the registration is said to be in Street Name. Street Name registration is used to simplify the transfer process by eliminating the need to re-register the traded security with a new beneficial owner.

Beneficial Owner

Street Side

A trade typically has two sides, and each side has two counterparties. The two sides of a trade are the customer side and the Street Side.

The customer side of the trade takes place between the customer and the broker. The Street Side of the trade occurs when the customer's broker does not have the desired security in their own inventory and a trade takes place between that broker and another broker who does have the security.

Customer Side, Buy Side, Sell Side, Counterparty

Stress Testing

Stress Testing can be either:

- Inserting a variety of assumptions into an investment model to see what the worst case outcome of a portfolio could be.
- Inputting a large number of transactions into a computer application to see if all of the components (application, hardware, telecommunications, people, etc.) can accommodate the peak volume within acceptable time frames. A stress test is usually performed after user acceptance testing, and usually before parallel testing.

Systems Development Life Cycle

Strike Price

The Strike Price is the pre-determined price of the underlying security at which a specific option can be exercised.

Exercise Price

Strip

There are two ways to use the term STRIP:

- A Strip, or a Separate Purchase of Registered Interest and Principal of Securities, is a derivative where the interest coupon of a US treasury bond has been removed from the promise to repay the principal.

  The interest coupon is traded separately as a strip, and the remaining principal is traded as a zero coupon bond. Strips pay interest semi-annually, and the stream of interest payments increases as the bond matures. Strips do not pay any principal.

- A STRIP is also an option strategy where the investor purchases two puts and one call on the same security.

Zero Coupon Bond, Derivative, STRAP

Student Loan Mortgage Association

The Student Loan Mortgage Association, also known as Sallie Mae, was established in 1972 to create a secondary market for securitized student loans.

Sub-Agent

See *Sub-Custodian*

Sub-Custodian

A Sub-Custodian is a local bank that clears and settles transactions in the local market on behalf of customers in other countries, typically through a global custodian.

Global Custodian

Subscription

A Subscription is an agreement to positively respond to an offering. Neither the offer nor the subscription is binding until it is accepted by an authorized issuer representative.

Subscription Agent

A Subscription Agent handles the activity that occurs when stockholders exercise their subscription rights.

Subsidiary

A Subsidiary is a company in which another company controls more than 50% of its voting stock.

Suitability

An investment's Suitability refers to its adherence to an investor's defined objectives. A broker is required to know their customer's investment suitability and objectives.

Know Your Customer

SuperDot

SuperDot is the New York Stock Exchange system for electronic order-routing that allows member firms to quickly and efficiently transmit market and limit orders of up to 30,999 shares. These orders are sent by SuperDot to the specialist post or to the member firm's booth for execution. When the trade is completed, the execution information is returned electronically to the member firm's office for their comparison.

The SuperDot system includes:

- The Display Book (Electronic Book)
- Opening Automated Report Service (OARS)
- Market Order Processing
- Limit Order Processing
- Broker Booth Support System (BBSS)
- Post Trade Processing
- Trade Reporting

Opening Automated Reporting System, Market Order Processing, Limit Order Processing, Broker Booth Support System, Post Trade Processing, Trade Reporting

Supermarket

A Supermarket is a program offered by brokerage firms whereby mutual funds offered by many different investment companies are available on a no-load, fee-only basis.

Supplemental Contract

The Supplemental Contract is issued by the NSCC as a portion of the Continuous Net Settlement process, and includes the:

- Total of the regular way contract
- Adjustments made through advisories
- Additions from seller processing
- Continuous Net Settlement

Support Level

The Support Level is the theoretical point at which a market stops dropping because buyers start to outnumber sellers.

Resistance Level

Surfing

When a person attempts to find information by moving from point to point on the internet, they are considered to be Surfing the net.

Internet, World Wide Web

Surveillance

See *Market Surveillance*

Swap

A Swap can be either:

- The sale of one security to purchase another with similar features. Swaps are frequently performed between an investment manager's accounts without tax consequences.
- The exchange of different futures instruments or similar futures instruments with different features. Swaps exchange one type of cash flow or asset for another with prearranged rules. For example, an interest rate swap is the exchange of a fixed rate obligation for a variable rate obligation, and an equity index swap could be the exchange of two independent stock market indexes.

Swap

See Interest Rate Swap.

Sweep

See *Cash Sweep*

SWIFT

See *Society for Worldwide Interbank Financial Telecommunication*

Swiss Exchange

The Swiss Exchange is a private organization with the legal status of an association comprised of the members of the previous exchanges in Basle, Geneva and Zurich.

Swiss Performance Index

The Swiss Performance Index is a stock index derived from equities listed on the Swiss Exchange.

Sydney Futures Exchange

The Sydney Futures Exchange (SFE) was established in 1960 as a physical exchange using open outcry and automated trading of financial and commodity futures and options in Australia.

Syndicate

A Syndicate is created when an investment bank brings together a group of other investment banks or brokerage firms for the purpose of underwriting a new issue.

Underwriter

Syndicate Manager

A Syndicate Manager is also called the managing underwriter or the lead manager.

Syndicate, Underwriter

Synthetics

See *Derivative*

System

A System is one or more applications that work together with their supporting hardware to meet a business need.

System Mapping

System Mapping is the process of diagramming the various hardware or software components of a system, and showing how they relate to each other.

Systemic Risk

Systematic Risk is the risk that if one firm is unable to meet its financial obligations, other firms participating in the same financial system will be affected and will also not be able to meet their obligations.

Systems Development Life Cycle

A Systems Development Life Cycle (SDLC) is a process that identifies the steps that are needed to define, design, develop, test and install a computer system. While there are several generic SDLC processes available, most firms create a customized version for their own firm.

Firms without an SDLC generally experience much higher development costs, longer development cycles, higher maintenance costs and higher project risk.

Project Risk, Testing

Systems Integrator

A Systems Integrator is a consulting firm that specializes in helping their customers connect their internal applications and to connect their systems to other firms.

The Summit Group

Systems Testing

Systems Testing is a full integrated test of an entire application and is usually conducted by the systems department before they deliver it to the users for the next step in the testing process.

Some development organizations do not fully test the system against the user requirements document and do not discover bugs or errors until user testing. This is very inefficient and leads to organizational disputes between the development organization and the user departments.

Testing, Systems Development Life Cycle

T Bills

See *Treasury Bill*

T+1, T+2, T+3

T+1, T+2, and T+3 refers to trade date plus 1 day, 2 days, 3 days, respectively.

Trade Date

TA General Index

The TA General Index Composite Index is a stock index derived from equities listed on the Tel Aviv Stock Exchange.

TAC

See *Targeted Amortization Class*

TAKASBANK

TAKASBANK is a clearing and settlement organization in Turkey.

Takeover

A Takeover occurs when one company acquires a controlling interest in another company.

Proxy, Proxy Fight

TAN

See *Tax Anticipation Note*

Tape

The term Tape is a holdover from when the stock exchanges distributed information about stock prices on a paper through a Ticker Tape machine. Today, the tape is an electronic distribution of trade information that is sometimes sequentially displayed as a series of data across a display board.

Ticker, Stock Exchange

Target

Target is the new central bank system for cross border payments within the European Monetary Union.

EMU

Targeted Amortization Class

A Targeted Amortization Class is a type of collateralized mortgage obligation that is designed to produce principal payments with a predetermined schedule and that has been developed by assuming that the underlying mortgages will prepay at a targeted rate rather than within a range of rates.

Planned Amortization Class, Derivative

TARS

See *Trade Acceptance and Reconciliation Service*

Task

A Task is an action that someone must perform in order to achieve a defined result.

Procedure

Tax Anticipation Note

A Tax Anticipation Note is a short term debt instrument issued by a municipality that is to be repaid by the revenues that will be received from a future tax period.

Tax Basis

The Tax Basis is the amount of taxable income that was claimed on a firm's tax return.

Tax Deferral Objective

An investor has a Tax Deferral Objective when they have a preference for investments that generate tax free or tax deferred income.

Tax Deferred

An investment is Tax Deferred when the earnings are not taxable until they are withdrawn by the investor.

Tax Exempt Bonds

Tax Exempt Bonds are municipal securities whose interest is free from federal income tax, and which may be free from state and/or local tax.

Tax Exempt Securities

Tax Exempt Securities are municipal securities whose interest is free from federal income tax, and which may be free from state and/or local tax.

Tax Identification Numbers

There are two major types of Tax Identification Numbers that are issued by the IRS to identify an entity for tax purposes:

- SSN - Social Security Number

- EIN - Employee Identification Number

EIN

Tax Impound

A Tax Impound occurs when a lender receives payments from a borrower and holds them in order to make periodic tax payments.

Tax Lien

A Tax Lien is a legal claim against a property for unpaid taxes.

Tax Lot

See *Tax Lot Accounting*

Tax Lot Accounting

Tax Lot Accounting is the accounting method that is used when a gain or loss on each security purchase can be separately reported.

First In-First Out, Last In-First Out

Tax Reclaim

See *Withholding Tax Reclaim*

Tax Reform Act of 1986

The Tax Reform Act of 1986 enacted legislation that restricted the deductibility of contributions to IRA accounts, eliminated preferential tax treatment for capital gains and put a maximum on the amount an employee can contribute to a 401(k) plan.

Tax Sale

A Tax Sale is the forced sale of property by a government because of the property owner's failure to pay applicable taxes.

Tax Shelter

A Tax Shelter is a type of investment that has been structured to reduce or defer taxes.

Tax Treaty

A Tax Treaty is negotiated between countries in order to define how much of the tax withheld on a cross border investment will be retained by the taxing country in which the investment is domiciled, and how much will be taxed by the investor's home country. A tax treaty is designed to prevent double taxation and provide withholding tax relief.

Withholding Tax

TBA

The letters TBA are used for different reasons, including:

- A trade for Mortgage Backed Securities that is made before the issue is released, and before it is completely identified with a unique pool number
- An abbreviation for To Be Announced, which is used to identify pending events or open positions on an organization chart

Mortgage Backed Securities

TBA Mortgage Backed Security

See *TBA*

TBD

To Be Determined

TCP/IP

TCP/IP stands for Transfer Control Protocol/Internet Protocol which is a way of defining the standard rules for how two networks can communicate with each other.

TD

See *Trade Date*

Technical Analysis

A Technical Analysis is a discipline that attempts to predict the price movements of equities by looking for various patterns such as historic price changes, rates of change, and changes in volume of trading and open interest. A technical analyst summarizes this information in the form of charts.

Fundamental Analysis

Teenie

See *Tick*

Tel Aviv Stock Exchange

The Tel Aviv Stock Exchange is the primary stock exchange of Israel.

www.tase.co.il

Telecommunications

Telecommunications is the process of sending data from one computer to another across telephone lines.

Telex

A Telex is a method of communicating typewritten instructions directly in real-time from one telex machine across a telephone line to a specific receiving telex machine. Telex is used less and less often today.

Ten Year Note

Government bond of ten year maturity.

Tender

A Tender occurs when a security is presented for sale to a party who has offered to buy it through a tender offer.

Tender Offer

Tender Agent

A Tender Agent administers the functions that are required in a tender offer.

Tender Offer

A Tender Offer is a formal offer by one company or individual to buy the shares of another company with cash, securities, or a combination of both. If either the corporation or the shareholders object, this is called an unfriendly takeover or a hostile takeover.

Hostile Takeover

Tennessee Valley Authority

The Tennessee Valley Authority (TVA) was established by the US government in 1933 to develop the resources of the Tennessee Valley region and to "strengthen the regional and national economy, and the national defense." TVA bonds are not obligations of the US, nor are they guaranteed by the federal government.

Tenor

The Tenor of a bond is the length of time between when it is issued and when it matures.

Terabyte

A Terabyte is a trillion bytes. Terabytes are a unit of measurement used to denominate a computer's storage capacity.

Byte

Term

The Term of a loan is the period of time between the beginning of a loan and the date on which the balance of the loan is due.

Term Mortgage

A Term Mortgage is a mortgage on which only interest is paid during the length of the loan. The term of the loan is usually for a period less than five years. At the end of the term, the entire principal amount is due.

Mortgage

Terminal

A Terminal is a screen-based computer access device. A terminal can either be a smart terminal, or a dumb terminal.

A smart terminal is one that has some internal intelligence and does some processing locally.

A dumb terminal does not have the capability of doing any local processing, and is used to send commands to the computer and display the information that is returned.

When a PC is used as a terminal to access a computer, it can be used as either a smart terminal, when some of its computing capabilities are used, or as a dumb terminal, when all of the processing is conducted by the computer.

Personal Computer

Terminal Based Interface

See *Text Based Interface*

Testing

Testing a computer system is usually done in several steps, as defined in a Systems Development Life Cycle:

- Unit Testing
- Systems Testing
- User Acceptance Testing
- Parallel Testing
- Stress Testing

Systems Development Life Cycle, Unit Testing, Systems Testing, User Acceptance Testing, Parallel Testing, Stress Testing

Text Based Interface

A Terminal Based Interface is the original method used by people to interact with a computer. The computer displays words or numbers as output, and a prompt identifies when the user must input a command by typing in words, letters or numbers.

Prompt, Graphical User Interface

Thailand Securities Depository Co., Ltd.

Thailand Securities Depository Co., Ltd. (TSD) is the central depository and securities clearing house of Thailand.

The Summit Group

The Summit Group provides support to banks, brokers, investment managers and other financial institutions through management consulting, market research and systems integration. Through its subsidiary, Securities Operations Forum, TSG trains over 2,000 people annually and publishes newsletters for the securities industry that are read by over 4,000 people worldwide.

www.tsgc.com

Securities Operations Forum

Theta

Theta is the measurement of the change in the value of an option relative to the continuous decrease in the time remaining to expiration.

Thin Market

A Thin Market is a market in which there are very few buyers or sellers or both. The term can be applied to a single security or the entire stock market.

Third Market

The Third Market is a way of trading listed securities in the over-the-counter market by broker/dealers. This over-the-counter trading of exchange listed securities is conducted by institutional investors and broker/dealers for their own accounts.

Primary Market, Secondary Market, Fourth Market

Third Market Trade Reporting

Third Market Trade Reporting is a system that collects and reports last sale prices of over-the-counter trades.

Third Market

Tick

A Tick is the smallest allowable price change of a security. Until recently, stocks traded on the major exchanges in eighths of a point, but now trade in sixteenths. A sixteenth is sometimes called a "teenie."

Up Tick, Down Tick

Ticker

The Ticker is the process by which the prices and volume of security transactions on the floor of a national exchange are immediately distributed to interested parties.

Ticker Symbol

A Ticker Symbol is the abbreviation that identifies each specific instrument on an exchange's ticker system.

Tape

Tickler

A Tickler is an automated reminder that something should be done at a certain time or by a certain date.

Tickler Category

A Tickler Category is any one of the different types of trigger events that can be initiated automatically by a system.

Tickler Date

The Tickler Date is used to denote when a certain event should take place.

TIFFE

See Tokyo International Financial Futures and Options Exchange

Tight Money

A condition of Tight Money exists when interest rates are high and credit is difficult to obtain.

TIGR

See *Treasury Income Growth Receipts*

Time and Sales Report

A Time and Sales Report can be provided to an investor who requests it from their broker when they feel that their trade was not accomplished in a timely manner. The report shows the trades that were made in the same security at the same time the investor placed their order.

Time Deposit

See *Certificate of Deposit*

Time Horizon

A Time Horizon is the length of time for which an investor plans to invest before starting to withdraw funds from the investment.

Time To Expiry

Time To Expiry is the period of time remaining until the expiration of a futures or an option contract.

Time Value

The term Time Value can be used in two ways:

- The Time Value of an option is that portion of an option's price that is attributable to the time remaining before expiration
- The Time Value of money is the current value of a dollar that will be received at some point in the future

Intrinsic Value

Time Value

The portion of the option premium that is attributable to the amount of time remaining until the expiration of the option contract. Time value is whatever value the option has in addition to its intrinsic value.

Timeliness

Timeliness is a percentage that identifies how well a particular timeliness indicator meets its anticipated level or a goal.

Timeliness Indicator

Timeliness Indicator

A Timeliness Indicator is used by managers to identify the processes that are being tracked relative to their anticipated timeliness or to a goal.

Timing

Timing is an investment strategy where an investor attempts to identify the exact moment to buy or sell a security to maximize their profit.

TIPS

See *Inflation Indexed Treasury Bonds*

Title

A Title is a document which proves the ownership of a property.

Title Company

A Title Company is a company that insures the title to land or a property.

TMTR

See *Third Market Trade Reporting*

Tokyo International Financial Futures and Options Exchange (TIFFE)

The Tokyo International Financial Futures and Options Exchange (TIFFE) was established in 1989 as a physical exchange with fully automated trading of financial futures and options contracts.

Tokyo Stock Exchange

The Tokyo Stock Exchange (TSE) was established in 1878, and is the primary stock exchange of Japan. The TSE is a physical exchange which provides fully automated trading of financial futures and options, and supports traditional trading in the underlying equity markets.

Tombstone

A Tombstone is an announcement in a newspaper of a new security issue. The announcement lists information such as:

- The Security
- Some specific information about the security
- The names of the members of the syndicate involved in selling the issue in the order of each members' importance

Toronto Stock Exchange

The Toronto Stock Exchange (TSE) is a Canadian stock exchange located in the province of Ontario.

www.tse.com

Total Return

The Total Return of a portfolio during a given period is the sum of the increase/decrease in the value of the securities in the portfolio, plus interest and dividends, less expenses, and adjusted for any changes in the value of the currencies in the portfolio relative to the base currency.

Base Currency, Market Action

Trade

A Trade is the result of matching a buyer and a seller of a security or a currency.

Trade Life Cycle

Trade Acceptance and Reconciliation Service

The Trade Acceptance and Reconciliation Service is an automated Nasdaq service that helps members reconcile uncompared trades.

Trade Amount

The Trade Amount is the total value of the trade, and is the price multiplied by the quantity.

Trade Date

The Trade Date is the date on which a transaction is executed.

Trade Date Inventory

Trade Date Inventory consists of all of the positions for each individual security at the start of the trading day which are available to be sold.

Trade Life Cycle

The Trade Life Cycle is the total of all processes involved in facilitating and serving a trade. There are several steps in the trade life cycle, sometimes also called the Trade Value Chain:

- Issuance
- Pre Trade
- Trade
- Post Trade
- Clearing
- Settlement
- Issue Servicing

Issuance, Pre-Trade, Trade, Post Trade Processing, Clearing, Settlement, Issue Servicing

Trade Matching

See *Matching*

Trade Netting

Trade Netting is a legally enforceable consolidation of individual trades into a net amount for cash and each involved security. Trade netting usually occurs between trading partners or among members of a clearing system.

Another form of netting, position netting, is not legally enforceable.

Position Netting, Netting

Trade Process

There are several steps in the Trade Process:

- Trade order - A buy or sell instruction is given to a broker.
- Order execution - An order is executed when a counterparty agrees to the trade. A trade date is established, and a contract defining settlement date, execution price, and counterparties is established.
- Trade confirmation – The confirmation contains the details of the trade. The confirm is normally sent electronically for institutional trades through the DTC ID system for DTC eligible securities. And on paper to retail clients. Operations departments match trade confirms with the trade orders.
- Trade Clearing – The netting of securities and money between brokers for the street side of the trade is the clearing process.
- Trade Settlement – The exchange of securities for money is the settlement. Individuals deal with brokerage firms on a cash basis, and institutions deal on a DVP basis.

- Trade Posting – Trades can be posted as a contractual settlement using settlement date accounting, or with trade date accounting for portfolio managers and institutional investors.

Cash Basis, Confirmation, Institutional Delivery System, DVP, Settlement, Clearing, Trade Life Cycle

Trade Publications

Trade publications are those that are designed to appeal to a specific group of people who usually are participants in the industry and who have an interest in learning more about their industry.

There are several trade publications that provide information to the securities operations professional:

- American Banker - Thomson Financial - Daily
- Pension and Investments - Crain Publications - Weekly
- Securities Operations Letter - The Summit Group - Semi-monthly
- Securities Industry News - Thomson Financial - Weekly
- Operations Management - Institutional Investor - Bi-weekly
- Trends Magazine - ABA - Quarterly
- Wall Street Technology - Miller Freeman - Monthly

Trade Registration System

The Trade Registration System (TRS) is a real-time trade matching and administration system which links the LIFFE trading floor to its members' back offices for post trade processing.

Trade Reporting

Trade Reporting is the process whereby brokers inform designated authorities of their trades. In most cases, the trades are captured electronically as they are made on an exchange or on Nasdaq.

SuperDot

Trade Shows

Trade Shows are events that are designed to bring together industry professionals and vendors who wish to discuss topics of common interest and to display new products.

There are several Trade Shows that are of interest to industry professionals, such as:

- NFSOC (American Banker's Association)
- BDUG
- Securities Operations Forum events
- SOD (Securities Industry Association)
- SIBOS (S.W.I.F.T.)

Trade Status Change Stream

The Trade Status Change Stream (TSCS) message system provides real time record transmission to the LIFFE members' computer systems. Every trade or position change generates a record which is transmitted via TSCS.

Trade-for-Trade

Trade-for-Trade is the MBSCC settlement system.

Trade-for-Trade Settlement

Trade-for-Trade Settlement occurs when each transaction between counterparties is settled individually. This is necessary for the customer side of a trade.

The street side is usually initially processed through a clearance system, such as the NSCC, and the net of the trades are settled at the end of the day. Brokers can settle the street side of individual trades on a trade for trade basis if they both agree.

Street Side, Customer Side

Tradepoint

Tradepoint is an order-driven screen-based market for UK equities that was started in 1995 to compete with the London Stock Exchange.

Trader

A Trader is an individual who actively buys and sells securities for his own account, for his firm's account or for his firm's customers. A typical trader does not hold securities for any length of time, and looks to make a profit on price movements.

Trader Assistant

A Trader Assistant provides the clerical support that is needed by the traders.

Trading

Trading is the process of buying and selling securities and can be conducted for a firm's account or for its customers. Trading is either conducted on an exchange or over-the-counter.

When trading for their own account, traders must be monitored via several risk monitoring limits, including position limits for:

- Trader (Daylight and overnight)
- Sector
- Counterparty
- Country

Trading Against the Box

See *Against the Box*

Trading Flat

Bonds are considered Trading Flat when they trade without accrued interest.

Trading Halt

A Trading Halt can be imposed by an exchange for various predetermined periods of time for various reasons, including:

- A security's issuer is disseminating material news
- The prices on an exchange are rapidly changing

Trading Panel

Equities that trade on the floor of the New York Stock Exchange are assigned to a centralized trading post and a specific Trading Panel. The panel is located on the trading post, and is where information such as the bid and ask, volume, etc., is displayed.

Trading Post

Trading Post

A Trading Post is any location that has been established on the floor of an exchange to buy and sell specific stocks. The New York Stock Exchange has 23 trading posts, each of which trade approximately 75 stocks.

Trading Panel

Trading Range

The Trading Range can be:

- The range of traded prices for a stock or a market during a given period.
- The trading limit that has been established by a commodities futures exchange on a given commodity.

Trading Systems

See *Order Management Systems*

Tranche

A Tranche is one segment of a collateralized mortgage. Each tranche contains mortgages that are expected to be repaid within a specific time period, giving an investor some indication of when they will be repaid. Any one tranche must be completely repaid before the holders of the next tranche receive any payments.

Collateralized Mortgage Obligation

Transaction

A Transaction is an event that includes purchases and sales, cash movements, transfers, corporate actions and payment of fees, etc.

Corporate Action, Transfer

Transaction Category

When developing a system, the Transaction Category identifies the various types of transactions that are available, such as:

- Add
- Change
- Delete

- Display
- Reverse

Transaction Status

When developing a system, the Transaction Status identifies the state of each transaction. Transactions can be:

- Entered
- Entered/Checked
- Entered/Checked/Authorized
- Entered/Authorized
- Reversed
- Reversed/Checked
- Reversed/Checked/Authorized
- Reversed/Authorized
- Cancelled
- Cancelled/Checked
- Cancelled/Checked/Authorized
- Cancelled/Authorized

Transfer

A Transfer is the process by which securities are registered in the name of the buyer by a transfer agent. In a transfer, the old certificate(s) are physically cancelled and subsequently destroyed, and a new certificate is issued to the buyer.

When shares are dematerialized in a depository and registered in nominee name, they do not have to be re-registered when they are bought and sold.

Nominee, Transfer Agent, Dematerialization

Transfer Agent

A Transfer Agent is a firm, usually a commercial bank, employed by a corporation, municipality or mutual fund to maintain the name and address records of the investors or holders of the issued stock. The transfer agent is also responsible for canceling and issuing certificates, and resolving problems with lost, destroyed, or stolen certificates.

Registrar

Transfer Tax

A Transfer Tax is applied in some countries by their regulating authority on purchases and sales of securities. The tax is paid when title passes from one owner to another.

Transparency

Transparency is the degree to which a market has promptly available and accurate price and volume information.

Transparent Market

A Transparent Market exists when trade and quotation information is made known to the public as it becomes available, and within the same timeframe as received by professional investors.

TRAX

TRAX is an electronic trade confirmation system offered by ISMA which mostly handles fixed income transactions in Europe.

ETC, ISMA

Treasuries

Treasuries are all securities (Bonds, Notes and Bills) that are backed by the issuing government.

See US Treasury Obligations

See UK Treasuries

Treasury Bill

See *US Treasury Bill*

Treasury Bill Auction

A Treasury Bill Auction is the process used to sell US Treasury Bills to dealers in the government segment of the industry.

The process works similarly to a Dutch auction, except that the treasury has a specific amount of bills to sell, and they will accept the highest bid first and then subsequently lower bids until all of their issue is sold.

Treasury Bond

See *US Treasury Bond*

Treasury Income Growth Receipts

Pronounced Tigers

Treasury Income Growth Receipts are Zero Coupon Bonds that have been issued by Merrill Lynch.

Zero Coupon Bond

Treasury Note

See *US Treasury Note*

Treasury Stock

Treasury Stock consists of shares of a company's stock that were repurchased by the issuing company. By repurchasing their own shares, often at a premium to the current market price, the company offers existing investors the opportunity to sell their shares and receive capital gains rather than dividends.

Trend

A Trend is the direction in the market or in the factors which influence business.

A market trend can be up, down, flat, oscillating, etc.

A business trend includes factors such as governmental regulation, economic forces, competition, etc.

Trésor Francais

See French Trésor

Treuhandanstalt

The Treuhandanstalt is the official German agency set up by the Government in 1990 to privatize former East German companies. It issued Treuhand bonds which carry the express guarantee of the German Government.

In 1994, the Treuhandanstalt was closed when its outstanding debt was passed to the 'Redemption Fund for Inherited Liabilities' (Erblastentilgungsfonds).

Trigger

A Trigger is a pre-defined event that, when recognized by a computer, causes the computer to take some specific action.

Trinidad and Tobago Stock Exchange

The Trinidad and Tobago Stock Exchange is the primary stock exchange of Trinidad.

TRS

See Trade Registration System

Trust

A Trust is a legal entity that requires an agreement defining the terms of the trust, a trustee who has specific responsibilities, and a beneficiary who has specific rights.
Trusts are used to provide a separate legal entity that will provide benefits to a beneficiary.

A Trust can be established for an individual (Personal Trust), for a pension fund (Institutional Trust), or for a security (Corporate Trust).

Trust Agreement, Trustee, Beneficiary, Personal Trust, Corporate Trust

Trust Account

There are three major types of Trust Accounts:

- Judiciary supervised accounts which include guardianships and estates
- Standard trust accounts
- Agency accounts

Trusts contain assets, which can include:

- Real Property
- Financial Assets
- Business

Trust Agreement

A Trust Agreement defines exactly how a Trust account will work. It defines:

- How funds will be received, invested and disbursed

- The role of the trustees
- Payment of legal, trustee, and other fees
- Liability of trustees
- Required reporting
- Trust, Trustee

Trust Fund

See *Trust*

Trust Indenture Act

The Trust Indenture Act, passed in 1939, requires a trustee for debt instruments. The Act was established to protect the rights of the bond holder, and it identifies what must be stated in an indenture. The indenture is a document that describes the role of the trustee, and prohibits conflicts of interest.

Indenture, Trustee

Trust Powers

Trust Powers identify the authorized activities of a trustee.

Trust Prohibitions

Trust Prohibitions are the transactions identified in the trust agreement that the trustee is prohibited from performing.

Trust Agreement

Trustee

A Trustee is an entity, typically a person, lawyer or a bank that has a fiduciary responsibility for a trust. The Trustee is responsible for receipts, disbursement, and investing the trust's assets.

As defined by ERISA, a fiduciary is "one who occupies a position of confidence or trust and who exercises any power of control, management, or disposition with respect to monies or other property of an employee benefit fund or who has authority or responsibility to do so."

ERISA, Trust

Truth in Securities Act of 1933

The Truth in Securities Act of 1933 was a Congressional response to the 1929 Stock Market Crash and is the primary regulation governing the US securities market. It was designed to protect investors from fraud that had existed with issuing and trading securities. The Act requires full disclosure requirements for security offerings, and established registration requirements for securities.

Truth-in-Lending Act

Enacted by Congress in 1968, The Truth-in-Lending Act requires a written disclosure of the terms of a commercial loan by a lender to a borrower.

TSCS

See Trade Status Change Stream

TSE

See Tokyo Stock Exchange

See Toronto Stock Exchange

TSE 300 Composite Index

The TSE 300 Composite Index is a stock index derived from equities listed on the Toronto Stock Exchange.

TSE Stock Index

The TSE Stock Index is a stock index derived from equities listed on the Taiwan Stock Exchange.

TSG

See *The Summit Group*

Turnover

Turnover is:

- The ratio of securities in a portfolio to the number of shares or bonds that were actually traded.
- The total value (unit of trading multiplied by number of contracts or shares) of all contract lots or shares that are traded on an exchange, for a specified period of time.

TVA

See *Tennessee Valley Authority*

Two-Dollar Broker

A Two-Dollar Broker, now often called an independent broker, is a floor broker who executes orders for other exchange members and charges a fixed fee for each trade. The name is derived from the two dollar commission that was typically paid to such brokers in the past for the buying or selling of 100 shares of a stock.

Independent Broker, Floor Broker

Two-Sided Market

The Two-Sided Market rule is the NASD's requirement for Market Makers to quote bid and asked prices for each security in which they make a market and to stand ready to execute orders at those prices.

UGMA

See *Uniform Gift to Minors Act*

UIT

See *Unit Investment Trust*

UK Treasuries

The UK government is the issuer of UK Treasuries, often called Gilts, which are fully guaranteed by the UK government. The UK bond market is one of the largest in the world, along with the US, Japan, Italy, Germany and France.

UN/Edifact

The UN/Edifact rules and standards have been established by the United Nations for commerce and transportation firms using electronic data interchange.

Unauthorized Trading

Unauthorized Trading occurs when securities are bought or sold in a non-discretionary investor's account without the investor's prior authorization.

Discretion

Uncovered Options

See Naked Options

Under Par

See *Below Par*

Underlying Security

The Underlying Security is the stock, commodity or other security that supports an options, derivatives or futures contract.

Option, Futures, Derivative

Undervalued

Undervalued securities are those that are selling for less than their value according to analysts.

Underwriter

An Underwriter is a brokerage firm, investment bank or commercial bank that distributes a new issue into the primary market by acting as a principal or as an agent to the trade. As a financial intermediary the underwriter can act as a principal or as an agent to support the seller of the issue.

- When acting as a principal, the underwriter assumes the risk of bringing a new issue to the market with the expectation of making a larger profit than if their firm acts as an agent. As a principal, the primary underwriter, also called the lead manager or lead underwriter, will either act alone or form a syndicate of other investment banks who become co-managers or co-underwriters. The single underwriter, or the syndicate, will buy the issue at a specific price from the corporation that is issuing the new stock or bond and will distribute the securities to individuals and institutions at whatever price they think the market will support. If the underwriter guarantees the sale of a certain number of shares to investors, it is a firm-commitment underwriting.
- When acting as an agent with best-efforts underwriting, the underwriter will not commit to any specific sale of securities, but will do their best to distribute the issue.

Best Efforts Underwriting, Investment Bank, Firm Commitment Underwriting, Principal, Primary Market, Syndicate

Underwriting

Underwriting is the process of bringing new security issues to the market.

There are two types of offerings:

- Private Placements vs. Public Offerings
- Initial Public Offerings (IPO) vs. Secondary Issues

Underwriter

Underwriting as Agent

An underwriter can function as a principal or as an agent in the IPO. Agency agreements include:

- Best efforts distribution (Compensated on a per share sold basis)
- All or none distribution (No compensation if all is not sold)

Underwriting Manager

The Underwriting Manager is either the single firm that is bringing the new issue to the market or the leading underwriter in a syndicate.

Syndicate, Negotiated Underwriting, Competitive Underwriting, Investment Manager

Underwriting Spread

The Underwriting Spread is the difference between the price an underwriter pays for a new issue, and the price at which it is offered.

Underwriter

Unfriendly Takeover

See *Tender Offer*

Uniform Gift to Minors Act

The Uniform Gift to Minors Act defines how an account can be administered for the benefit of a minor.

Uniform Net Capital

According to the Uniform Net Capital rule, brokers are required to maintain a certain level of capital to ensure their viability as principal to the trades that are conducted in the securities market.

15c3-1

Uniform Practice Code

The NSCC has established the Uniform Practice Code to define its rules to its members. It has another set of rules called the Fair Practice Rules that deals with customers.

Fair Practice Rules

Uniform Submission Agreement

A Uniform Submission Agreement is a document that is signed by both parties to an arbitration process. It indicates their concept to be bound by the determination of the arbiter.

Un-issued Stock

Un-issued Stock is stock authorized for sale by the Board of Directors, but which has not as yet been issued to investors.

Unit

A Unit is a category of instrument that contains two or more classes of instrument, but trades as one security. The components could be separated at some future point if allowed in the terms of the instrument.

A common form of unit is the combination of a bond and a warrant at issuance, which can be traded as a unit or separated and traded independently.

Unit Investment Trust

A Unit Investment Trust (UIT) is an investment company that offers a stake, denominated by units, in a fixed portfolio of securities that never change over the life of the trust. The securities are usually self-liquidating and do not have to be managed, lowering the cost of administering the portfolio.

UITs have become very popular in Europe.

Unit Testing

Unit Testing is the first step in the testing process, and is usually conducted by a programmer to ensure that a program operates as required by the user.

Testing, Systems Development Life Cycle

United States Postal Service

The United States Postal Service (USPS) was established in 1971 as an independent business within the executive branch of the US government. The USPS is authorized to issue debt to finance capital expenditures and current operations.

Universal Bank

A Universal Bank is a European style bank that combines commercial and investment banking in one organization.

Glass-Steagall Act

Universal Exchange Corporation Limited

Universal Exchange Corporation Limited (UNEXcor) is a recognized clearing house in South Africa.

Universe

In performance measurement, a Universe is a structured group of securities that should behave in a predicted way. A Universe is used as the base against which a portfolio's performance is measured.

Unlisted Securities

Unlisted Securities are those which do not trade on any organized stock exchange. Unlisted securities usually trade over-the-counter, or are closely held and not traded anywhere.

Unrealized Losses

An investor is said to have Unrealized Losses when the current market value of a position is lower than its cost basis. Once a security is sold, the loss is considered realized.

Realized Losses

Unrealized Profits

An investor is said to have Unrealized Profits when the current market value of a position is greater than its cost basis. Once a security is sold, the gain is considered realized.

Realized Profits

Unrelated Business Income

Unrelated Business Income is a trust's income which is derived from any unrelated trade or business in which the trust is engaged. While dividends, interest, capital gains, etc. are not taxable, unrelated business income is taxable.

Trust

Unsecured Debt

Unsecured Debt is that which is not backed by collateral.

Debenture

Unwind

To Unwind is to engage in the process of reversing a transaction.

Up Tick

An Up Tick is an upward movement in the price of a listed security.

Tick

Upstairs Trader

An Upstairs Trader is a firm's trader who remains in the trading or dealing room, and does not trade on the floor of an exchange.

Downstairs Trader

US Treasury Bill

US Treasury Bills are short term instruments issued by the US government. T-Bills, as they are also called, are issued at a discount from their face amount, and do not exceed terms of one year, with three-month (90-day) or six month (180-day) issues typical.

T-Bills are offered in bearer form in amounts of $10,000 and greater, in multiples of $5,000, and are not registered in any legal name.

Yield is calculated on a 360-day basis, versus 365 days for interest-bearing securities, and uses the actual number of days remaining until maturity.

Bearer, Yield

US Treasury Bond

US Treasury Bonds are long term debt issued by the US government. Bonds are issued with interest paid for periods of 10 to 30 years.

US Treasury Note

US Treasury Notes are an intermediate debt obligation of the US government, usually issued for one to 10 years.

T-Notes, as they are also called, are issued at par, in coupon form, with interest paid semi-annually and are actively traded.

Par, Coupon

US Treasury Obligations

US Treasury Obligations are negotiable debt obligations that are issued by the US government and backed by its full faith and credit.

US Treasury Obligations include:

- Treasury bills
- Treasury notes
- Treasury bonds

US Treasury Bill, US Treasury Bond, US Treasury Note

US Working Committee

Firms in the US established their own Working Committee to define how the US could best implement the recommendations of the Group of Thirty.

Group of Thirty

Usable Bond

A Usable Bond is one that can be used along with a warrant to purchase shares of common stock. The bond, warrant and stock must all be issued by the same firm, and the bond's face value can be used as cash to purchase the shares allowed by the warrant.

USD

USD is the abbreviation for US dollars, the currency unit of the United States.

User Acceptance Testing

User Acceptance Testing is a very critical stage of the testing process since it is managed by the users to determine if the application meets the terms of the requirements document.

This test should consist of a series of predetermined tests, with defined expected results, that will validate the functionality of the system and ensure that the users can work with the system as it has been designed.

User acceptance testing is often the first step in user training on the new system.

Systems Development Life Cycle, Testing

Usury

Usury laws identify the maximum amount of interest that can be legally charged on a loan.

Utility

A Utility can be:

- A firm that produces a product such as electricity.
- A department that delivers a service that is expected to be standardized and continuously available, such as a data center.
- Software that is used to help make a computer or an application run more efficiently.

Utility Bonds

Utility Bonds are those that are issued by regulated utilities to finance their construction activities.

VA Loans

See *Veteran Administration Loans*

Vaerdipapircentralen

Vaerdipapircentralen (VP) is the central depository and securities clearing house of Denmark.

Valley

A Valley is a temporary period of reduced activity. It could refer to a decrease in transaction volume, a decrease in errors, or low stock prices.

Peak

Value Added Service

A Value Added Service is one that goes beyond the traditional services offered by a financial firm. These services are usually premium priced.

Premium Price

Value Chain

There are several steps involved from the time a trade is considered through to final settlement, and different suppliers of services add value along the way. The following steps constitute the Trade Value Chain:

- Pre-Trade
- Trade
- Post Trade
- Clearance
- Settlement
- Issue Servicing
- Trade Life Cycle

Value Date

The Value Date is the date that a transaction becomes effective. A transaction can be forward valued or back valued.

Available Date, Cleared Date

Vancouver Stock Exchange

The Vancouver Stock Exchange is a Canadian stock exchange.

www.vse.com

Vaporware

Vaporware is the name applied to vendor software that has been promised or announced, but is not yet ready for delivery to customers, and which may never be delivered.

Hardware, Software

Värdepappers-centralen

Värdepapperscentralen (VPC) is the central securities depository of Sweden.

Variable

A Variable is a symbol, used in a computer program, that represents a number or text that can be different for each transaction or in each record.

Record

Variable Annuity

A Variable Annuity is a mutual fund within an insurance policy. The purchaser of the insurance policy will have some insurance coverage during the life of the annuity and will then receive the income resulting from years of investment by the mutual fund.

Annuity

Variable Rate

A Variable Rate is an interest rate that changes periodically and which is usually based upon the movement of an index.

Variable Rate Bond

Variable Rate Bonds are instruments that do not have a fixed interest rate. Instead, the rate changes based upon the movement of a commonly used index such as the Consumer Price Index or the Prime Rate.

Consumer Price Index, Prime Rate, Fixed Rate Bond

Variable Rate Instruments

See *Variable Rate Bond*

Variable Rate Mortgage

A Variable Rate Mortgage (VRM) is similar to a Renegotiable Rate Mortgage in that there is no fixed interest rate. However, a VRM does not have a fixed expiration date.

After a specified period of time the VRM interest rate can be annually raised or lowered. The new rate is defined in the mortgage agreement and is often tied to an index such as Federal Home Loan Bank Cost of Money Index.

Adjustable Rate Mortgage

Variance

A Variance is:

- A statistical measure of variability based on squared deviations of individual observations from the mean value of a distribution. The square root of the variance is the standard deviation.
- An operation measurement that defines the magnitude of deviation from the expected results, goals, and standards of a plan

Plan, Standard, Goal

Variance to Standards

A Variance to Standards occurs when the actual results of a process differ from the predefined standards. A variance can be better or worse than the standard, unless the standard is 100%.

Goal

Vault

A Vault is a safe that is secured against fire and theft and which is used to store valuable assets. Custodians, brokers and depositories use vaults to safekeep physical securities.

Vega

Vega is the measure of change in the value of an option compared with a change in the volatility of that option.

Venture Capital

Venture Capital consists of funds that are invested in new firms that may have a high degree of risk. When a person or a firm makes a venture capital investment, they take a large risk, expect to receive a significant share of equity in the firm, and anticipate a high profit.

Verdipapirsentralen

Verdipapirsentralen (VPS) is the central depository and securities clearing house of Norway.

Verification of Deposit

A Verification of Deposit (VOD) is a document that is signed by a borrower's bank and which shows the borrower's account balance and history.

Verification of Employment

A Verification of Employment (VOE) is a document that is signed by a borrower's employer to verify the borrower's position and salary.

Vertical Merger

A Vertical Merger is a merger between two firms involved in the same industry but which offer different products or serve a different client base.

Vertical Spreads

A Vertical Spreads is an option strategy that combines the purchase and sale of two puts (bear put spread) or two calls (bear call spread) with different strike prices on the same underlying security.

Vesting

Vesting is the process of making certain benefits irrevocable. Benefit rights can become vested after employees work for a firm for a specific number of years, reach a certain age, or complete other requirements.

Veteran Administration Loans

VA Loans are fixed-rate loans that are guaranteed by the US Department of Veterans Affairs, and which are designed to make housing affordable for eligible US veterans. The maximum VA loan amount is currently $203,000.

Vienna Stock Exchange

The Vienna Stock Exchange is the primary stock exchange of Austria.

apollo.wu-wien.ac.at/ cgi-bin/boerse1.pl

Voice Recognition

Voice Recognition is the process of converting the spoken word into data that can be stored and manipulated by a computer.

Volatility

Volatility is the degree of price fluctuation for a given asset, rate, or index over a defined period of time, usually the daily price history over the last year.

Beta

Volume

Volume can be:

- The total number of contracts, shares or currency units that are traded on a specific exchange during a given period of time
- The total number of transactions processed by a firm or an operations unit

Volume Insensitive

A process is Volume Insensitive when it will not have more errors, cost more or function more slowly when volume increases substantially.

Volume Sensitive

Volume Sensitive

A process is Volume Sensitive when additional volume will probably increase errors, costs and processing time.

Volume Insensitive

Voluntary Corporate Action

See *Mandatory Corporate Action*

Voting Right

A Voting Right is a stockholder's right to participate in the affairs of the company. Voting rights can be delegated to another party through a proxy.

Proxy

VSE Composite Indicator

The VSE Composite Indicator is a stock index derived from equities listed on the Vancouver Stock Exchange.

VSE Share Index

The VSE Share Index is a stock index derived from equities listed on the Vienna Stock Exchange.

W-2

See *IRS FormW-2*

W-4

See *IRS FormW-4*

W-9

See *IRS FormW-9*

Waiver

A Waiver is a voluntary release or surrender of some right or privilege.

Wall Street Technology Association

The Wall Street Technology Association, a non-profit association, was founded in 1967, and currently represents the interests of over 165 member firms from the greater New York financial community, and provides educational opportunities for more than 1,200 members.

WAN

See *Wide Area Network*

Warrant

A Warrant is a certificate, similar to an option, that is issued to stock/bond holders, usually as an inducement to purchase the associated bond or equity. A warrant is a negotiable instrument that can be detached and traded separately from its associated security.

Warrants have a long expiration period, usually 10 to 20 years, and allow its holder to purchase the issuing corporation's stock at a certain price over the stated period of time.

Negotiable, Unit

Warsaw Stock Exchange

The Warsaw Stock Exchange is Poland's primary stock exchange.

info.fuw.edu.pl/pl/gielda.eng.html

Warsaw Stock Exchange Index

Warsaw Stock Exchange Index (WIG) is a stock index derived from equities listed on the Warsaw Stock Exchange.

Wash Sale

A Wash Sale occurs when an investor sells and then repurchases a specific security within a thirty day period. In this circumstance, the IRS will not allow a capital loss deduction.

Weak Market

A Weak Market is a market that is tending to go lower because sellers generally outnumber buyers.

Bear Market

WEBS

See *World Equity Benchmark Shares*

Weighting

Weighting is a statistical technique that is used to maintain some consistency of data or to make data elements more comparable.

Wells Fargo

Wells Fargo is a US-based bank.

www.wellsfargo.com

When Issued

When Issued is the short form of "when, as, and if issued," that is used for securities that are about to be issued and whose settlement date is not set. The term is used to indicate the conditional nature of the trade since the security has not actually been released, and therefore, the transaction can only settle if the security is issued.

Common stock that is issued by a rights offering trades When Issued.

Treasury Bills auctioned on Tuesday but settled on Thursday will also trade When Issued.

White Knight

A White Knight is a person or a firm that makes an offer to acquire a company that is "in play." The White Knight may actually acquire a firm that is being sought by another, or it may change the way people see the firm, making additional offers by other parties more likely.

In Play

White Label

Banks provide a White Label service when they act as the back office for other banks, in the name of the other bank. The services include back office operations and technology, and complete accounting and reporting services.

Private Label

White Paper

An opinion developed by an individual or a group that describes how things should be is called a White Paper. White Papers are frequently written to describe an ideal situation without considering existing conditions or constraints.

White Room

When developing a new product, process or system, managers may elect to establish a work area in a totally new environment that is not bound by any existing conditions or constraints. This is a White Room.

Wide Area Network

A Wide Area Network is a group of computers over a broad geographic area, connected by telecommunication lines.

Wilshire 5000

The Wilshire 5000 is a capitalization weighted index of all US companies, which currently number approximately 7,000 firms.

Window

A Window is a view of information provided by a graphical user interface. A window can be opened, moved, resized and closed, and it is used to enter and retrieve the data stored in a computer.

Graphical User Interface

Windows

Windows is the name of the operating system developed by Microsoft. It is a graphical user interface

Graphical User Interface, Operating System

Wire House

A Wire House is a broker with multiple branch offices that are linked by a telecommunications system. The term originated when brokerage offices communicated via Western Union telegrams.

Withdrawal Penalty

A Withdrawal Penalty is the charge that is made on an investor who withdraws from an investment before the agreed upon time.

Withdrawal Plan

A Withdrawal Plan is a process whereby investors receive regular payments from their mutual fund account. It is a way of extracting cash from the account over a period of time for living expenses.

Withholding Tax

Withholding Tax is a process required by government regulation to ensure that the government receives tax payments up front. The US government and governments around the world require financial institutions to withhold tax for interest and dividends in certain circumstances.

Withholding Tax Reclaim, Tax Treaty

Withholding Tax Reclaim

A Withholding Tax Reclaim is a form and a process that is used by an investor in one country, or a financial institution on behalf of an investor, to reclaim all or part of a tax that was withheld by another country's government.

Withholding Tax, Tax Treaty

Workflow

Workflow is:

- The way that transactions are processed by a firm
- A type of an application that can be used to document existing processes and to automate portions of it

Workstation

A Workstation is similar to a PC in that it usually is dedicated to the need of a specific person, but historically has had far more processing power than a PC.

PC

World Equity Benchmark Shares

WEBS are mutual funds that are designed to reflect the performance of specific Morgan Stanley Capital International Indexes.

WEBS began trading on the Amex on March 18, 1996, and currently allow investors to invest internationally in 17 different countries.

World Wide Web

The World Wide Web is a method of organizing the information on the internet. If documents are placed on the internet in a hypertext format, they can be reviewed by a browser. Documents can contain pointers to other documents so that a user can "surf" from place to place on the internet.

Browser, Hypertext, Internet

WORM

See *Write Once Read Many*

Wrap Account

See *Wrap Fee Account*

Wrap Around Mortgage

A Wrap Around Mortgage is a refinancing method that is used as interest rates are rising, whereby the lender assumes payment of the existing mortgage and issues a replacement mortgage with a higher principal and interest rate to the borrower.

As a result, the new mortgage wraps around the original mortgage, but is subordinate to the original lien.

Wrap Fee Account

A Wrap Fee Account is an investment program that bundles several services, including advisory services, research, account management, brokerage, etc., into a single fee that is based on the value of assets in the account.

The account may also allow multiple money managers to manage separate portfolios within the same account structure.

Write Once Read Many

A Write Once Read Many (WORM) data storage device is one that has been designed to be created at one point in time and read many times thereafter. A vendor's CD ROM with an application on it is a WORM storage media.

Writer

See *Option Writer*

WSJ

Abbreviation for The Wall Street Journal

WSTA

See *Wall Street Technology Association*

www

See *World Wide Web*

WYSISYG

Pronounced Wizy-wig, and short for What You *See* Is What You Get.

This is a term that is used to establish that what a user sees on the screen is what they will see when the screen is printed on paper.

XML

Abbreviation for Extensible Markup Language

Y2K

See *Year 2000*

Year 2000

The Year 2000 problem is one where a firm's computer code may not function correctly on January 1, 2000 because programmers used to minimize data storage by only putting the last two digits of the century in their computer programs. Therefore, in the year 2000, computers would only see 00 and think that year was less than 99. This problem must be resolved before computer applications begin processing transactions involving dates after January 1, 2000.

Year-To-Date

Year-To-Date is the period from the beginning of the calendar year to the reporting date.

Yen

The Yen is a unit of Japanese currency.

Yield

The Yield is the rate of return on an investment, which is a ratio of the instrument's return compared to its cost. Two commonly quoted yields are current annual yield and yield to maturity.

A bond's yield is inversely related to its price and therefore varies in relation to any changes in price. When a bond's yield drops, the price of the bond rises.

Current Yield, Yield to Maturity

Yield Curve

The Yield Curve is a graphical view of how interest rates relate to time, often from three months to thirty years. The most used yield curve is for the 30 Year Treasury Bond. However, separate yield curves can be constructed for each category of fixed income instrument, based upon their relative risk.

The yield curve is generally upward sloping where longer times to maturity are positively correlated with higher yields.

Yield Spread

The Yield Spread is the difference between any two groups of fixed income securities.

Yield to Call

The Yield to Call is the yield on a security that has been calculated by assuming that interest payments will be paid until the first possible call date, when the security will be redeemed at the call price.

Yield to Maturity

A Yield to Maturity is the total annualized amount of interest earned over the life of an instrument, adjusted for the purchase premium, and divided by the amount invested.

Yo-yo Stock

A Yo-yo Stock is a volatile equity that rises and falls quickly.

YTD

See Year To Date

Zagreb Stock Exchange

The Zagreb Stock Exchange is the primary stock exchange of Croatia.

Zero Coupon Bond

A Zero Coupon bond, also known as a Zero, is a derivative created by removing the interest coupon of a US treasury bond from the promise to repay principal. The interest coupon is traded separately as a Strip, and the remaining principal is traded as a Zero. Zeros are usually traded at a discount that decreases as the instrument approaches maturity and do not pay any interest.

Strip

Zero Coupon Notes

See Zero Coupon Bonds

Zero-Hour Rule

The Zero-Hour Rule is included in the bankruptcy laws of many countries. The rule states that a bankruptcy is considered to have been declared at 0.00 AM of the same day.

Zimbabwe Industrial Index

Zimbabwe Industrial Index is a stock index derived from equities listed on the Zimbabwe Stock Exchange.

Zimbabwe Stock Exchange

The Zimbabwe Stock Exchange is Zimbabwe's primary stock exchange.